Light Railway Transit Circulation

LRT Track with
stations at 3
segment intervals

LRT Track
zone B

Primary Circulation

Pavilions

Japanese Vertical Pavilion

Vertical Pavilion

Tertiary Circulation

Primary Circulation

Secondary Circulation

Vertical Access Systems

Circulation Systems

Continuous Ramps

Continuous Pedestrian
Ramp as main boulevard

Boulevards In The Sky

International
Pavilion Zone
@ 50 segment

International
Pavilion Zone

Reinventing the Skyscraper

REINVENTING
THE
SKYSCRAPER

A Vertical Theory of Urban Design

by Ken Yeang

WILEY-ACADEMY

Acknowledgements

I would like to record my gratitude and thanks to Maggie Toy, Abigail Grater, Mariangela Palazzi-Williams and Wiley-Academy in the realisation of the publication.

Published in Great Britain in 2002 by Wiley-Academy, a division of John Wiley & Sons Ltd

Copyright © 2002

John Wiley & Sons Ltd, The Atrium, Southern Gate, Chichester, West Sussex PO 19 8SQ, England
Telephone [+44] 1243 779777

Ken Yeang,
8, Jalan 1, Taman Sri Ukay,
68 000 Ampang, Selangor, Malaysia
Telephone [+603] 4257 1966

Email (for orders and customer service enquiries): cs-books@wiley.co.uk
Visit our Home Page on www.wileyeurope.com or www.wiley.com

Other Wiley Editorial Offices

John Wiley & Sons Inc., 111 River Street, Hoboken, NJ 07030, USA

Jossey-Bass, 989 Market Street, San Francisco, CA 94103-1741, USA

Wiley-VCH Verlag GmbH, Boschstr. 12, D-69469 Weinheim, Germany

John Wiley & Sons Australia Ltd, 33 Park Road, Milton, Queensland 4064, Australia

John Wiley & Sons (Asia) Lte Ltd, 2 Clementi Loop #02-01, Jin Xing Distripark, Singapore 129809

John Wiley & Sons Canada Ltd, 22 Worcester Road, Etobicoke, Ontario, Canada M9W ILI

ISBN 0-470-84355-1

Book Design by Yenniu Lim, Ridzwa Fathan, Shahrul Nizam and Renee Lee for ADF Management Sdn. Bhd.

Printed and bound in Malaysia by EHT Creative & Graphic Services

Contents

Reinventing the Skyscraper

Contents ▷ 004|005

Foreword

How can we make working, living and all aspects of our life in the high-rise building more palatable? Today this is the one of the most compelling questions confronting our politicians, city planners, urban designers, architects, investors, sociologists and all those concerned with the planning, design and development of, and investment in our cities.

While on the one hand many of them will vehemently decry the desirability of the tall building as a built form, citing a multitude of reasons why we should not build upwards, at the same time they have to ruefully conclude that the adoption of the tall building as the urban built form of choice is inevitable. Simply stated, unless an alternative equivalent built form presents itself that can economically and physically be a more viable solution to the intensification of our cities' land use (as a consequence of urban growth), then tall buildings will remain with us for a while.

004

▷ **006|007**

008

033

056

072

088

101

126

138

148

173

180

193

212

218

220

Presented here is a new approach to the tall building, where its design and planning are perceived as a form of urban design which takes precedence over its architectural form-making. The outcome of this approach is a built milieu that is more physically and socially comprehensive; a high-rise built environment that is more humane and more habitable; a built environment that should be a replication of, and where possible significantly improve on the ideal and pleasurable life that we currently enjoy, and have always enjoyed, at the ground plane.

The ideas and propositions presented here will lead to a more livable intensive urban environment, if taken to their logical conclusion, they should eventually become the fundamental bases for the planning and building codes governing the design of future high-rise buildings and the development of our cities.

Ken Yeang
2002

... Their basic planning remains the same. Whether in concrete or in steel, most are still nothing more than a series of stacked trays piled homogenously and vertically one on top of the other, while at the same time seeking to optimise net-to-gross area spatial efficiencies ...

004

006

▷ **008 009**

033

056

072

088

101

126

138

148

173

180

193

212

218

220

... The consequence is a demeaning and alienating form of high-rise existence for their inhabitants, that ultimately only expeditiously satisfies the real estate developer's financial returns on his investment ...

Premises for a Vertical Theory

Contemporary lifestyles and the increasing combined pressures of urbanisation and population growth on our cities demand a redefining of our conventional perceptions of working and living in high-rise structures in the city. Today, many of the world's predominantly low- and medium-rise cities such as London are in the process of transforming into high-density, high-rise living and working environments. The question now confronting designers of these high-rise buildings is whether the current approaches for high-rise design adequately provide the occupiers of those buildings with an acceptable quality of urban life in the sky.

△ Most skyscrapers today are nothing more than a series of stacked plates one on top of the other.

△ Analogous to a stack of books or magazines, the floor plates can only pile-up so high beyond which the height becomes structurally problematic.

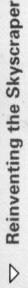

004

006

▷ **010|011**

033

056

072

088

101

126

138

148

173

180

193

212

218

220

◄Typical floor, plan of Chrysler Building, New York [completed 1930].

Typical floor plan, of Mellon Bank Center, Philadelphia [completed 1991] showing that skyscraper design has changed little since its invention in the 1930s.

◄ Skyscrapers could be designed as a series of vertical events like a superburger, with a variety of spatial delicacies at each level.

Skyscraper architecture has remained essentially unchanged since its invention. Of course its technology and engineering have become far better and much more sophisticated, but most, if not all, of the skyscrapers constructed today remain fundamentally the same in built configuration. Their basic planning remains the same. Whether built of concrete or of steel, most are still nothing more than a series of stacked trays piled homogeneously and vertically one on top of the other, while at the same time seeking to optimise net-to-gross areal spatial efficiencies. The consequence is a demeaning and alienating form of high-rise existence for their inhabitants, that ultimately only expeditiously satisfies the real estate developer's financial returns on his investment.

Premises for a Vertical Theory

What is crucially needed is a redefinition for more satisfyingly habitable working and living urban environments: more diverse; greater multiplicity; certainly less regimented; with networks of plazas, parks and enclosed spaces in the sky. Simply stated, an environment that recreates those fulfilling aspects of our life on the ground. What we need is a new skyline, for the prevalent one (found in most of our cities' Central Business Districts today) consists of skyscraper architecture that is ubiquitously repetitive in all its internal spatial dispositions; this is eminently visible through its very thin facades.

▷ We need to design pleasurable places in the sky like those found on the ground. [BATC Tower Kuala Lumpur, 1997]

▷ We need to provide large parks in the sky like those found in our major cities. [BATC Tower, Kuala Lumpur, © TR Hamzah & Yeang, 1997]

▷ Chapter 01

Reinventing the Skyscraper

▷

As cities and their business and residential precincts become considerably denser, we need to approach skyscraper design in such intensive urban localities as more of an urban design proposition and not just as an architectural design for a building type. The rationale is that, as an urban design proposition, we would be required to regard the skyscraper as a vertical extension of the city and to carry out its design in considerably more complex and inclusive terms. This is new territory that deserves critical exploration. For instance, we would need to design the skyscraper's external, internal and transitional spaces to be similar to those successful urban spaces found in many of our cities, but at the same time take into studied consideration the needs of its current and future users.

▽ We need to recreate public realms like Venice's Piazza San Marco in the sky.
[Source: *Design of Cities*, Edmund M. Bacon, 1967]

△ We need to provide within skyscapers a
◁ multiplicity of land uses and a greater
◁ complexity in their movements systems.
[BATC Tower, Kuala Lumpur, © TR Hamzah & Yeang, 1997]

004
006
▷ 012|013
033
056
072
088
101
126
138
148
173
180
193
212
218
220

Premises for a Vertical Theory

The proposition that skyscraper design should be urban involves an integration of socio-economic-political-environmental and physical concerns with the architectural concerns of building design. The multidisciplinary concerns include economics, ecology, sociology, environment, psychology, technology, urban geography, cultural theory and real estate, all of which will be seen to affect the design of the new skyscraper.

N
Scale 1:1500

Level 65

Level 29

Level 60

Level 24

Level 55

Level 19

Level 50

Level 14

Level 45

Level 9

Level 40

Level 35

Level 4

▷ Floor plans for the BATC Signature Tower.
[© T. R. Hamzah & Yeang, 1997]

■ Tennant Space

■ Special Functions

■ Sky-courts/Public Spaces

Structure + Core: walls, columns, plant rooms, stairs and lifts, WCs, lobbies
Primary circulation: main corridors, horizontal routes required for escape in case of fire
Fit factor: space that is unusable because of building peculiarities
Support space for all the building: cafeteria, library, reprographics, conference suite
Ancillary space: for departments or groups: group files, local copier, project area
Work space: desks, offices and the local circulation to reach them

▷ Multiplicity of land uses can be planned like layers within the skyscraper.

⬅ The floor plates need not be regular but should be articulated to provide spaces and places in the sky.

004

006

▷ 014|015

033

056

072

088

101

126

138

148

173

180

193

212

218

220

Generally stated, the objectives of urban design, now applied to skyscraper design are to:

- design and create a place with its own character and identity;
- ensure an urban continuity and enclosure in providing a place where public and private spaces are clearly distinguished;
- provide quality public realms as places with attractive, successful and accessible outdoor areas;
- provide ease of movement by creating places that are easy to get to and move through;
- design for legibility so that places are easy to understand and have a clear image;
- design for adaptability as places can change easily;
- provide diversity by creating places with variety and choice.

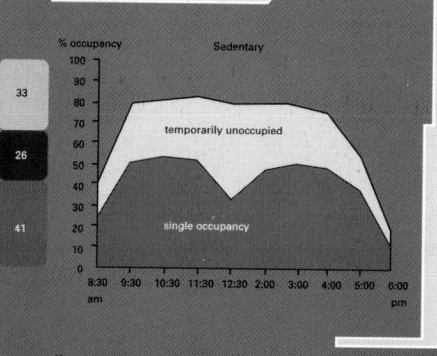

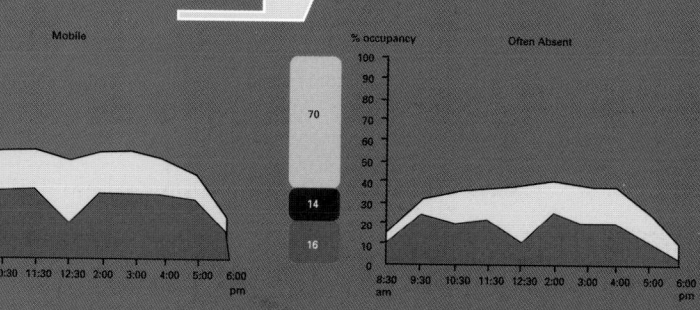

⬆ People do not remain in one place in the skyscraper. They move about within their spaces over the working day and require a diversity of internal environments:
[Source: Alexi Marmot Associates, space-occupancy studies for various organisations]

Premises for a Vertical Theory

Urban design also determines the very shape of the streets and public spaces that make up our urban areas. It influences how easy and pleasant it can be to move from one area to another, how much daylight, landscape and beauty we can enjoy. All these aspects should be part of the influence on the design of the new high-rise. What is crucially needed is a theory for skyscraper design that is equivalent to a vertical theory of urban design, which would radically revise our existing spatially and socially demeaning approaches to the creation of the skyscraper's built form.

The compelling imperative for the theory is, of course, driven by the skyscraper's own reason for its existence: its sheer spatial and population intensity.

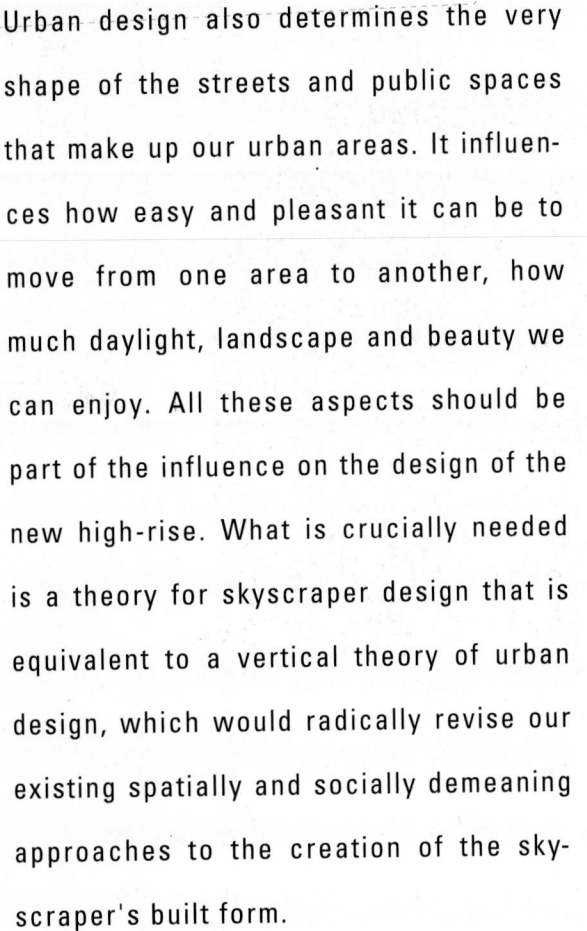

▽ The bland skyscraper that signifies a monotonous and impersonal pattern of life and dreary use of spaces.

▷ The skyscraper should have within it a series of small squares as public refuge zones within a dense urban realm. Example: Public squares as found in European cities such as London.

004

006

▷ **016|017**

033

056

072

088

101

126

138

148

173

180

193

212

218

220

◁ Some of the successful urban landscaping design solutions at the ground plane can be adapted for the upper levels of the skyscraper. Example: Central Park, New York.

◁ Centralized planting within the city [eg. New York]

This intensity is inevitable. The world is intensively urban because towers and cities offer substantial benefits over other forms of settlement. The advantages that people derive from densely aggregating together are greater than those when they settle and disperse.

Park encompasses several levels in the skyscraper linked by ramps.

◁ The equivalent of a central park in the skyscraper is a multilevel interconnected park that encompasses several floors within its built form.

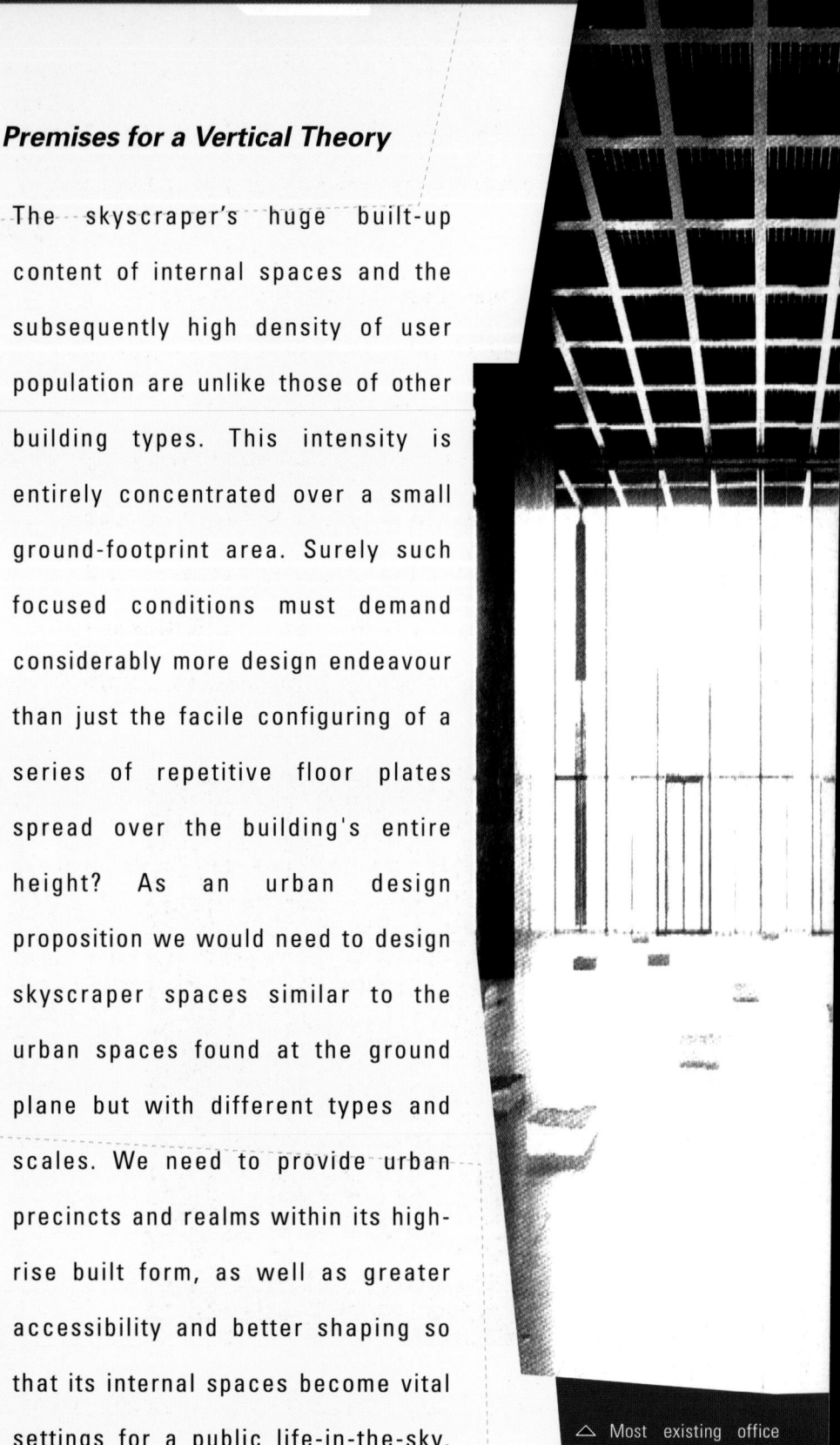

Premises for a Vertical Theory

The skyscraper's huge built-up content of internal spaces and the subsequently high density of user population are unlike those of other building types. This intensity is entirely concentrated over a small ground-footprint area. Surely such focused conditions must demand considerably more design endeavour than just the facile configuring of a series of repetitive floor plates spread over the building's entire height? As an urban design proposition we would need to design skyscraper spaces similar to the urban spaces found at the ground plane but with different types and scales. We need to provide urban precincts and realms within its high-rise built form, as well as greater accessibility and better shaping so that its internal spaces become vital settings for a public life-in-the-sky. This endeavour should also include the provision of breathing open spaces within the skyscraper's built

△ Most existing office floor plates in today's skyscrapers are bland and devoid of any visual interest.

form as public realms, and spaces of a scale to nurture civic consciousness within its inhabitants.

004

006

▷ 018|019

033

056

072

088

101

126

138

148

173

180

193

212

218

220

To illustrate we can take, for instance, a skyscraper of 20 storeys with an average typical floor-plate area of about 1400 square metres. The concentration of built-up space within its towering built form amounts to a gross area (if it was flattened out horizontally) equivalent to about 2.8 hectares of landed surface area, and it has an internal population of about 2000 persons (at an

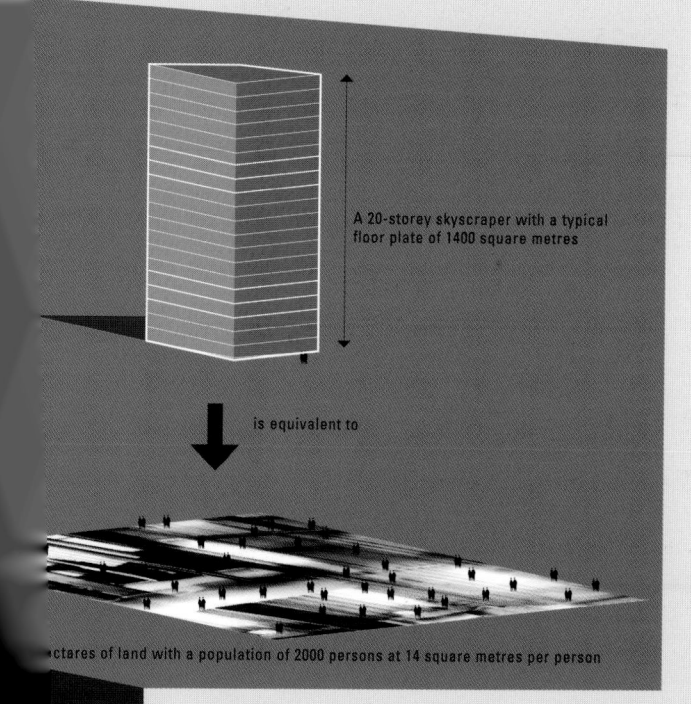

A 20-storey skyscraper with a typical floor plate of 1400 square metres

is equivalent to

ctares of land with a population of 2000 persons at 14 square metres per person

might be
artificial
cal real

average of one person per 14 square metre gross area).

Premises for a Vertical Theory

▽ Skyscraper typology reused ironically as the facade for the casino. Example: Las Vegas.

Too much skyscraper design effort today goes into the facade design as a form of △ corporate packaging.

Unfortunately, when designing such an intensive building most architects tend to ignore the urbanistic consequences of the significant areal magnitude. Commonly, the designer is misled by design precedents into thinking that his design effort starts with the configuring of the building's typical floor plate as a standard plan, and then afterwards extrudes this as a repeated plan upwards over its entire height.

Configuring a floor plate of only 1400 square metres might be regarded as comparable to designing a smallish building.

004

006

▷ 020|021

033

056

072

088

101

126

138

148

173

180

193

212

218

220

For many designers, once they have determined the general disposition of the essential components for this typical floor plate (such as the elevator core position, the main and escape staircases, plant rooms, riser duct locations, and the delineation of the structural grids), their attention gets redirected to the facade design and other technical and engineering aspects of the skyscraper. In some instances there might perhaps be some limited design variations, such as the articulation of the ground-floor-plan and the lower-floor-plan configurations and the provision of special uppermost penthouse floors. Aside from these insignificant variations, the bulk of the floors remains the same.

◁ The skyscraper has a reduced footprint on the ground compared to the extensive footprint of low- rise and medium-rise buildings. In this regard, its real impact on the ecosystem is less than that of a sprawl configuration.

Premises for a Vertical Theory

Unfortunately, most skyscraper designs tend to be just this – a typical floor repeated mindlessly over all the building's height. Further design efforts, if any, instead become focused on improving net-to-gross usable area ratios and the functionalism this demands results in an obsession with efficiency. It is this design facileness that makes so much of current skyscraper design spatially simplistic and internally unsatisfactory to the building's occupants. In contrast, what is needed are spaces-in-the-sky that will give a quality of life and vitality that will make high-density urban living desirable, and which will be attractive places in which to live and socialise.

We might contend that designing a building that contains within it such a huge built-up area would surely involve much more urbanity than just this simplistic shaping and planning of a standard extruded plan. For instance, have we considered the communal facilities at the upper floors and whether these are adequate for such a large population of occupants?

△ The regimented repetitiveness of the conventional office skyscraper needs to be reconfigured.

gross area

stairs

elevators

custodial restroom

usable area

rentable area

net area

maintenance

In skyscraper design too ▷ much attention has been diverted to improving net-to-gross efficiencies in order to enhance returns on investments. [Source: McDamacion, *Office Access*, 1992]

core & shell

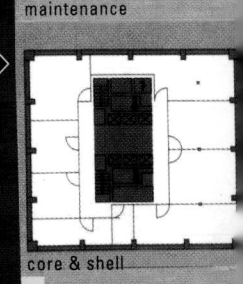

Would all the occupants of the high-rise have to make their way down to the ground plane or to the podium levels to find the basic amenities necessary to make their lives complete and diverse; and would these amenities be adequate to meet the multitude of needs of this sizable population? Has adequate attention been paid to the usual preoccupations of urban designers, such as the provision of public realms, greenery, linkages, place-making, neighbourhoods, etc? These are the essentially unanswered questions posed by most of the skyscrapers built today.

◁ The ubiquitous glass-box sky-scraper

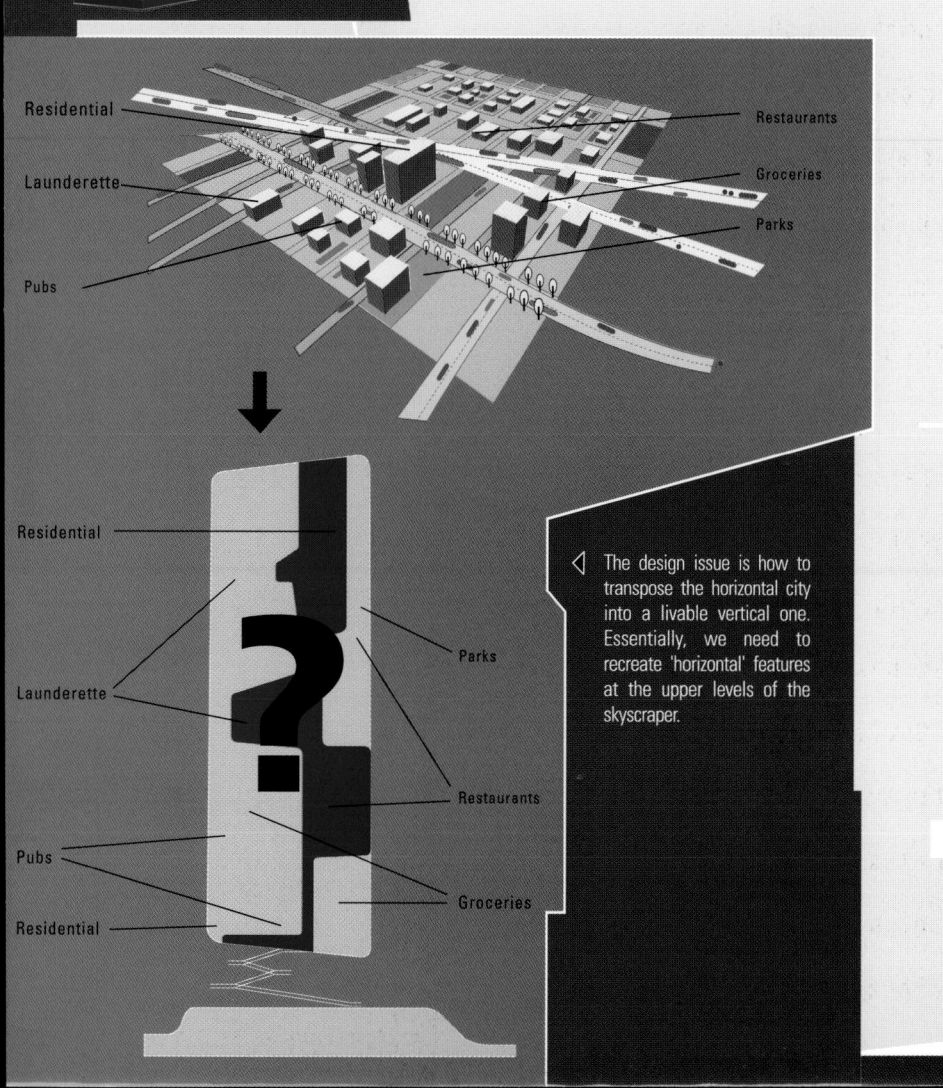

Residential

Launderette

Pubs

Restaurants

Groceries

Parks

Residential

Launderette

Pubs

Residential

Parks

Restaurants

Groceries

◁ The design issue is how to transpose the horizontal city into a livable vertical one. Essentially, we need to recreate 'horizontal' features at the upper levels of the skyscraper.

004
006
022|023 ▷
033
056
072
088
101
126
138
148
173
180
193
212
218
220

Premises for a Vertical Theory

As an urban design proposition, the communal concerns of the skyscraper generally are better addressed. In this case, urban design propositions are equally applicable to skyscraper design. The key difference is that the urban spaces and features at the ground plane need to be reinterpreted within the skyscraper's vertically built form.

▽ How high can we stack the floor plates before the cookie skyscraper tumbles down? Instead of pursuing increasing height we should pursue increasing habitability.

HOW HIGH CAN YOU STACK?

WIN A $20,000 SAVINGS BOND

If, for instance, we regard the skyscraper's built content to be equivalent to an area of 8.8 hectares located within the city's business district, the design endeavour would certainly require careful attention in order to integrate the skyscraper's design within the context of the existing urban fabric and circulation linkages,

004

006

▷ **024|025**

033

056

072

088

101

126

138

148

173

180

193

212

218

220

in order to link with the existing urban networks and systems surrounding the site, to create new public realms and urban places within the overall plan, and to attend to many of the usual social and physical considerations inherent in any urban planning and design situation. These considerations must be similarly crucial for the skyscraper, even though its huge content of built-up spaces is vertically segmented and stacked.

▽ Lessons in designing a skyscraper can be learnt from the aircraft carrier, which is a total floating city with a multitude of urban amenities within it. Its length exceeds 300 metres equivalent to a 90- to 100- storey skyscraper.
[Source: *Yomiuri Weekly*, Oct 2001]

approximately 220 metres

Premises for a Vertical Theory

The dreaded spatial homogeneity and design facileness in many of the skyscrapers built today already suggest the need for an urgent rethink of current approaches to the design of tall buildings. This need must now be all the more crucial since large numbers of these building types are being built worldwide, and these numbers are increasingly likely to increase.

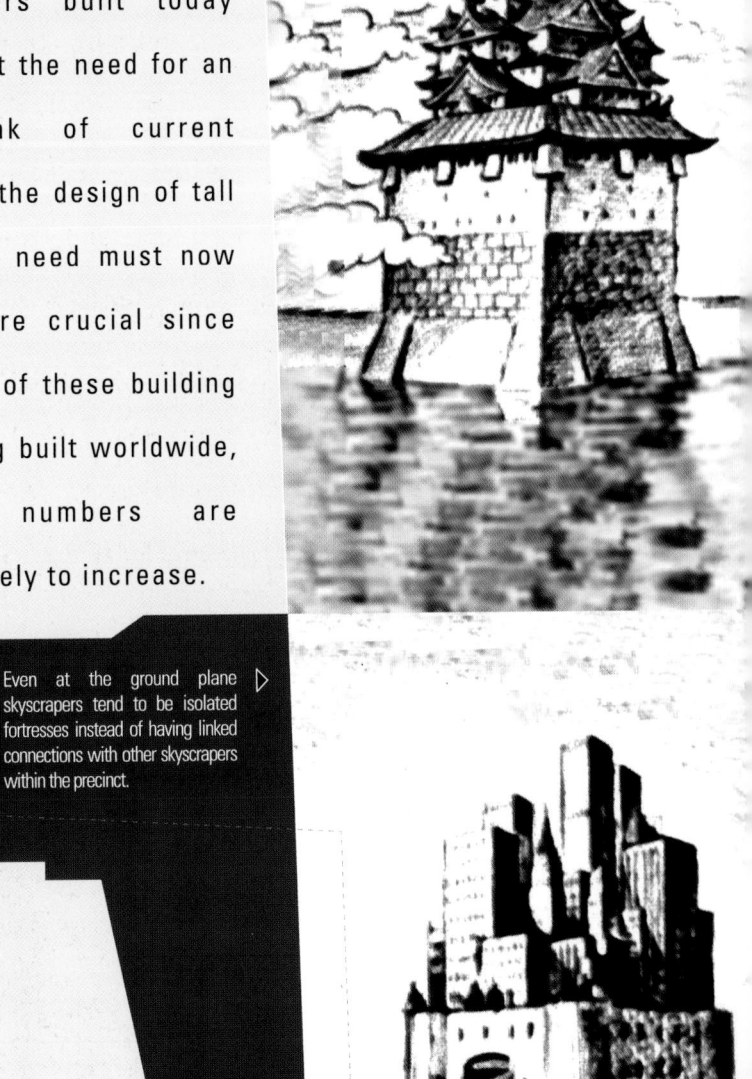

Even at the ground plane skyscrapers tend to be isolated fortresses instead of having linked connections with other skyscrapers within the precinct. ▷

Such a vertical theory is, of course, noticeably non-existent currently. That it should exist becomes vitally important for not just skyscraper designers but also for investors. For it will provide them with the basis for the design of a more humane, more socially and physically acceptable tall building. It will enable the reformulation of the changing urbanistic role of the skyscraper and its definition as being simply just a building. It should be better perceived as a precinct-in-the-sky. Designing the skyscraper as urban design offers a greater set of opportunities for reforming its built form and, in effect, for rediscovering the many hidden opportunities in its built form. For the investor, usually the person who makes the ultimate commercial decisions on the skyscraper's design, it could increase the range of marketing features, to enhance sales or rentability and the building's long-term asset value.

004

006

▷ 026|027

033

056

072

088

101

126

138

148

173

180

193

212

218

220

viewing deck

◁ In future skyscrapers the viewing deck of the Empire State Building should be repeated at regular intervals over the length of the building and expanded to create public realms.

Premises for a Vertical Theory

It is understandable that commercial pressures tend to focus a tall building's design primarily on the optimisation of its floor plate's net-to-gross efficiency (to perhaps 80 percent and above), and subsequently ensure that this space-use efficiency is maintained mindlessly upwards. Unfortunately, this is exactly what has happened with most tall buildings, their designers afterwards expecting the occupants to enjoy the internal life, perhaps ameliorated in selective up-market instances by elaborate interior furnishings. This might explain why so many people have such an aversion to this building type, and why many simply detest the very idea of working and living in high-rise structures.

The skyscraper is a massive commercial investment and high net-to-gross efficiencies and accurate timing are imperatives for the developer.

In recent years skyscrapers have been built as speculative buildings with no committed purchasers or tenants. They become financial Trojan horses for high-rise corporate investors.

As we begin to critically rethink the design of the tall building, it is clear that this has to depart radically from the current Modernist concept of what is a skyscraper. The one-liner obviousness of its design as a series of repeated floors, with the predictable provision of vertical connections by elevator shafts and staircases and its built form wrapped by an external skin, has to be reconstructed. We must now see the skyscraper more organically, as a built form that requires a greater level of spatial articulation and reassembling. It should be designed as an urban design exercise, as though its built space had been flattened out on the ground plane, and then reassembled in the sky into a high-rise built form, with critical attention paid to all aspects of its urbanity and denseness, and within it the provision and shaping of its internal common spaces and public realms should be more communally driven. Simply stated, the basis for the vertical theory of urban design is the recreation, up in the sky, of ideal habitable urban conditions found at ground level.

004

006

▷ 028|029

033

056

072

088

101

126

138

148

173

180

193

212

218

220

Height 72m [keel to funnel] equivalent to a 23-storey building

Length 345m equivalent to a 86-storey tower

△ The *Queen Mary* is like a horizontal floating skyscraper or "seascraper". The new high-rise should be a vertical version of this. [Source: "The World's Largest Liner", *Straits Times*. 19 January, 2002]

Premises for a Vertical Theory

We need to look in greater detail at the conventional theories and ideas in urban design, and critically assess what these would mean or how they could be reconfigured laterally and transposed vertically. Urban design concepts meant for the horizontal plane will be flipped to a high-rise condition and reinterpreted as vertical propositions.

We might consider, for instance, what 'place-making' will mean spatially and aesthetically in the case of the skyscraper. How do we create successful places-in-the-sky on the upper parts of a building as we have done on the ground? How can these places be made to be public, memorable and evocative of a sense of place, as are some of those successful places created at the ground?

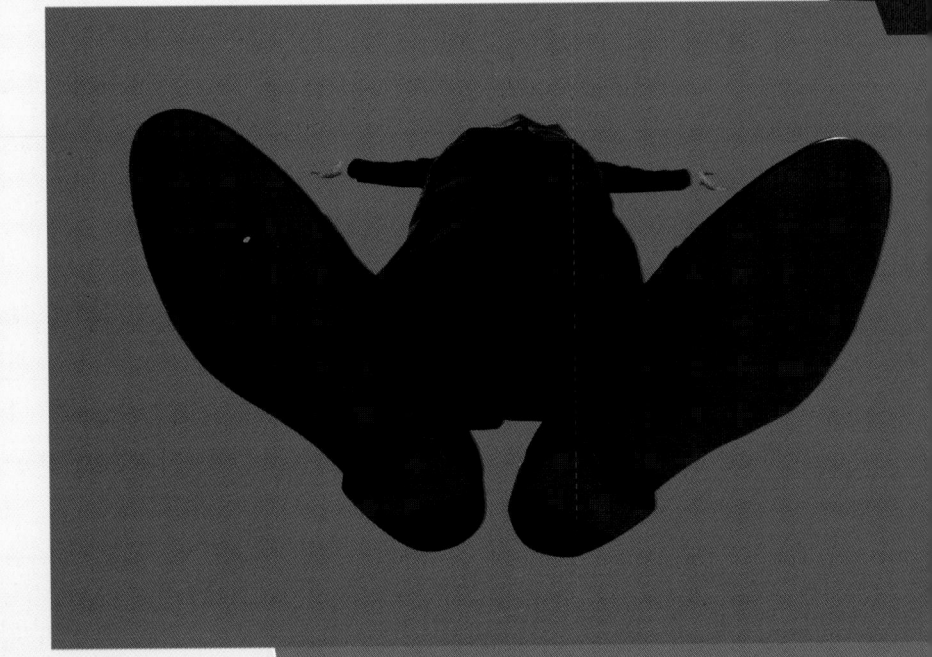

▲ The relationships of the ground plane to the skyscraper's upper levels are crucial.

004

006

▷ **030|031**

033

056

072

088

101

126

138

148

173

180

193

212

218

220

How would landscaping and the provision of communal open spaces appear in the case of the tall building?

Why do we neglect providing these facilities within the upper parts of the skyscraper's built form, and instead place so much dependency on their being provided at the ground or podium levels?

September 11 is a reminder ▽ of the need to provide multiple fire-rated access systems.

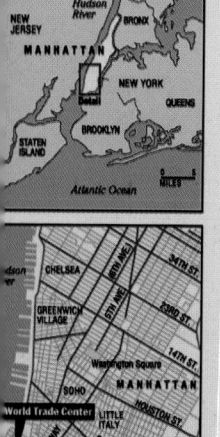

[Source: *The Washington* ▲ *Post*, 2001]

Could not providing them be imposed now as mandatory planning conditions for the skyscraper's upper levels, as happens with other planning conditions that are imposed on all new developments in urban planning? How do we design the provision of multiple accessibility and higher complexity of linkages, which can be favourably compared to the multiplicity and complexity of accessibility at the ground at the upper parts of the skyscraper? Can we create pleasurable boulevards and avenues-in-the-sky?

Premises for a Vertical Theory

Those people and inhabitants unhappy with high-rises, and those others who rail against the high-rise built form, are often those who find their own experiences of life and work in the high-rise unbearable because of the poor comparison with the pleasant or ideal conditions found when inhabiting low- and medium-rise buildings. In this regard the design endeavour to make the high-rise habitable must possess similar ideals and favourable conditions similar to those enjoyed by these people at the ground plane. By re-examining the existing concepts of conventional (horizontal) urban design and planning, and then reapplying these – now reinvented – to new vertical contexts and conditions, we have the vertical superimposition of preferred urban design ideals from the ground plane onto the skyscraper's vertical built form. By doing this, we will find emerging before us the concept of a new skyscraper built form and the development of a new approach to its design. Starting as an urban design endeavour at the onset, skyscrapers can become more humane, more communally focused and more salubriously acceptable and habitable environments for the new denser urban communities within our cities. With this endeavour we will be better prepared to meet the increasing intensification of our cities with a more compatible and urbanistic approach to articulating the conditions essential for a more habitable life-in-the-sky.

20
1:12

17
1:10

13
1:8

10
1:6

6
1:4

3
1:2

The skyscrapers built form is inevitable on sites with land areas of less than 2000 square metres with plot ratios above 1:6 and with site coverage of 65 percent.

... The skyscraper as a possible solution to urban growth and intensification is likely to continue to be perpetuated in great numbers in all the world's major cities. If the size of population is any guide, then living in an urban environment seems to have a greater appeal than residing in the countryside

...

The Tall Building Typology and Cities

| Singapore | Kuala Lumpur | Sydney |

For many who dislike skyscrapers, the prevalent question is why build tall anyway? What is the justification for the skyscraper? Is the tall building the best or the most appropriate built form to accommodate land intensification? Do we really need tall buildings? Could we not achieve the same high density in medium-rise built forms, thus saving our cities from the high-rise scenario?

Our intention is not to advocate the tall building per se, but simply to propose that this built form should be designed and adopted only if it is inevitable. If an alternative, less imposing but fulfilling built form is more suitable we should not consider the tall building in the first instance. It is a built form to be adopted only if there are mitigating conditions and

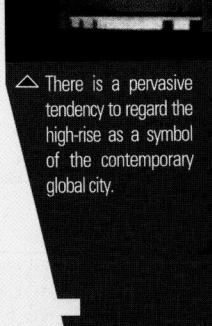

△ There is a pervasive tendency to regard the high-rise as a symbol of the contemporary global city.

004

006

008

034|035

056

072

088

101

126

138

148

173

180

193

212

218

220

The skyscraper built form has proliferated globally giving the impression that it is the inevitable typology for city centres and the indicator of the ultimate in urban achievement.

Hong Kong   New York City

mitigating conditions and reasons that make it inevitable.

In many central city locations the high-rise exists for totally commercial reasons. In such circumstances the high-rise is the result of high land prices. In order to compensate for the high cost of land, the cost needs to be apportioned to as much new built-up space as permitted until the potential income from rental or sales gives a profitable return over the total costs of land, development and finance per square metre of net area.

◁ Cities are dense social zones where a complement of communal facilities and public realm places is crucial. These need to be provided not just at the ground plane and podium levels but also at the other levels in the city's buildings.

The Tall Building Typology and Cities

Nor are we advocating the high-rise built form as the panacea for the spatial problems of urban growth, or as the inevitable consequence of the intensification of land use and urban density. However, it is clear that, unless we have another economically viable physical alternative to this built form (for instance, in the future the digital revolution could well render the skyscraper built form obsolete), the skyscraper as a possible solution to urban growth and intensification is likely to continue to be perpetuated in great numbers in all the world's major cities. If the size of population is any guide, then living in an urban environment seems to have greater appeal than residing in the countryside. The number and size of cities and the rate by which many of them are growing suggest that most people find them highly attractive and acceptable forms of settlement.

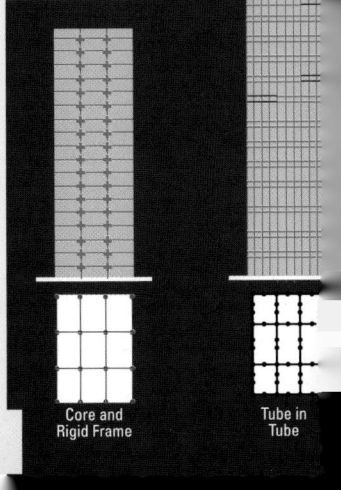

Staggered Truss

Trussed Frame

Suspended

Flat Slab

Belt-Trussed Frame and Framed Core

Interspatial

Core and Rigid Frame

Tube in Tube

004

006

008

▷ 036|037

056

072

088

101

126

138

148

173

180

193

212

218

220

[Parallel]
Bearing Walls

Cores and
Bearing Walls

Boxes
[Self Support]

Cantilevered
Slab

Core and
Rigid Frame

Tube in
Tube

Studies have shown that the resultant built form that results from land intensification need not be the tall building's built form. Early land use and built-form studies (Martin et al, 1967) demonstrate that it is possible to achieve high-density or high land-use plot ratios through using courtyard layout built forms. However, to achieve high-density, medium-rise development using courtyard built forms the land lots must be of sufficient aggregate land area and configuration (ie. squarish) to enable such layouts. If land acquisition does not present itself as a problem in land development, then such built forms should most certainly be considered as possible design solutions. To achieve such layouts, we need land lots of over 2000 square metres. Unfortunately, most land lots in city centres are less than 2000 square metres whereupon, in most instances, the high-rise built form becomes inevitable.

△ Aside from other human-safety factors, the
◁ structural system becomes one of the key constraining factors in articulating the spatial configurations in the high-rise as vertical urban design.
[Source: *High-Rise Building Structures*, Schueller, 1977]

The Tall Building Typology and Cities

One dysfunctional aspect of skyscraper architecture that is found in most buildings is their homogenous regular and repeated floor plates. These, of course, suit most engineers and builders as they make construction simple. The more repetitive elements there are, the lower the cost and the faster the construction. These aspects also make the conventional high-rise layouts attractive to the real estate developer, as they lead to gross design simplifications, high floor-use efficiency and eventually greater profitability.

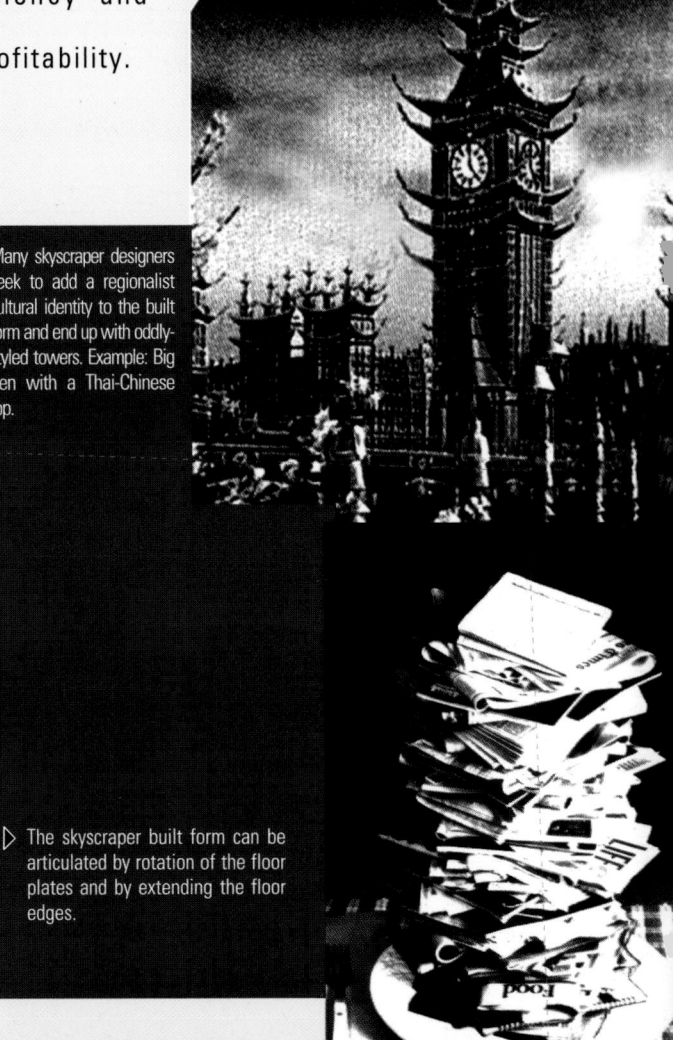

▷ Many skyscraper designers seek to add a regionalist cultural identity to the built form and end up with oddly-styled towers. Example: Big Ben with a Thai-Chinese top.

▷ The skyscraper built form can be articulated by rotation of the floor plates and by extending the floor edges.

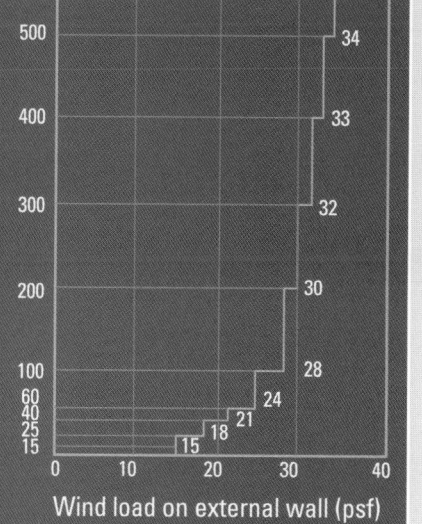

Wind loads are not critical for low-rise buildings but become key constraints in skyscraper design. Minimum wind loads for rectangular buildings in New York state.
[Source: *High-Rise Buildings Structures*, Schueller, 1977]

The torsional effect of wind on the high-rise built form is another constraining factor.
[Source: *High-Rise Buildings Structures*, Schueller, 1977]

Of course it can be argued that post-construction customisation of the homogenous floor plates and the uniformity of their interior spaces can be effected through good interior design, but surely this is seeking to solve the problem after it has been created? We need to reverse the homogenisation or ideological colonisation that has led to this pervasive sense of placeness within the skyscraper, generated by the standardisation and universality of spaces within its internal and transitional spaces. The politics of universalism in design should yield to the politics of differentiation and interdependence, and to the multiple rather than the singular. We need to create a diversity of spaces and internal environments in the high-rise and enable greater opportunities for the colonisation and customisation of its spaces.

004
006
008
▷ 038|039
056
072
088
101
126
138
148
173
180
193
212
218
220

The Tall Building Typology and Cities

It is also projected that our future human experience will become an increasingly urban one. As has been contended, the high-rise's built form (in the current absence of another economically viable alternative) is likely to be with us for some time. If this is the case, it is certainly even more timely that we now radically revise our approach to tall building design.

Research on the demography of urbanisation indicates that the world's urban and rural populations will be generally equal by 2007, and that by 2010 70–80 per cent of the world's population will be living in its cities and urban conglomerations. In such a scenario the tall building may well become the usual built form, not by choice but by default.

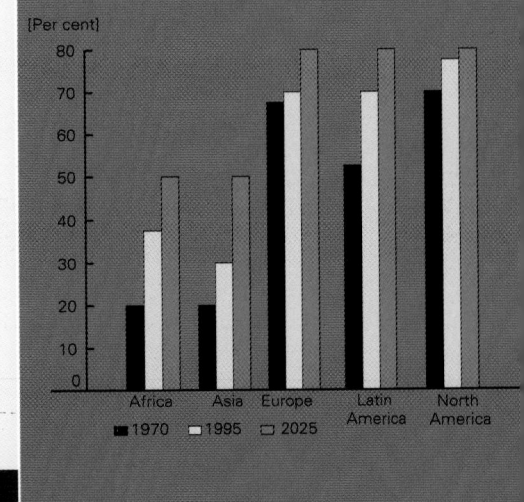

▷ It is expected that by the year 2025 over 80 per cent of the population in Europe and in the Americas willbe living and working in cities. In which case the high-rise may become the inevitable built form by default.
[Source: UN New York, 1995]

004

006

008

▷ 040|041

056

072

088

101

126

138

148

173

180

193

212

218

220

The number of cities with populations above 10 million has already risen from six to 19 in the past 40 years, and will continue to rise. Such 'megacities' include some of the most horrendously overcrowded ones: Lagos, Karachi, Mumbai. Even in cities of fewer than one million inhabitants, these existent urban areas will absorb half of the world's increase in urban population over the next three decades. Despite forebodings that cities' populations will decrease as business can be located anywhere due to the digital economy, it is important to note that, at the millennium's end, the two largest metropolitan regions, New York and Los Angeles, led the USA in aggregate payroll and job creation respectively.

▽ Le Corbusier's vision of Paris with high-rise towers. The contention is that the ground plane is freed for recreation and parks.
[Source: *Design of Cities*, Edmund N Bacon, 1967]

smaller footprint

space for greenery and recreational

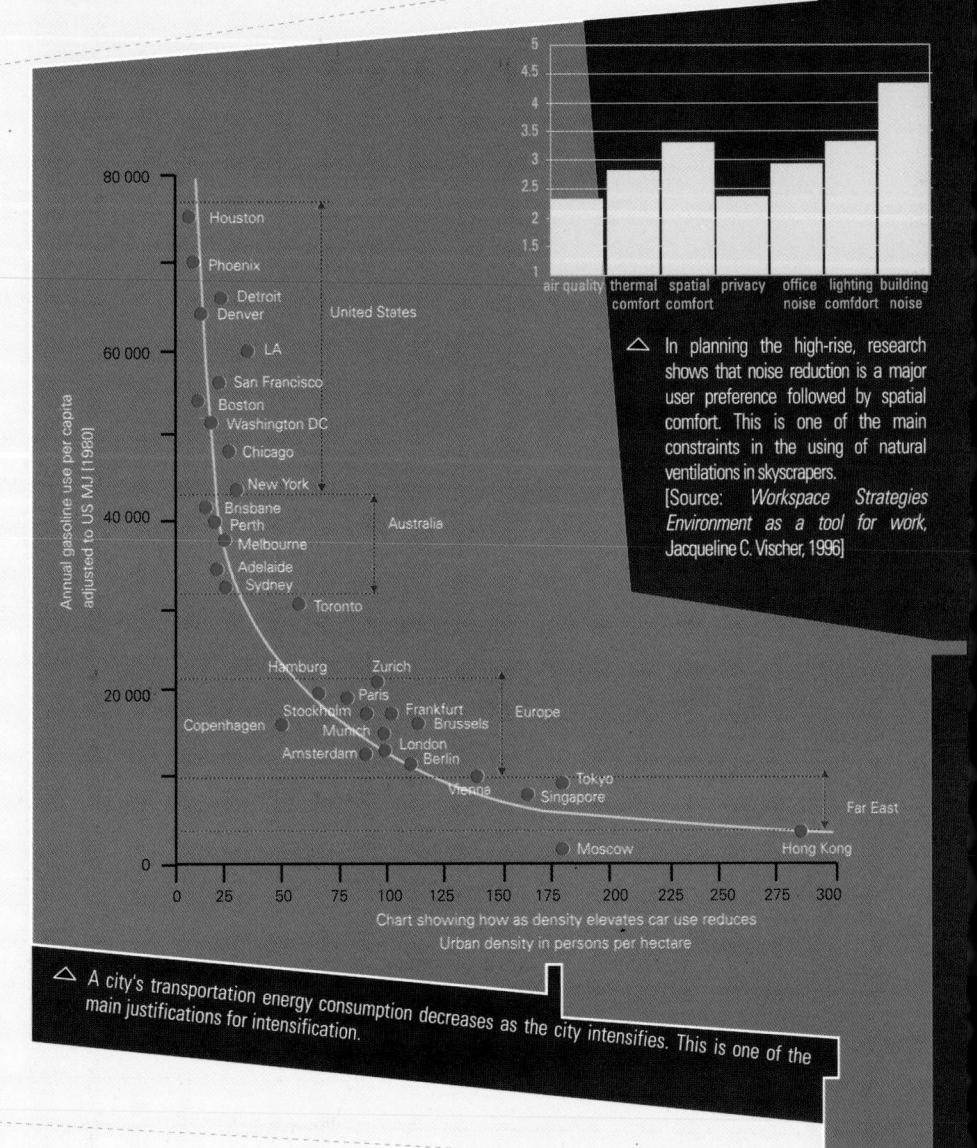

△ In planning the high-rise, research shows that noise reduction is a major user preference followed by spatial comfort. This is one of the main constraints in the using of natural ventilations in skyscrapers.
[Source: *Workspace Strategies Environment as a tool for work*, Jacqueline C. Vischer, 1996]

Chart showing how as density elevates car use reduces
Urban density in persons per hectare

△ A city's transportation energy consumption decreases as the city intensifies. This is one of the main justifications for intensification.

What, then, could be our land-use options to accommodate this huge increase in urban population and to handle the problem of urban growth? All cities grow. Decisions have to be made on when to call a halt. For instance, the 'green belt' around London persists as a mechanism to control sprawl and outward growth. But in order to accommodate growth, a strategy for planning new growth points is required. One solution is to locate these growth the city boundary, as a series of new towns linked by high-speed rail.

Option for accommodating this growth range from expanding the city boundaries to increasing the metropolitan areas. This means opening up more of the peripheral surrounding land for development or, as in the case of London's new towns, building satellite townships around existing urban conurbations which surround the existing city and link them by rapid mass-transit systems. In both these cases, the land-use consequences mean significant building on existing vegetated, forested or arable land located at the peripheries of these cities, and in many instances will involve expensive acquisition of suburban land and increased transportation energy consumption. The countryside can only retain its intrinsic qualities if the city adheres to a more compact form to contain urban sprawl.

004
006
008
042|043
056
072
088
101
126
138
148
173
180
193
212
218
220

	Factor/Issue	Average Petrol Use [US MJ (1980)]	Factor Score	Variation in Factor & Fuel Saving
Intensity densities	Cities with lowest land-use intensity	49 990	25	
	Cities with highest land-use intensity	7 785	169	7 x factor variation / 6 x reduction in fuel
Provide alternatives	Cities least orientated to non-car use	59 455	34	
	Cities most orientated to non-car use	4 215	233	7 x factor variation / 15 x reduction in fuel
Restrain car use	Cities with least restrained traffic	49 732	20	
	Cities with most restrained traffic	12 748	99	5 x factor variation / 4 x reduction in fuel
Urban clustering	Cities with lowest degree of centralisation	53 142	17	
	Cities with highest degree of centralistion	14 736	84	5 x factor variation / 3 x reduction in fuel
Performance public modes	Cities with worst performing public transport systems	66 467	21	
	Cities with best performing public transport systems	10 395	157	7.5 x factor variation / 6 x reduction in fuel

◁ This chart uses data from 32 cities to indicate how fuel use can be reduced in relation to improving five key factors. Note that the chart is factored from real data.
[Source: Newman & Kenworthy, 1989, from their classic study of 32 cities around the world]

The other obvious option is to retain the city's existing limits and boundaries and to intensify development within the city itself, optimising the existing land use within its limits through identifying left over spaces, utilising brown field sites and any other under developed land, and renewing worn-out suburbs. With this latter option, the intensification of development would in most instances mean building more efficiently and building upwards (rather than expanding sideways as would be the case with the other options).

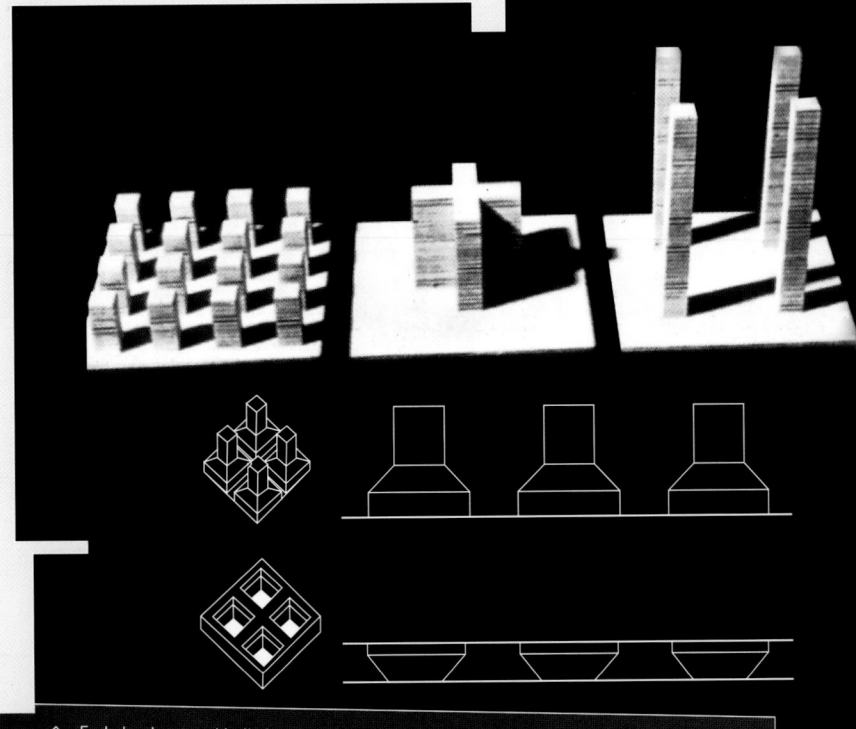

△ Early land use and built form studies by Martin et al [1967] show that high density can be
▷ achieved using courtyard layouts. However subsequent studies (Yeang, 1999) show that
this can only be achieved with land lots larger than 2000 square metres.

044|045

Diagram of the form of the typical American city. The high-rise core (hatched area) is surrounded by a belt of parking lots and highways created during urban renewal (stippled areas) a ring of lost space that segregates downtown from residential neighbourhoods. Similar lost spaces can be found at the upper levels of the city and not just at the ground level. In contrast, the existing skyscraper built form is too compact and has no provision for transitional spaces.
[Source: *Finding Lost Space*, Trancik, 1986]

004
006
008
056
072
088
101
126
138
148
173
180
193
212
218
220

It is the latter solution of intensifying the use of the city's existing land area through optimised land use that is held by many city fathers to be the more viable option. There are, of course, other considerations, such as the constraining thresholds of the city's existing infrastructural systems (physical, economic, social and administrative) which limit the extent of intensification. These in effect constitute its economic and physical limits.

The Tall Building Typology and Cities

Current worldwide interest in the high-rise built form has not abated. Urban areas throughout the world continue to expand upwards. As city authorities and councils evaluate their range of options for meeting the future expansion needs of their communities, they continue to pursue interests towards the skyscraper

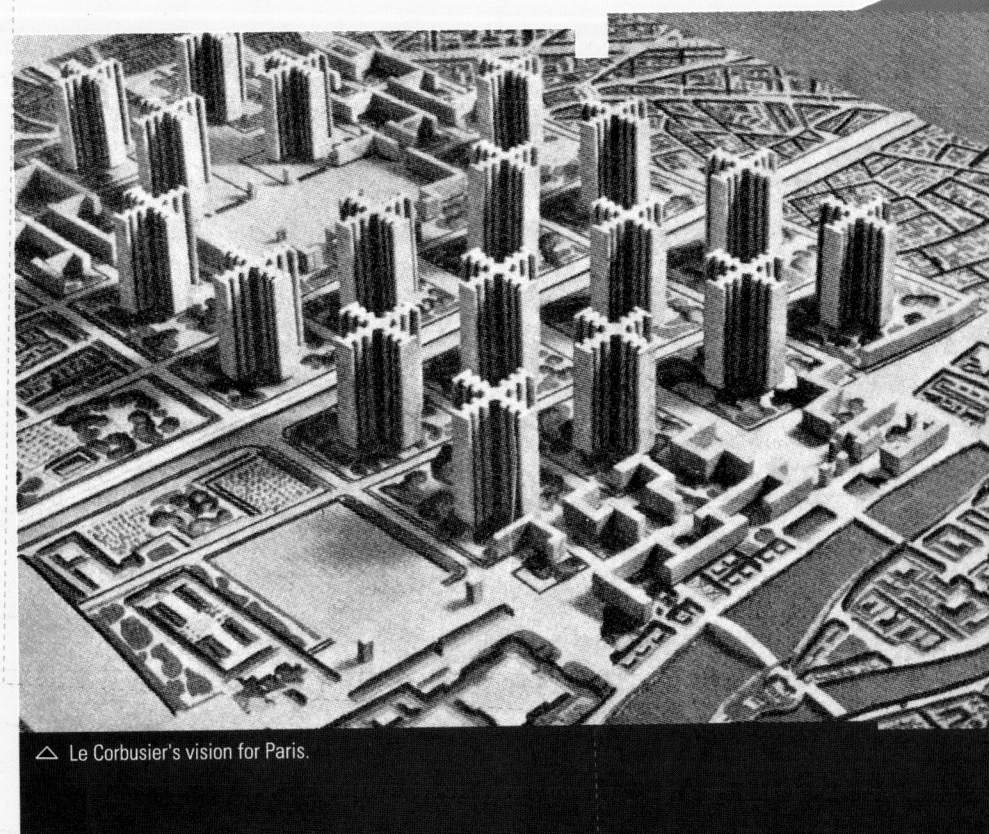

△ Le Corbusier's vision for Paris.

typology or the tall building's built form as the seemingly inevitable solution to urban growth, albeit now with greater concern for security and safety.

Costs per person

All activities
Transport [Private]
Transport [Public]
Education
Rapid Transit
Power

1000   10 000   100 000   1 000 000   10 000 000
Population

004

006

008

046|047

056

072

088

101

126

138

148

173

180

193

212

218

220

There are obviously thresholds to the continued intensification of our cities beyond which their cities' infrastructures become inadequate and overly stressed.

Many people regard the expansion of their cities upwards in order to optimise the city's metropolitan land area as the most viable economic and ecological option. Throughout Europe (for instance, London, Cologne, Frankfurt, Stuttgart, etc), city centre planners are proposing increased intensification of their CBDs (Central Business Districts) and building over their cities' railway lines, but clearly this expansion has to be well managed and relate to the projected built-stock requirements of each individual city's economic growth and built space absorption rates.

Studies have shown that the greater the intensification of urban population, the lower the energy consumption per inhabitant for travel by car. Indeed, there appears to be a geometrical relationship between the reduction of energy consumption through transportation and the increase in building density.

Le Corbusier's Plan Voisin. Paris, 1925.

The Tall Building Typology and Cities

The transportation issue provides a crucial justification for dense building development, for the existence of cities and for intensive urban buildings such as the skyscraper. Furthermore, this lower-energy justification applies not just to horizontal transportation systems but to vertical transportation systems as well. For example, elevators in skyscrapers are estimated to be 40 times more energy efficient and 10 times more materials efficient than an average 1995 automobile (Von Weiszacker et al, 1997, p 94). But it is only when we consider how the building is used, and not just what it is, that these environmental and energy costs become clear. Automobiles consume land in highways, and in feeder roads and parking areas that are entirely dedicated to them. They also consume the majority

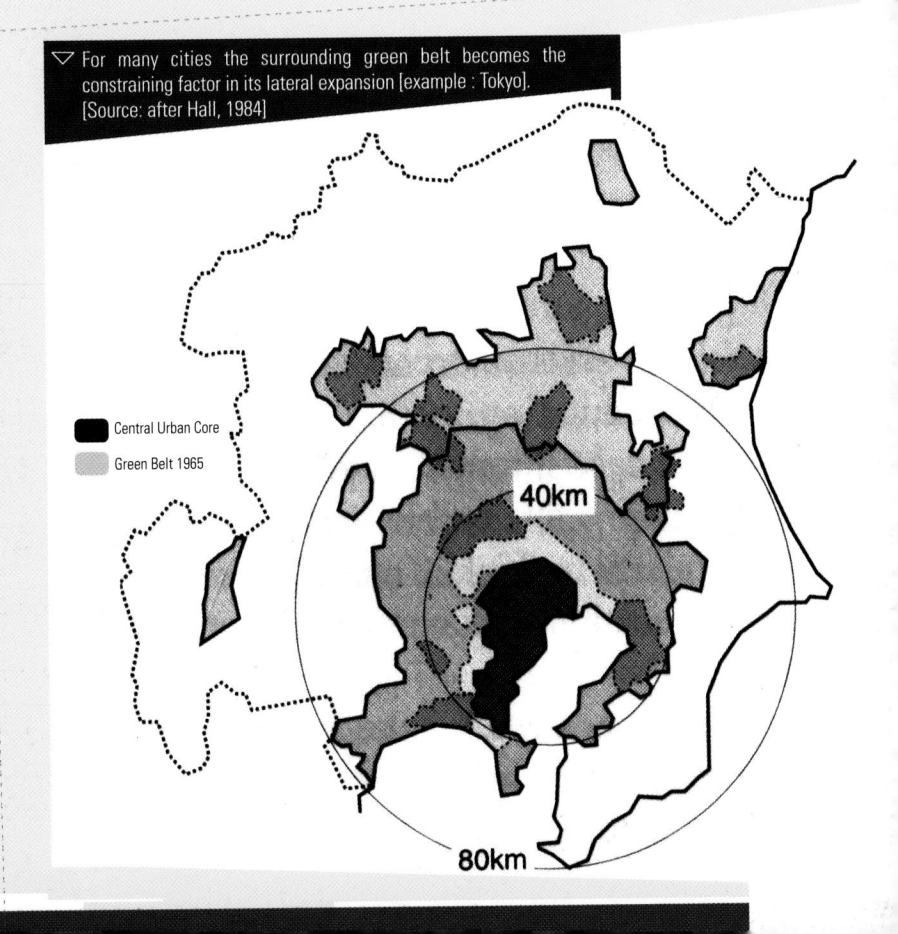

▽ For many cities the surrounding green belt becomes the constraining factor in its lateral expansion [example : Tokyo]. [Source: after Hall, 1984]

Central Urban Core

Green Belt 1965

40km

80km

The constraining Green Belt to the city's lateral growth.

M25

Green Belt

Suburbia

Middle Core

Middle Core

Inner Core

Middle Core

Suburbia

North

Green Belt

The green belt around London.

004

006

008

▷ 048|049

056

072

088

101

126

138

148

173

180

193

212

218

220

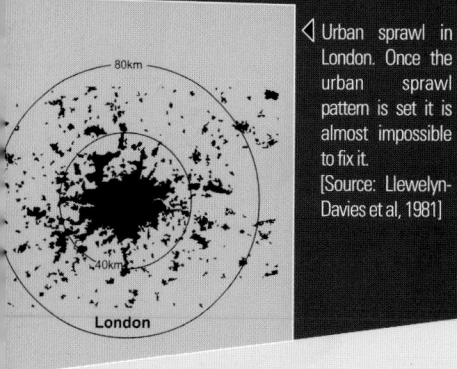

80km

40km

London

◁ Urban sprawl in London. Once the urban sprawl pattern is set it is almost impossible to fix it. [Source: Llewelyn-Davies et al, 1981]

of the street space that was originally given to pedestrians. Of urbanised land, 25–35 per cent is given to streets and roads, and another significant percentage is given to inter urban travel. For every car that leaves for work, the area needed for parking equals the footprint of an average house.

The intensification of cities as compact urban centres means an increase in built area and residential population densities; an intensification of the urban economic, social and cultural activities; and the management of urban size, form and structure and settlement systems in pursuit of the environmental, social and sustainability benefits derived from the concentration of urban functions. Urban compaction enables residential uses to be located within, or close to, the central areas and allows residents easy access to the various urban facilities and amenities.

The Tall Building Typology and Cities

Most urban centres with a strong historical core are likely to survive and to grow in the future. They will continue to be where businesses want to locate their headquarters and where face-to-face contact remains a deciding factor. It is unlikely that even the most sophisticated video-conferencing systems will replace this. The traditional core area will have the capability of offering a rich variety of supporting elements – shops, cultural activities, restaurants and hotels – which cannot be found elsewhere in a defined area, and increasingly in the future more people will choose to live there as the quality of the environment improves.

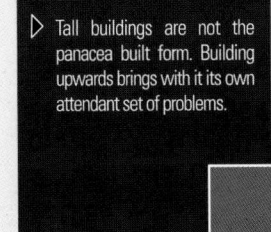

▷ Tall buildings are not the panacea built form. Building upwards brings with it its own attendant set of problems.

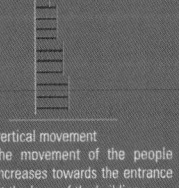

torsion and wind forsec
Wind forces twist the tower. The torsion is greatest at the base where the tower is restrained, reducing with height.

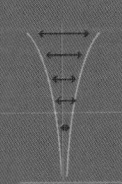

vertical movement
the movement of the people increases towards the entrance at the base of the building.

horizontal sway
as the wind passes around the tower the pressure disbalance causes the tower to sway.

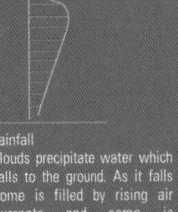

rainfall
clouds precipitate water which falls to the ground. As it falls some is filled by rising air currents and some is evaporated so that its intensity is reduced.

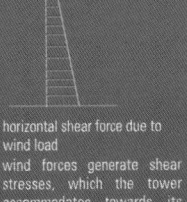

concentration of pollution
the main sources of pollutants are from vehicles and industry. Vehicles deposit more pollutants at ground level, whereas industry deposits it at high level.

horizontal shear force due to wind load
wind forces generate shear stresses, which the tower accommodates towards its base where the shear forces are the greatest.

horizontal direction
as the wind hits the tower it deflects. The greatest deflection is the furthest point from the supports at the ground.

ground noise
street noise for example, is less noticeable beyond five storeys.

004
006
008
050|051
056
072
088
101
126
138
148
173
180
193
212
218
220

nal changes

wind velocity
the friction of the earth's
surface and building landscape
reduce airflow

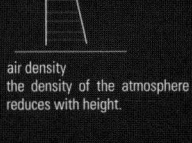

ty
ty varies throughout the
owever it is the greatest
und level and within cloud

air density
the density of the atmosphere
reduces with height.

e predictability
e is a compiled
tion of the atmospheric
of radiation, air-
ent and atmospheric
e. Near the sun's face,
climatic forces become
fluential and the global
tanding become less
able.

views
surrounding buildings at low
level obstruct views. At higher
level cloud cover will also
reduce visibility.

air pressure
as the density decreases with
height, so does its air pressure

perature
mperature drops with

elocity
ction of the earth's
and building landscape
irflow

bending stresses due to
horizontal wind loads
wind bend twist the tower. The
bending stresses are the
greatest at the base where the
tower is strained, reducing with
height.

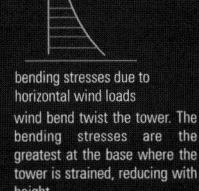

iation
un's rays pass through
osphere its energy is
However, as it hits the
evel it is reflected,
ing radiation towards
r at lower levels.

speed of climatic change
the ground provides a source of
thermal inertia, moderating
sudden climatic variations.

The costs of office space in ▷ these central areas will be high and ultimately, as land becomes scarce, more new developments utilising air-rights are likely over railway land where the stations provide good access. High-rise development will put pressure on the need for good-quality access by public transport, with a lessening demand for car access as traffic congestion rises. The design of the movement systems will have to give direct access from subway platforms to offices above. This stresses the importance of siting high-rise offices and residences adjacent to subway stations.

The Tall Building Typology and Cities

Together with the growth of offices in the core area will come the need for more residential apartments within walking distance. In order to survive, future city centres must house more people in the common areas. This will help reduce pressure on the transport system and give life to the centres, particularly at night. There is a real need for affordable living space for 'dinkies' (dual income, no kids) who prefer the buzz of a city rather than the peace of a suburb. Developers now want to combine office development with other uses, such as hotels and apartments, with shops and restaurants at ground level, previously never considered economic.

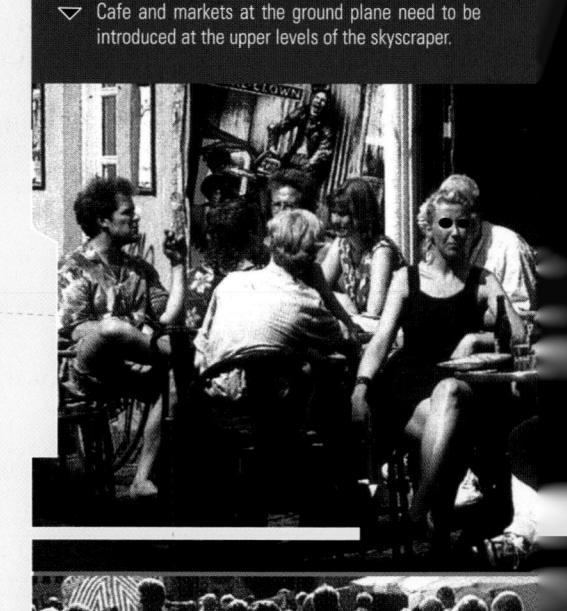

▽ Cafe and markets at the ground plane need to be introduced at the upper levels of the skyscraper.

△ Office-apartment-workshop in the high-rise residential skyscraper.
[Source: *Benkei in New York*, Jinpachi Mori & Jiro Taniguchi, 1996]

004

006

008

▷ **052|053**

056

072

088

101

126

138

148

173

180

193

212

218

220

There is now a realisation that the environment at street level is important, and has an effect on the value of the properties, and that traffic must be tamed.

Future city centres must therefore be planned for a much greater mix of use than existed in the past. Electronic technology is unlikely to make them obsolete. With more people working from home several days a week, offices in the centres will be not only places for their 'hot desk', but somewhere where they will meet their fellow workers – if only to compare notes and socialise.

◁ Office-apartment-den. Working from the high-rise home.
[Source : *Frame*, Jan/Feb 2002]

The Tall Building Typology and Cities

As a building type, the skyscraper's built form exists as a consequence of high land prices and economically optimised land use. These commercial considerations engender in the skyscraper other roles, such as its symbolic role in signaleing the city's contemporary technological superiority, its maturity, its economic and geographical control over its hinterland.

Will the demolition of the two World Trade Center towers in New York on 11 September 2001 affect the future of the high-rise built form? The contention here is that it will not. It is likely that high-rise buildings will continue to be built, but perhaps the super tall ones (ie. over 60 storeys) will be curtailed. Future skyscrapers will continue to be built, but with more stringent safety and security features.

▷ Downtown New York. The towers are disparate and connected only at the ground plane.

004

006

008

▷ 054|055

056

072

088

101

126

138

148

173

180

193

212

218

220

0 - 19.9	△ Predicted percentage of urban
20 - 39.9	population in 2025.
40 - 59.9	
60 - 79.9	
80 - 100	

▽ The Kuala Lumpur twin towers with a mid level connecting bridge. Further upper-level linkages will enhance accessibility opportunities for the towers' inhabitants.

As the skyscraper typology is likely to remain with us for some time, what we need is a critical rethinking of its built configuration, its planning and its design in a way that better responds to its intensity and to the urbanistic needs of its inhabitants.

... Current skyscraper buildings consist of a series of chopped-up compartmentalised spaces, vertically stuck back together ...

... These internal spaces are rigidly stratified and totally contained, some even with unopenable windows ...

Decompartmentalising the Skyscraper's Built Form

We might start by looking at the spaces within the skyscraper's built form. Current skyscraper buildings consist of a series of chopped-up compartmentalised spaces, vertically stuck back together. These internal spaces are rigidly stratified and totally contained, some even with

△ Unfortunately most skyscrapers, whether residential or office, treat their inhabitants as items for shelving. Occupants are placed in tidy cellular compartments or at regimented workstations.

unopenable windows. The simple fact is that most skyscrapers today are essentially nothing more than vertical piles of identical regular compartmentalised internal spaces that are straitjacketed as neatly gridded series of vertically stratified containers.

▷ The typical skyscraper floor can be spliced and linked by bridges to provide spatial variations in moving from one zone to another. Example: National Library, Singapore.
[© T. R. Hamzah & Yeang, 2002]

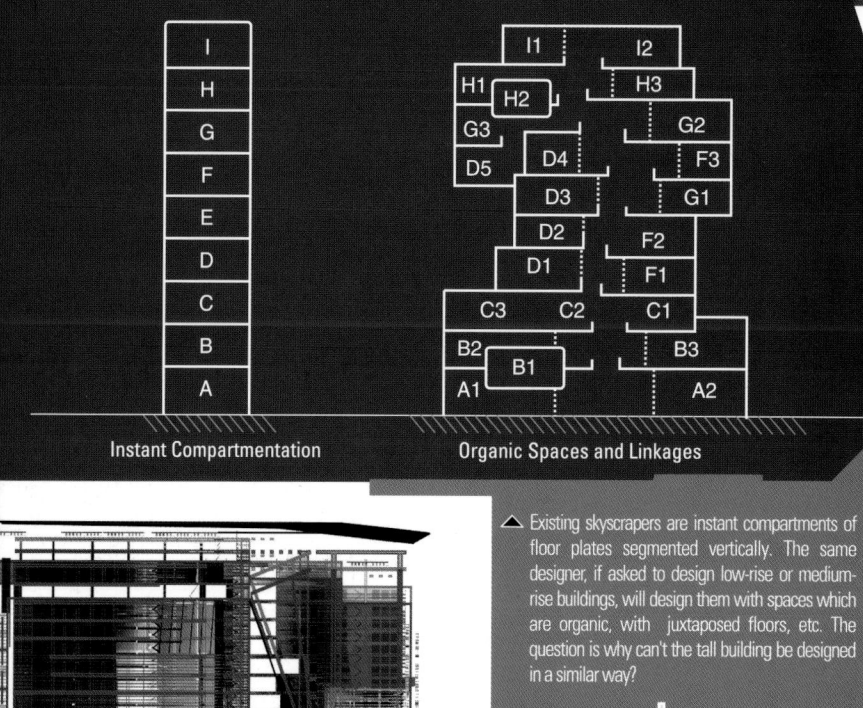

Instant Compartmentation	Organic Spaces and Linkages

004

006

008

033

▷ 058|059

072

088

101

126

138

148

173

180

193

212

218

220

△ Existing skyscrapers are instant compartments of floor plates segmented vertically. The same designer, if asked to design low-rise or medium-rise buildings, will design them with spaces which are organic, with juxtaposed floors, etc. The question is why can't the tall building be designed in a similar way?

◁ The creation of organic spaces within the high-rise built form.

What we have today in these tall buildings is an instant condition of spatial segregation. For instance, all their floor plates are spatially noncontiguous and are physically segmented-off one from the other. Their spaces are no longer linked or interactive, but are isolated, homogeneous enclaves devoid of the diversity and richness of life that exists at the ground plane. This isolation exacerbates feelings of social alienation in its inhabitants. The desire for engineering expediency in the skyscraper's design and construction has undermined the potential for the diversity and richness of urban life in the building. It is this compartmentalisation and confinement of spaces that make the skyscraper such an unsatisfactory built form and unpleasant environment for its users.

Decompartmentalising the Skyscraper's Built Form

These spaces become zones of containment, spaces without any physical context other than through the views from the windows. Many workers in commercial offices live in a totally artificially controlled environment. In some, because of their floor layouts, a large number of the inhabitants do not even have a window to look out of or to receive daylight through.

△ Solutions to provide sky courts in the skyscraper as potential expansion zones and opportunities for inhabitants to have contact with the outside environment. Reference: Menara Mesiniaga, Subang Jaya, Malaysia [© T. R. Hamzah & Yeang, 1992]

In current urban design conditions we find that the motorcar's impact on the city is similar to that of the elevators on the high-rise. In both instances, we end up with built spaces that have little or no relationship to each other. In the case of the high-rise, the spaces are connected only through the fire-compartmentalised staircases and the elevators.

An atrium can be inserted between floors to vertically decompartmentalise the high-rise.

Example:
National Library, Singapore.
[© T. R. Hamzah & Yeang]

How do inhabitants in the high-rise move from one floor (compartment) to another? They can walk upwards (or downwards, as the case maybe) using the main or escape staircases; and this can be tiresome after several floors. Most commonly they enter the common space called the 'elevator lobby'. They then press a button (designated up or down) and, magically, a metal cabin (the elevator car) appears with opening double doors. Next, the skyscraper's inhabitants step in, press another button to indicate the selection of their next destination and the doors close, further isolating them. In most instances this metal cabin (the elevator car) travels in a windowless, artificial, claustrophobic condition and, like a mini subway carriage, along tracks (albeit not horizontally, but vertically upwards or downwards) within its confining shaft to reach that desired next destination and compartment. The journey is a totally disjointing and disorientating experience devoid of any spatial continuity. At least all subway trains in the cities have windows so the passengers can see the walls of the subway tunnels.

▷ 060|061

072
088
101
126
138
148
173
180
193
212
218
220

Decompartmentalising the Skyscraper's Built Form

This mechanistic (and strange, to those unfamiliar with it) way of travelling from one space to another is in sharp contrast to our ability to move virtually freely through spaces horizontally when we are at or nearer the ground. At ground zero the spaces are certainly not so rigidly compartmentalised. In most instances there is a physical and visual contiguity of space from one area to another, generally multidirectionally free, and maybe even flowing in an orderly progression as in the case of any well-planned urban precinct. It is these conditions at the ground that we should now design into the skyscraper.

We find that, in stark contrast to the inhabitants of skyscrapers, the occupants of low- and medium-rise buildings are able to move about freely through their spaces without the need for elevators, and without the rigid compartmentalisation or with, at least, a minimal sense of spatial segregation.

▽ We could make greater use of escalators on the upper floors of skyscrapers for interfloor accessibility. They provide visual linkages absent in the case of elevators.

△ Addition of internal secondary staircases provide a sense of spatial continuity between floors.

We find that the movements between spaces and floors in most low- and medium-rise buildings are in most instances by visually evident routes: by passageways or bridges, or stairs or even ramps.

004

006

008

033

▷ 062|063

072

088

101

126

138

148

173

180

193

212

218

220

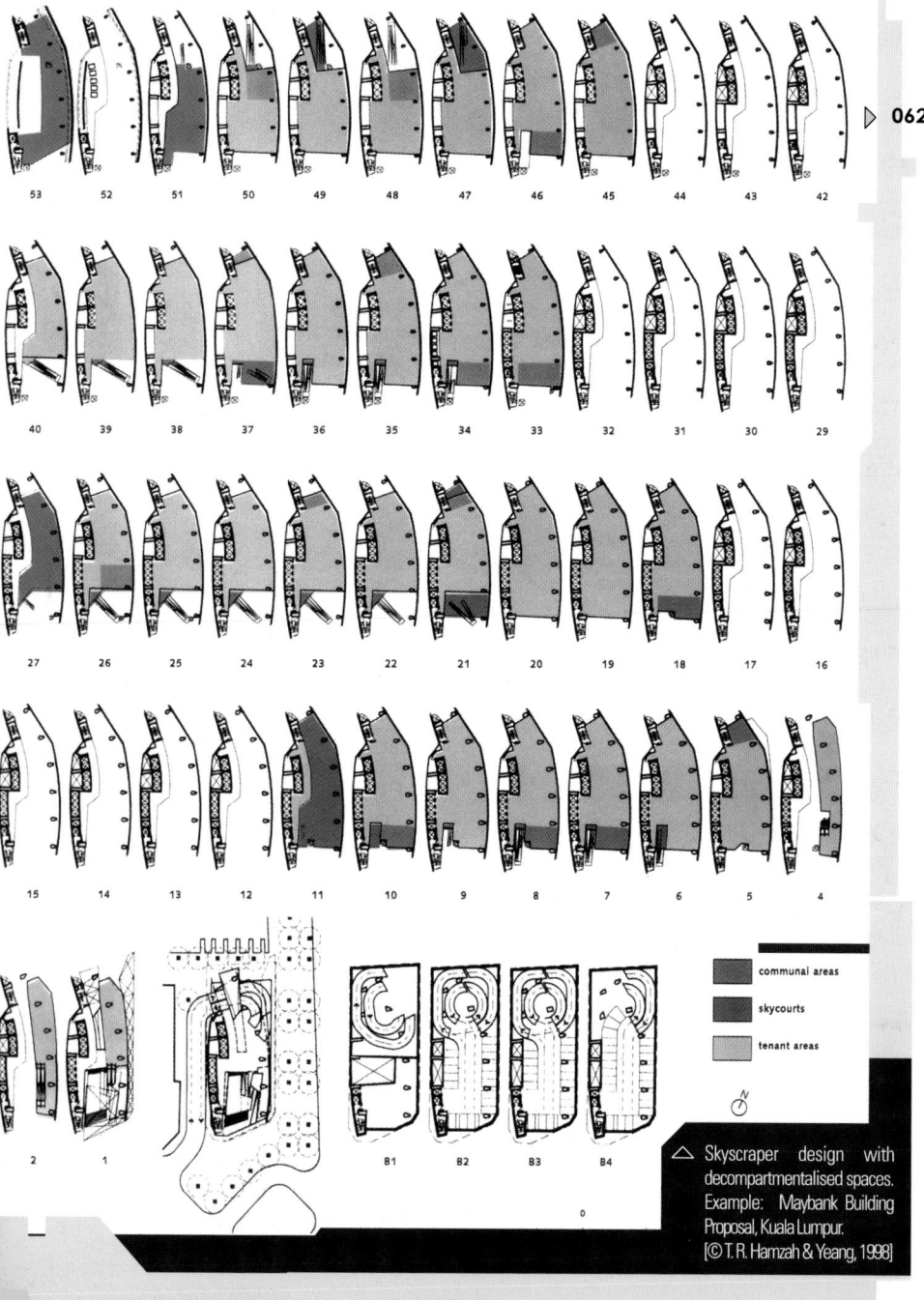

▨	communal areas
▨	skycourts
▨	tenant areas

△ Skyscraper design with decompartmentalised spaces. Example: Maybank Building Proposal, Kuala Lumpur. [© T. R. Hamzah & Yeang, 1998]

Such multiplicity of accessibility (and, generally, often good visual coherence and way-finding) are either nonxexistent or restrictive in the case of the high-rise.

Decompartmentalising the Skyscraper's Built Form

In many low-rise and medium-rise buildings there will very often also be transitional spaces (eg, atriums) to enable users to experience a contiguous organic spatial relationship between the variety of spaces. Users in these conditions also enjoy a greater and freer sense of access as they are generally able to move more easily through one space to another, whether through open stairs, ramps, bridges or corridors. As fire-protection conditions in low-rise and medium-rise buildings are less stringent, the stairs and passageways are not often fire compartmentalised.

We find such openness in multilinkages, and multichoices in accessibility to be generally nonexistent in most high-rises.

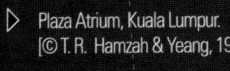

▷ Plaza Atrium, Kuala Lumpur.
[© T. R. Hamzah & Yeang, 1985]

Instead, what we have is a condition of access that is dictated by the main banks of elevator cores, by a fire-compartmentalised main staircase and by escape stairs. The experiences of movement are thus limited, often noncontiguous, visually segmented vertically and unpleasant; and there is the ▷ **064|065** mechanistic compartmentalised experience of travelling between floors in the elevator cars.

We also find that, in great contrast to the conditions in most skyscrapers, the inhabitants of low- or medium-rise buildings (unless, of course, they are in prison or some similarly spatially confining buildings where segregation is necessitated by its internal function), enjoy a considerably greater spatial freedom between internal spaces, and freer opportunities for traversing from internal to external spaces, which is generally much more pleasant. The designer will generally find that it is at these transitional sites within buildings and at their edges (such as circulation routes, passageways, staircases, stairwells, lobbies, public reception areas, etc) that design opportunities can be found to create novel spatial experiences for the building's users. It is in these parts of the high-rise that we need to find opportunities to reconstruct its built form.

Example of faceting the transitional spaces at the facade and intergrating these with photovoltaic panels and vegetated floors. Reference: EDITT Tower, Singapore.
[© T. R. Hamzah & Yeang Sdn. Bhd]

072

088

101

126

138

148

173

180

193

212

218

220

Decompartmentalising the Skyscraper's Built Form

Of course, the question that is posed is whether we can design tall buildings in a similar way that is as structurally and economically justifiable and as spatially exciting as the design of low- and medium-rise buildings. Can we design tall buildings to have the same level of visual and spatial connectivities and complexities with unique articulation of transitional spaces- to be spatially organic environments with the greater contiguity and other spatially stimulating internal environments that we would find in most low- and medium-rise buildings? Can we design the skyscraper as an urban design with the accompanying creation of urban spaces-in-the-sky?

The internal spaces can be installed as colonised spaces and inserted pods within the framework of the building envelope. Reference: MCA Building Renovation, Kuala Lumpur.
[© T. R. Hamzah & Yeang, 2001]

The answer must be a resounding yes, of course we can, but many designers do not do it, simply because of an inhibiting perception of past conventions that dictate that they must not do so. Designers need to step out of this self-imposed conceptual box.

Within the high-rise built form we need to reconsider its internal and external spaces and their borders and edges. By intentionally designing to blur and dissect the borders and edges, and boundaries between these spaces, we can create pleasurable crossings across the spatial borders as one of the decompartmentalise ways to the rigid stratification of the conventional high-rise. The intention is to derive a less spatially – confining skyscraper architecture.

◁ An example of decompartmentalising the skyscraper built form. Reference: BATC, Kuala Lumpur.
[© T. R. Hamzah & Yeang, 1997]

004
006
008
033
072
088
101
126
138
148
173
180
193
212
218
220

We might regard the design of the skyscraper's currently vertically segmented floors now as 'folded spaces', to deny the very idea of framing and rigid compartmentalising in favour of a temporal modulation. The idea of spatial folding in the high-rise's internal and transitional spaces holds out the promise of generating field organisations within its built form that can both negotiate between the constricting tyranny of the vertical grid (existent by virtue of the high-rise built form), and depart from the hierarchical heterogeneity of finite geometrical patterns of plan and section.

△ The inclusion of 'in-between' spaces at the upper levels of the residential skyscraper.
Reference : MBF Tower, Penang.
[© T. R. Hamzah & Yeang, 1990]

MBF Tower, Penang.
[© T. R. Hamzah & Yeang, 1990]

004

006

008

033

▷ **068|069**

072

088

101

126

138

148

173

180

193

212

218

220

The endeavour enables the creation of more flexible, and more unpredictable, local connections within the high-rise's built form is therefore enabled.

The spatial transitions within the skyscraper's built form might be designed to be capable of spatially 'bending' rather than 'breaking' and 'separating'. Designing the spaces to break away from the existent segmented compartments within its built form can also be achieved, by inserting secondary spaces and by organically linking the vertically stacked spaces. In doing so, we will find that within the borders and in the junctions between the spaces there exist design opportunities for creative cultural production and refutation of the traditional high-rise pristine form.

Decompartmentalising the Skyscraper's Built Form

The avoidance of compartmentalisation can also be achieved by having internal or transitional spatial volumes (such as atriums), with the other internal spaces volumetrically connected to it, spatially, visually and organically. Another way is to have half-floors, split-level floors or secondary spaces inserted between floors, spaces that are juxtaposed or spaces that are detached and connected by bridges and ramps.

The stepped or set-back section and the inverted set-back profile could also be used to break down the regularity of the form.

The vertical slab.

The flat slab/shed

△ The homogeneous slab, whether
▷ vertical in the skyscraper built form
or horizontal as a flat slab built form
remains monolithic.

All these enable us to break away from the tyranny of the horizontal stratification and enable new concepts for internal environments that would more greatly resemble the spatial and other conditions pleasurably experienced at the ground plane. We therefore need to depart from the current inhibiting state of spatial compartmentalisation. What is clear is that we need a high-rise design with greater spatial and environmental diversity for its occupants, one that better resembles the high level of spatial and environmental contiguity and diversity existent in the more familiar habitable conditions that we find at the ground.

Spatial articulation within floors.

Articulation of lower floors and linkages.

△
▷ The spatial diversification of built form in low-rise and medium-rise buildings in the city can be recreated vertically within the skyscraper built form.

004
006
008
033
▷ 070|071
072
088
101
126
138
148
173
180
193
212
218
220

... Current theories of urban design and planning have perhaps not anticipated the implosion of high-rise construction and the sudden huge intensification of our cities ...

004

006

008

033

056

▷ **072|073**

088

101

126

138

148

173

180

193

212

218

220

... Fundamentally, their inadequacy lies in their not regarding skyscrapers as high-rise precincts within the city, or as high-rise suburbs within the city, but simply as just another built form as one building typology out of many in the morphology of the built environment ...

△ Vertical urban design might be regarded as designing within a three-dimensional matrix.

It is clear that current urban design and planning strategies are inadequate to deal with urban precincts of significantly high density and intensity within today's cities. Their concepts tend to be outdated propositions that were adopted when the city's precincts were essentially still sites of low plot ratios and low densities. They remain in sharp contrast to what is prevalent today.

Current theories of urban design and planning have perhaps not anticipated the implosion of high-rise construction and the sudden huge intensification of our cities. Fundamentally, their inadequacy lies in their not regarding skyscrapers as high-rise precincts within the city, or as high-rise suburbs within the city, but simply as just another built form; as one building typology out of many in the morphology of the built environment. In many of today's significantly denser CBDs and other precincts in the major cities in the world the new and plot ratios and residential densities make traditional urban design and planning concepts totally outmoded and invalid.

For instance, current floor area to plot ratios in some of the major cities in the world are above 1:12, and the residential densities are in excess of 400 persons per acre. With such high intensities, the planning area becomes no longer the land area for the development but the entire built-up area and the volume of potentially buildable vertical space above it. Under such conditions urban design now should be reconsidered as a form of high-rise, three-dimensional planning and design. Here, we are no longer planning on a flattened ground plane resulting in a two-dimensional urban design land-use plan with the towers as extrusions at selected locations.

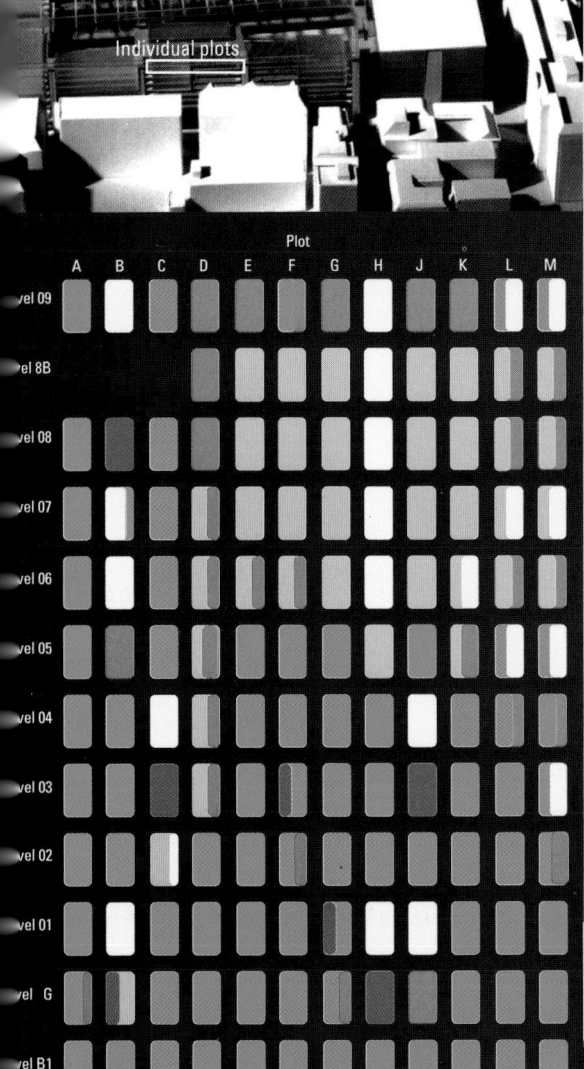

Individual plots

Plot

△ The land-use mapping of the high-rise can be in the form of a three-dimensional matrix. Reference: Marsham Street development, London.
[© TR Hamzah & Yeang, 1996]

Legend
Retail Residential Office Office Space

004
006
008
033
056
▷ 074|075
088
101
126
138
148
173
180
193
212
218
220

Urban Design Framework and Vertical Land-Use Mapping

We are now designing and planning within a three-dimensional high-rise spatial matrix, as a framework that contains the key urban design principles in a vertical form of land-use planning which is vertically located over the precinct. This framework consists of vertically occupied as well as potentially occupiable spaces. Urban places and connectivities at such dense locations within our cities, and in effect the entire urban design and planning of these high-intensity locations, now have to be conceived within a three-dimensional context.

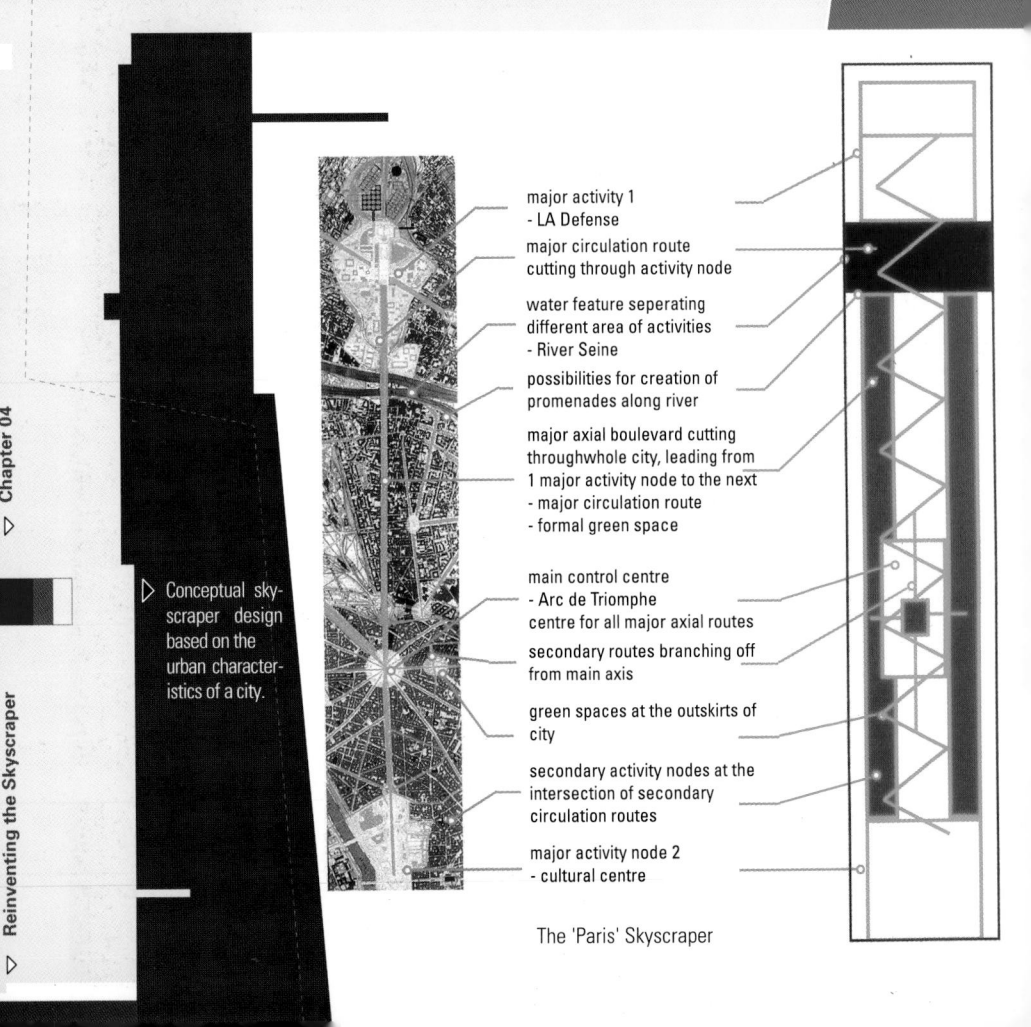

▷ Conceptual skyscraper design based on the urban characteristics of a city.

major activity 1
- LA Defense

major circulation route cutting through activity node

water feature seperating different area of activities
- River Seine

possibilities for creation of promenades along river

major axial boulevard cutting throughwhole city, leading from 1 major activity node to the next
- major circulation route
- formal green space

main control centre
- Arc de Triomphe
centre for all major axial routes

secondary routes branching off from main axis

green spaces at the outskirts of city

secondary activity nodes at the intersection of secondary circulation routes

major activity node 2
- cultural centre

The 'Paris' Skyscraper

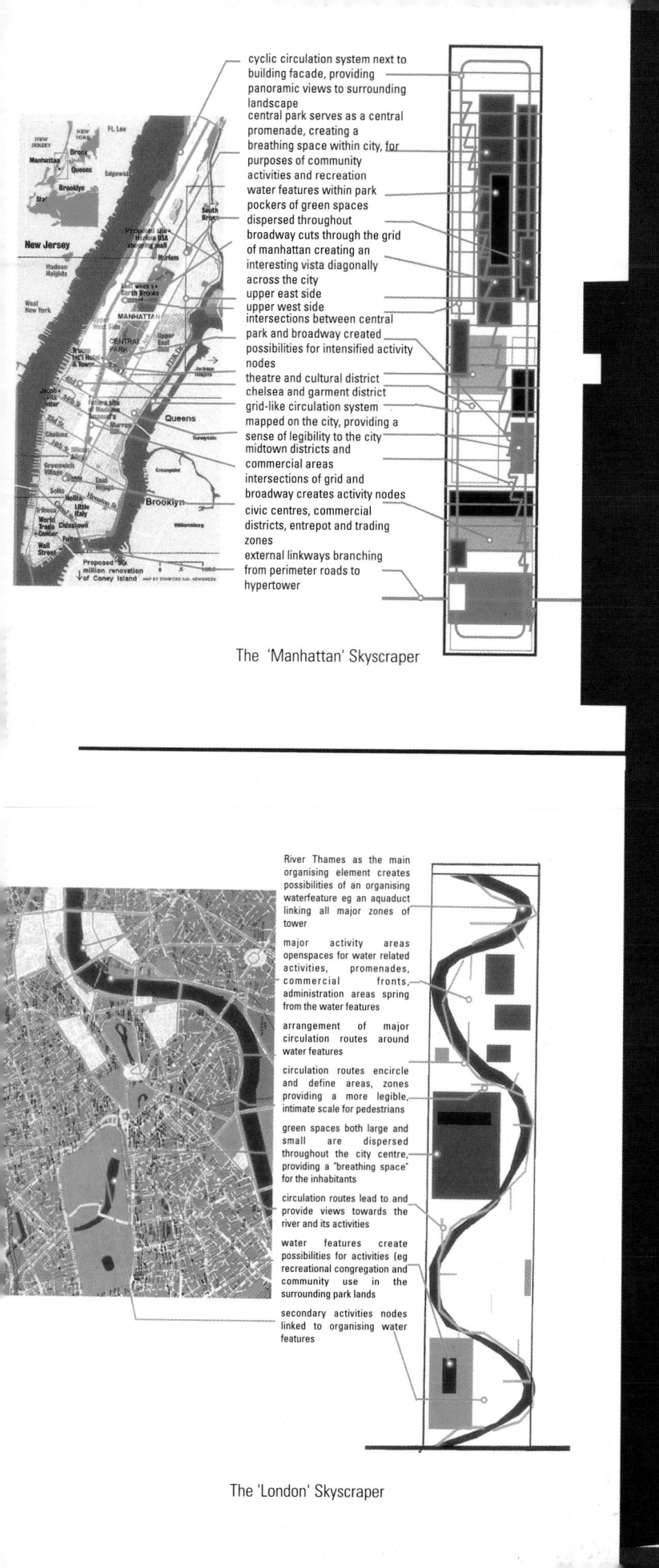

cyclic circulation system next to building facade, providing panoramic views to surrounding landscape

central park serves as a central promenade, creating a breathing space within city, for purposes of community activities and recreation

water features within park

pockers of green spaces dispersed throughout

broadway cuts through the grid of manhattan creating an interesting vista diagonally across the city

upper east side

upper west side

intersections between central park and broadway created possibilities for intensified activity nodes

theatre and cultural district

chelsea and garment district

grid-like circulation system mapped on the city, providing a sense of legibility to the city

midtown districts and commercial areas

intersections of grid and broadway creates activity nodes

civic centres, commercial districts, entrepot and trading zones

external linkways branching from perimeter roads to hypertower

The 'Manhattan' Skyscraper

River Thames as the main organising element creates possibilities of an organising waterfeature eg an aquaduct linking all major zones of tower

major activity areas openspaces for water related activities, promenades, commercial fronts, administration areas spring from the water features

arrangement of major circulation routes around water features

circulation routes encircle and define areas, zones providing a more legible, intimate scale for pedestrians

green spaces both large and small are dispersed throughout the city centre, providing a "breathing space" for the inhabitants

circulation routes lead to and provide views towards the river and its activities

water features create possibilities for activities (eg recreational congregation and community use in the surrounding park lands

secondary activities nodes linked to organising water features

The 'London' Skyscraper

004
006
008
033
056
▶ 076|077
088
101
126
138
148
173
180
193
212
218
220

Urban Design Framework and Vertical Land-Use Mapping

We might contend that urban space, whether in the high-rise or at the ground, is turned into 'place' through our acts of discursive representation. Generic space is turned into the particularities of place through our acts of description and evaluation. The conventions of forms of urban representation include the naming of cities, the mapping of urban areas, written and spoken descriptions, and so on. Such systems of representation are discourses of meaning which include whole sets of ideas, words, concepts and practices and in this instance, a new concept of vertical urban design in a three-dimensional framework.

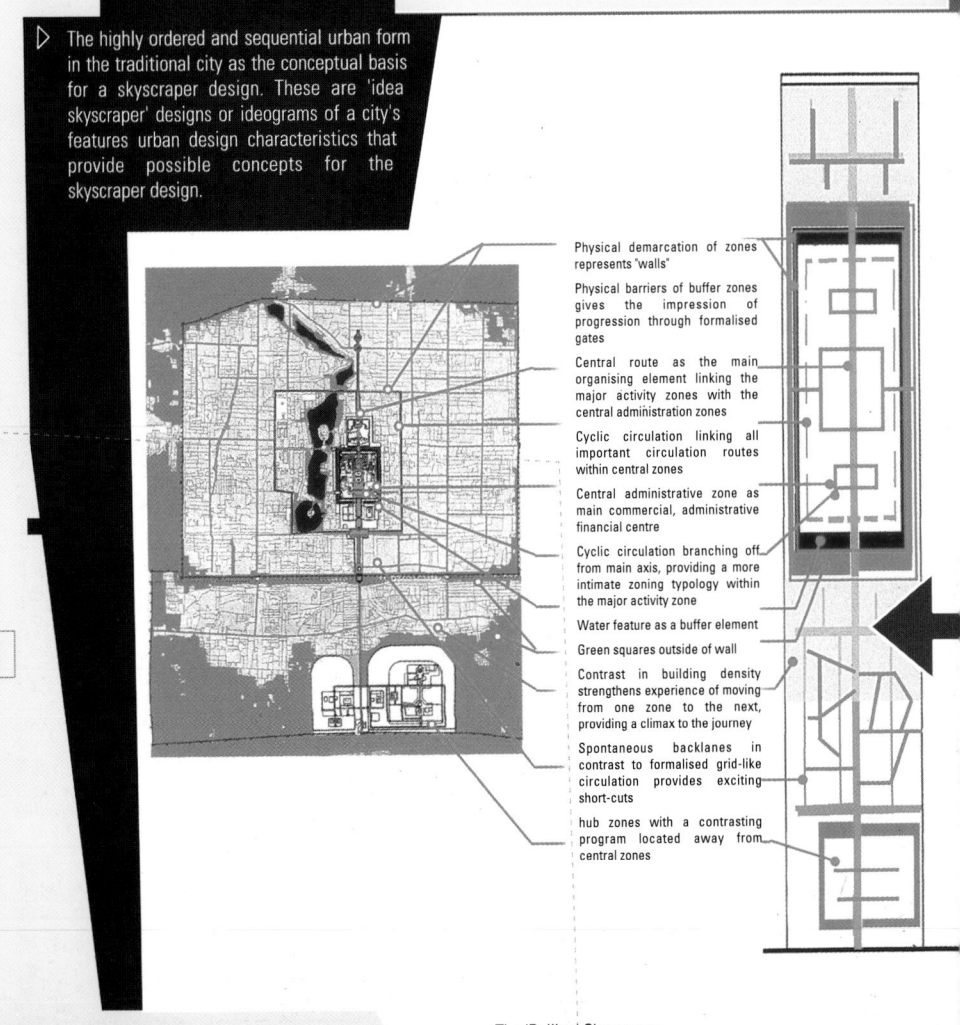

▷ The highly ordered and sequential urban form in the traditional city as the conceptual basis for a skyscraper design. These are 'idea skyscraper' designs or ideograms of a city's features urban design characteristics that provide possible concepts for the skyscraper design.

Physical demarcation of zones represents "walls"

Physical barriers of buffer zones gives the impression of progression through formalised gates

Central route as the main organising element linking the major activity zones with the central administration zones

Cyclic circulation linking all important circulation routes within central zones

Central administrative zone as main commercial, administrative financial centre

Cyclic circulation branching off from main axis, providing a more intimate zoning typology within the major activity zone

Water feature as a buffer element

Green squares outside of wall

Contrast in building density strengthens experience of moving from one zone to the next, providing a climax to the journey

Spontaneous backlanes in contrast to formalised grid-like circulation provides exciting short-cuts

hub zones with a contrasting program located away from central zones

If we take for instance, a city's Central Business District (CBD) with an area of 20 hectares and a height limit of 30 storeys (or 120 metres assuming a typical floor height of four metres), the planning study area is in effect the entire three-dimensional spatial matrix over the 20 hectares land area up to a height of 120 metres. The expanded urban planning area becomes a three-dimensional zone above the land area. Planning is no longer on the horizontal plane, with extruded high-rises linked essentially at the lower levels or at the ground plane, but the entire spatial zone that extends vertically above the site. This zone has a network of potentially linkable "places-in-the-sky" that will have their own complex set of planning and urban design rules.

004

006

008

033

056

▷ 078|079

088

101

126

138

148

173

180

193

212

218

220

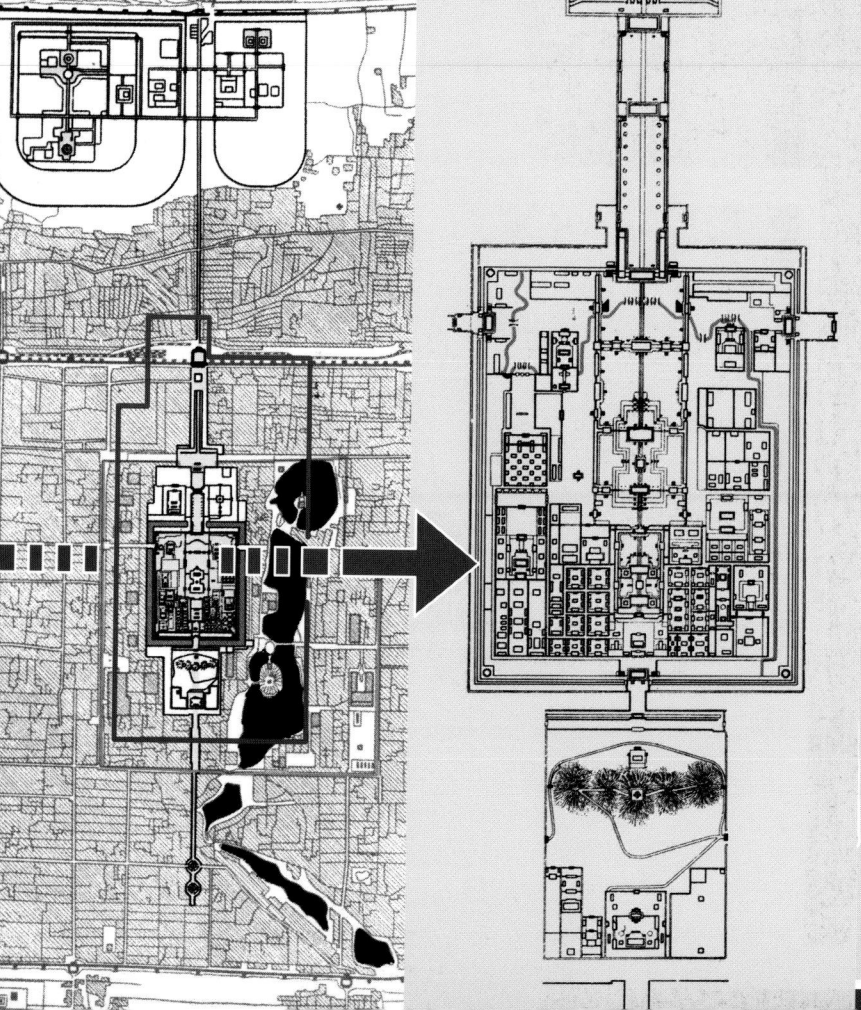

Urban Design Framework and Vertical Land-Use Mapping

▽ Summary of floor plans of the Gamuda Building as the formal basis for the mapping studies.

Social

Offices

Offices

Commercial

Parking

Parking

Artery (Atrium)

R   R
        11
10   10
9   9
8   8
7   7
6   6
5   5
4   4
3   3
2   2
1   1
P2   P2
P1   P1

―――― pedestrian (horizontal)   ―――― service line (auto)
―――― pedestrian (vertical)   ―――― main line (general lift)
―――― emergency line   ―――― secondary line (parking lift)

Mapping of the circulation system : examples of the generic mapping of △
the skyscraper's circulation system for the Gamuda Building analogous
to the mapping of the city's subway system.

Model of the Gamuda Building,
Shah Alam, Malaysia
[© T. R. Hamzah & Yeang, 1996]

▽ Mapping of population density
The mapping of population density in the Gamuda
Building high-rise informs us of floors that have
inadequate provision of communal facilities, open spaces,
etc., especially the more highly populated one which have
large numbers of workstations compared with the low
density top executive floors.

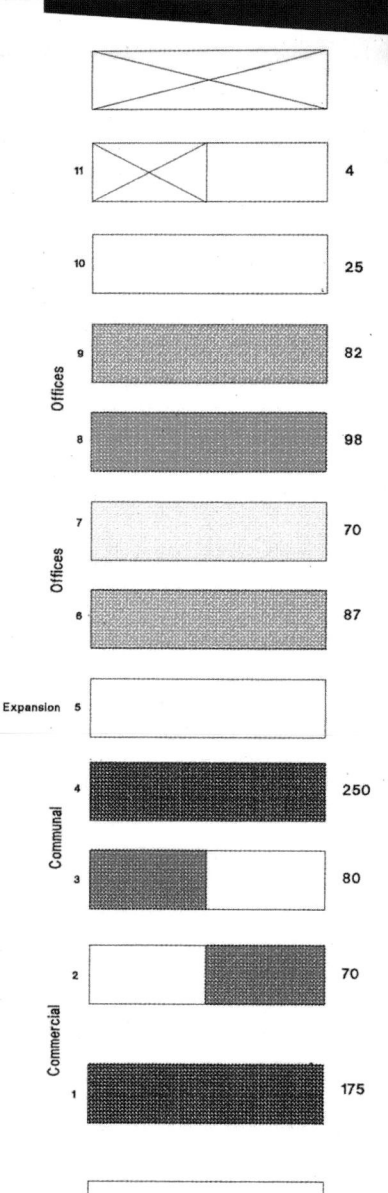

Floor	persons/sq m
11	4
10	25
Offices 9	82
8	98
Offices 7	70
6	87
Expansion 5	
Communal 4	250
3	80
Commercial 2	70
1	175
Parking P2	
P1	

persons/sq m

☐ < 0.003   ■ 0.05 - 0.1

☐ 0.01 - 0.02   ▨ 0.03 - 0.04

▨ 0.04 - 0.05   ■ > 0.1

☐ 0.02 - 0.03

With this approach to urban planning, the planning area is not just a land surface area of 'x' hectares of landed area but a multilevel planning endeavour in a spatial matrix developed from the configurations at the ground plane and within the boundaries of the study area. This is an approach that requires careful multilevel spatial differentiation. It is contended that the need for a new vertical theory of urban design becomes even more crucial for such intensive localities, as the imperative for a vertical theory is now driven not by the sheer intensity of the spatial content within a skyscraper's built form (as argued earlier), but by location because of the exceptionally high intensities on the urban sites themselves.

056

▷ 080|081

088

101

126

138

148

173

180

193

212

218

220

Urban Design Framework and Vertical Land-Use Mapping

Current high intensities within many of the world's major cities further affirm the urgent need for this vertical theory of urban design, not just to enable designers to revise skyscraper design as argued earlier, but to enable planners and urban designers to effectively and strategically handle high-intensity precincts within cities.

In the 1950s, as cities started going high-rise, it was found that the push towards verticality destroyed the integrity of the street space at the ground (which was essentially horizontal and low-rise). With the development of high-rises those parts of the city with towers became removed from street life. To worsen this condition, the use of raised or sunken plazas and internalised malls further undermined the traditional social functions of the street. Of course this happened in existing city conditions where the focus of the

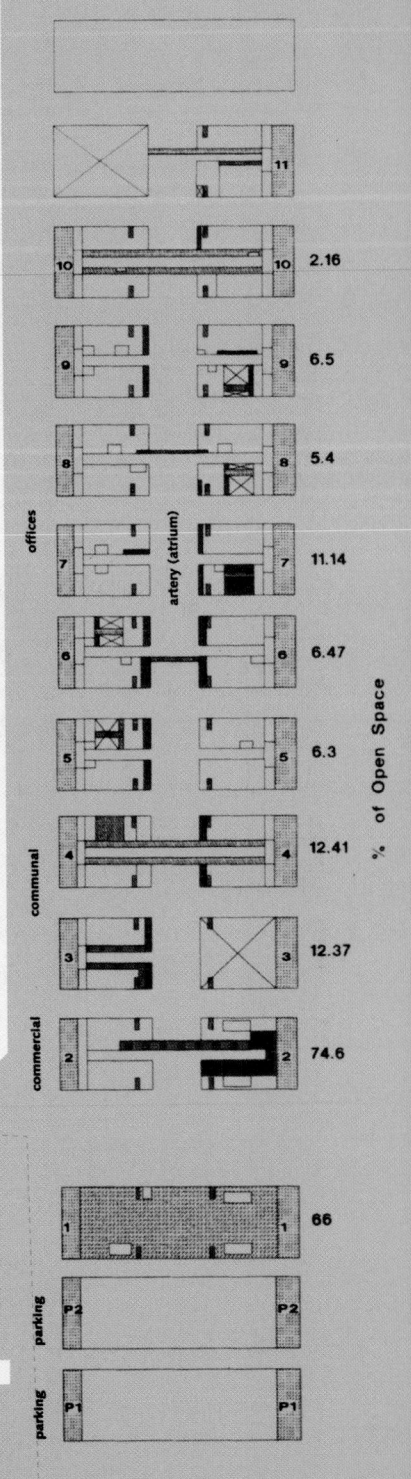

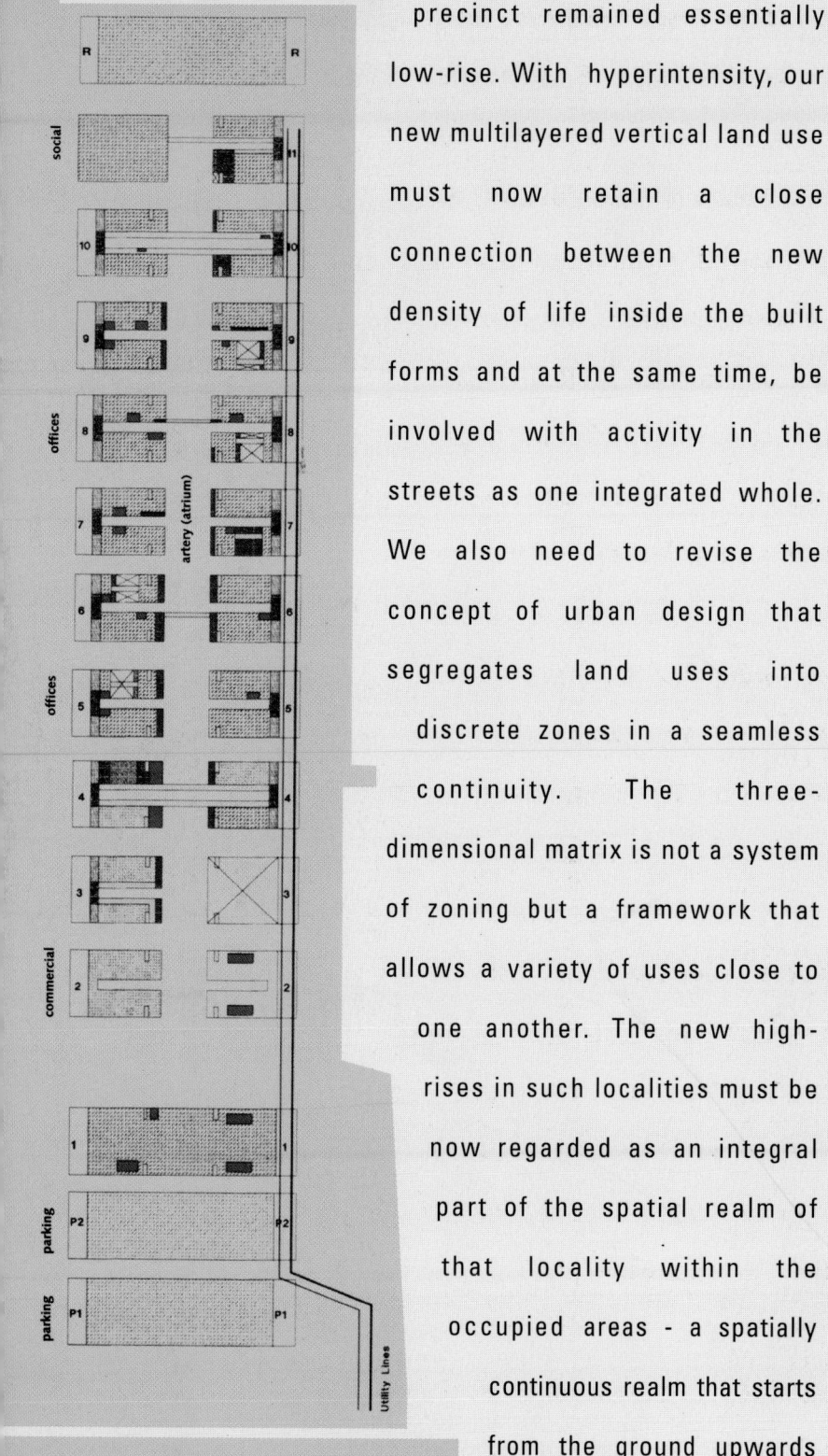

Mapping of Land use in the ▽
Gamuda Building, Shah Alam,
Malaysia.

Legend:
- ⊠ void space
- service zone
- communal zone
- office zone
- ■ social zone
- business zone
- office space
- □ circulation zone
- climatic buffer zone

rest of the urban life in that precinct remained essentially low-rise. With hyperintensity, our new multilayered vertical land use must now retain a close connection between the new density of life inside the built forms and at the same time, be involved with activity in the streets as one integrated whole. We also need to revise the concept of urban design that segregates land uses into discrete zones in a seamless continuity. The three-dimensional matrix is not a system of zoning but a framework that allows a variety of uses close to one another. The new high-rises in such localities must be now regarded as an integral part of the spatial realm of that locality within the occupied areas - a spatially continuous realm that starts from the ground upwards within the three-dimensional planning matrix.

004
006
008
033
056
▷ **082|083**
088
101
126
138
148
173
180
193
212
218
220

Urban Design Framework and Vertical Land-Use Mapping

A criticism of many of today's urban design projects is that they rarely correspond in spatial structure to the evolved community they replaced, nor do they correspond to the social relationships that gave meaning to the community's existence. Neither have the newly designed spatial structures been effective in creating a new viable community. In this regard, the new matrix must be aware of this and counter it with a system of continuous spaces and relationships from the ground to the sky, integrating buildings and linking spaces and places-in-the-sky into a new vertical equivalent of an urban fabric and social relationships.

Thus, if the skyscraper is to be effectively regarded as three-dimensional occupied spaces within the matrix, in principle we should be able to map its features, characteristics and systems in the same way that we are able to map similar planning considerations in conventional urban design and planning for purposes of urban analysis. We should be able to map vertical land-uses, for instance, in terms of office use, open space (terraces), sky courts (parks), retail (commercial), etc. We should be able to map other

▷ Central Plaza Build
  Kuala   Lump
  Malaysia
  [© T. R. Hamzah
  Yeang, 1992]

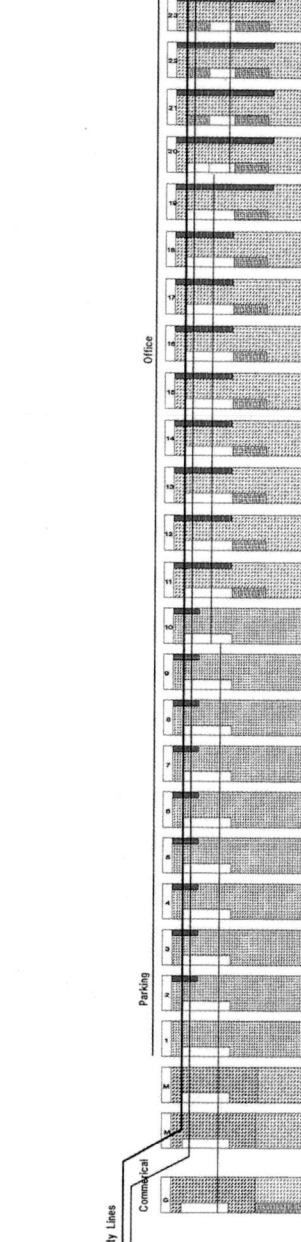

▷ 084|085

Summary of floor plans and mapping of land use for the Central Plaza Building.

aspects such as space and green areas, infrastructures, population density, income levels and so on as the basis for designing these as an urban design endeavour. These help us to 'read' the vertical built environment and understand what makes it work, or why it doesn't work; and to look at a streetscape or park or square or ensemble in its new intensity and location in the upper parts of the site, and analyse the qualities of good public space-in-the-sky with an understanding of, and feel for, the new vertical city of memory, 'desire', and 'spirit'.

088

101

126

138

148

173

180

193

212

218

220

Business Zone
Circulation Zone
Service Zone
Green Zone
Communal Zone
Climatic Buffer Zone
Office Zone
Social Zone

Urban Design Framework and Vertical Land-Use Mapping

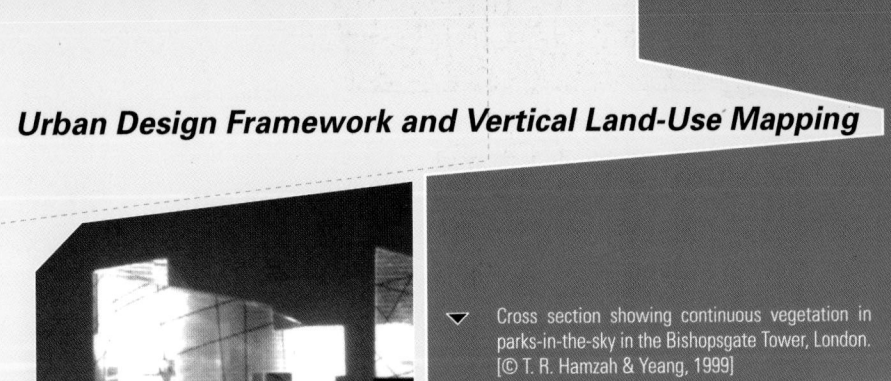

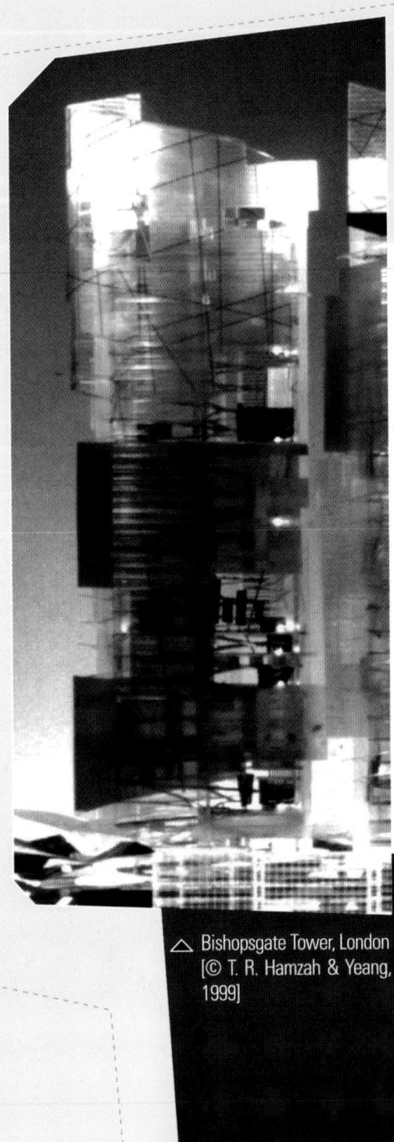

Bishopsgate Tower, London [© T. R. Hamzah & Yeang, 1999]

Cross section of Bishopsgate Tower.

Cross section showing continuous vegetation in parks-in-the-sky in the Bishopsgate Tower, London. [© T. R. Hamzah & Yeang, 1999]

Common Garden
Internal Atrium
Spiral Landscape Ramp
Structural Transfe Level & garden
Commercial / Retail Program
Residential

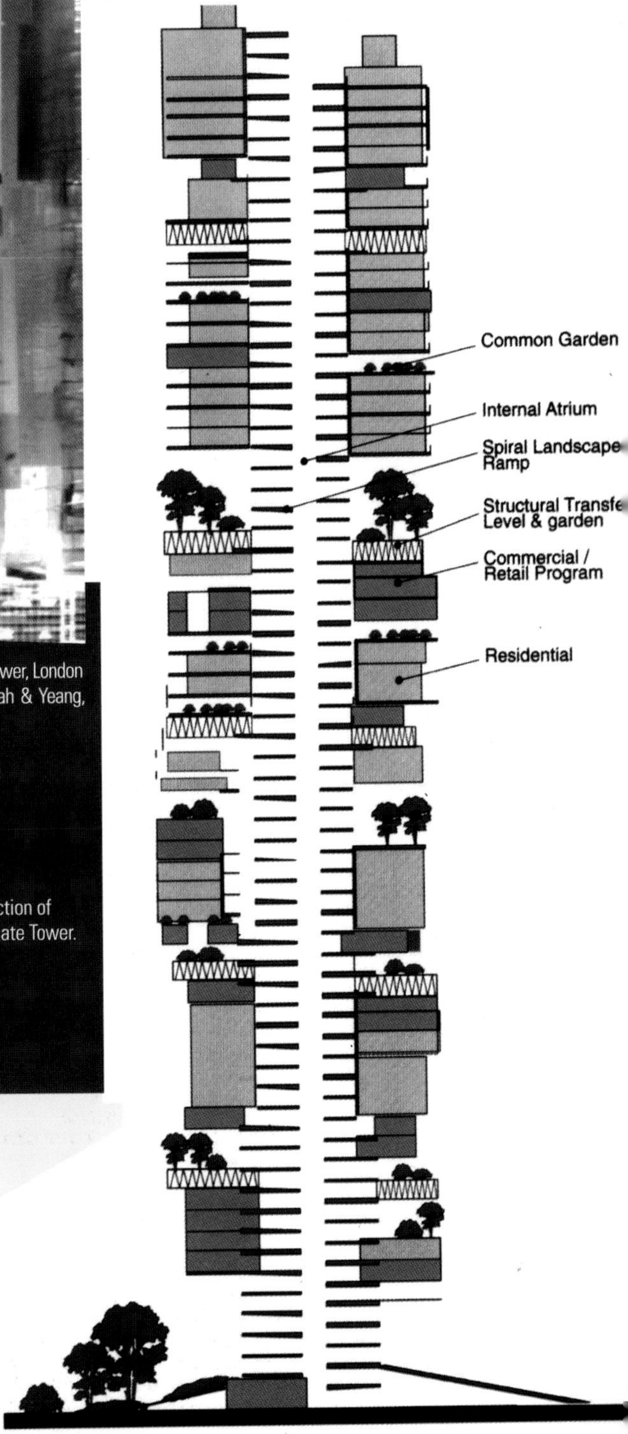

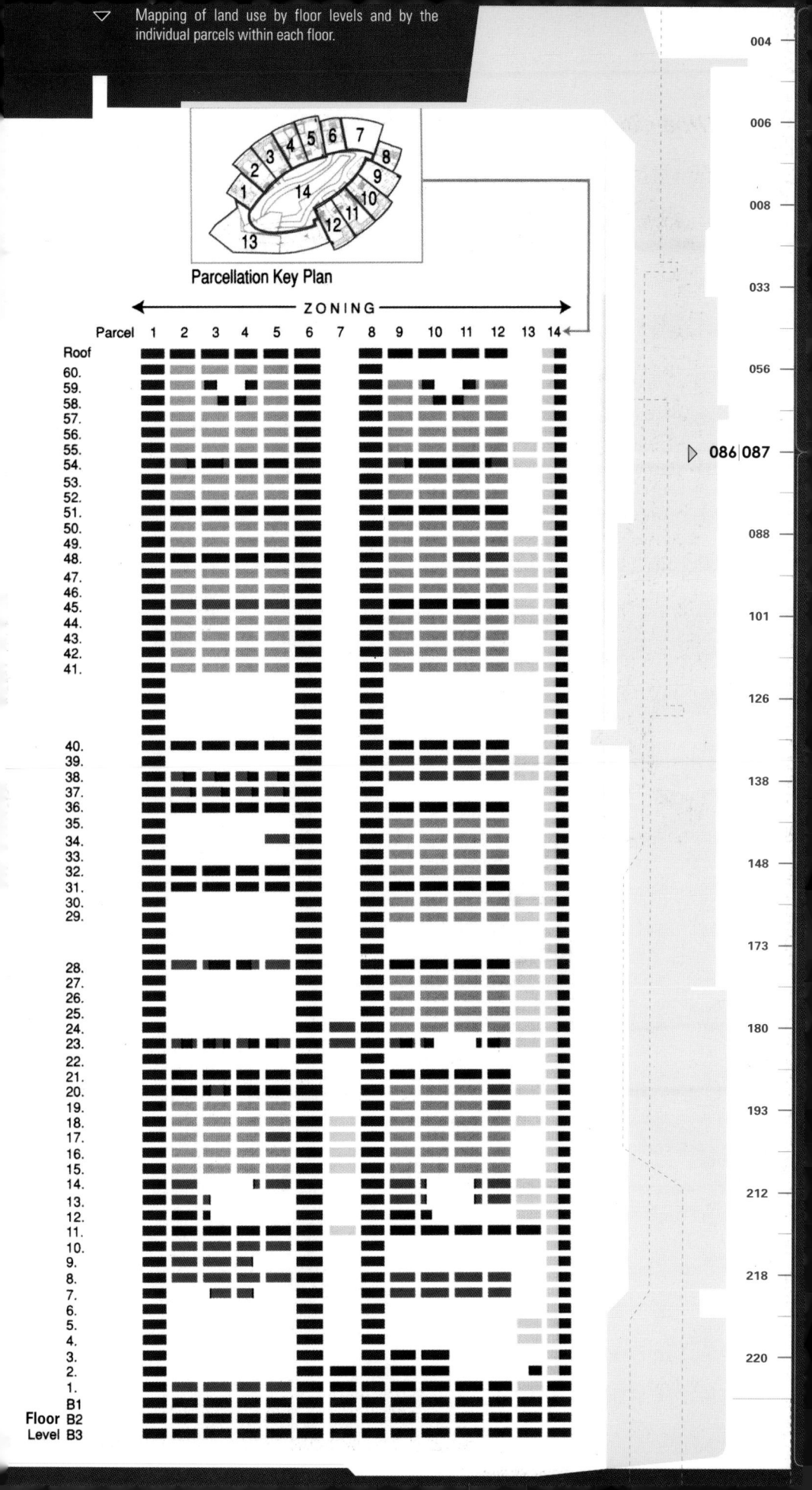

Parcellation Key Plan

Urban Design Framework and Vertical Land-Use Mapping

By analogy the skyscraper's elevatoring system becomes the equivalent of the city's subway system and can be mapped in a similar way as the city's subway map. As the skyscraper's built form becomes more articulate, the elevator stops become equivalent to subway-station stops in horizontal underground conditions.

Mapping of the transit circulation system in the high-rise can be compared with the map of a city's underground system.

In high-rise offices we will find that although the floor plates may have the same net area, they do not all have the same density of population per floor. Floors with executive rooms and boardrooms obviously have very low population density (eg c. 300 sq metres per person) whereas "beehive" floors consisting of mainly workstations may be as dense as 100 to 150 sq metres per person. As in any urban design for those precincts with higher urban population densities, these precincts need to be designed with higher provisions of public amenities and open spaces. Similarly, the denser floors in the high-rise should have more communal amenities, services, toilet provisions and accessible public spaces and terraces. The urban mapping of the skyscraper serves two purposes. First, it provides a means of graphically representing the skyscraper as an urban plan, which will facilitate its generic performance and adequacy as an urban design proposition in comparison with other skyscrapers. Second, it facilitates analysing it as an urban plan and leads to the discovery of its designs strengths and weaknesses as a work of urban design. Indeed, if we are to regard our design of the new high-rise as a form of urban design, the mapping of the high-rise's generic urban design functions in a way that is zonally and systemically similar to the mapping and analyses in conventional horizontal urban design and is a crucial factor.

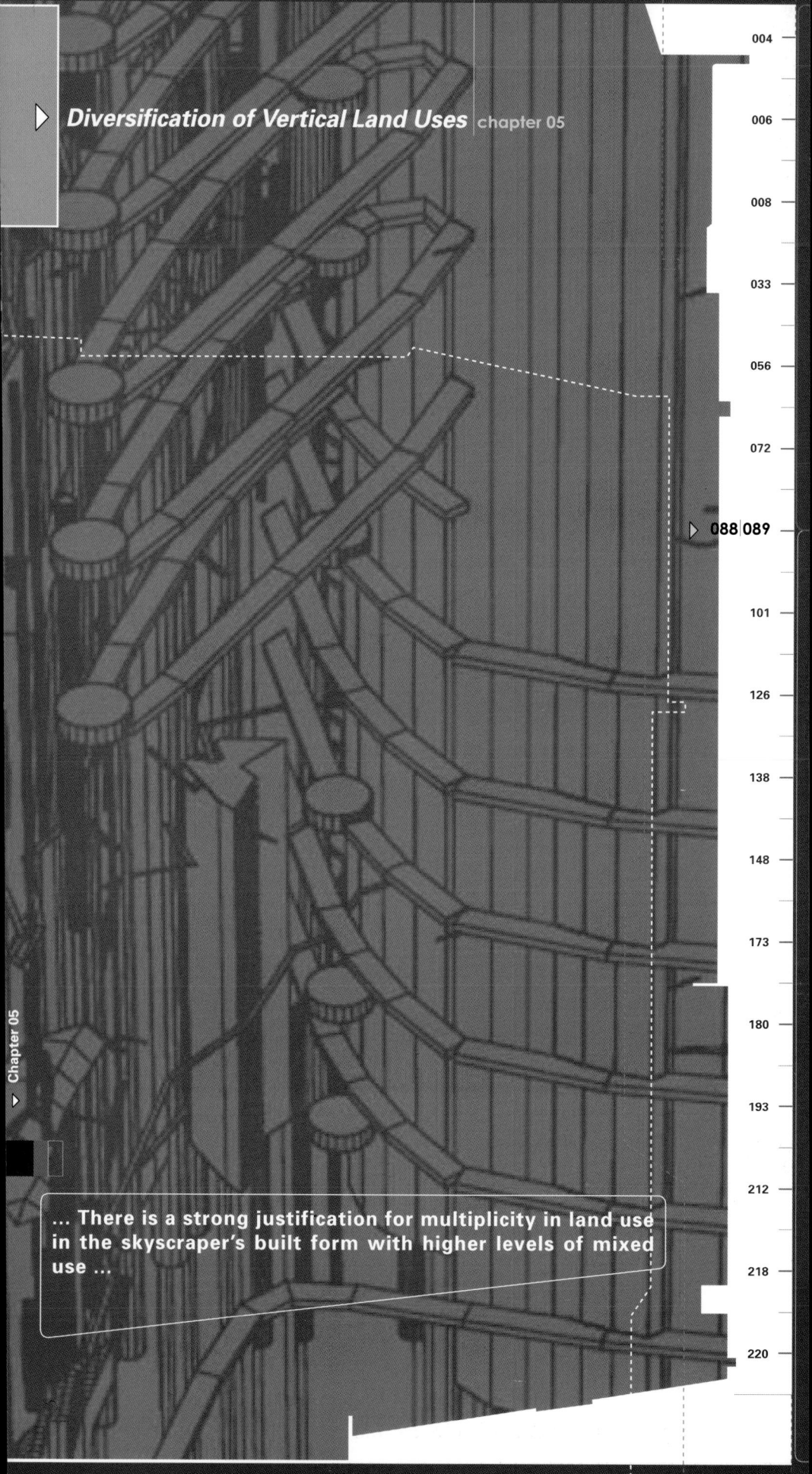

004

006

008

033

056

072

▷ **088|089**

101

126

138

148

173

180

193

212

218

220

▷ Chapter 05

... There is a strong justification for multiplicity in land use in the skyscraper's built form with higher levels of mixed use ...

Diversification of Vertical Land Uses

The traditional high-rise is a product of the Moderns, and hence its spatial assemblage is a universal product within a neutral space. The obvious response is an immediate retreat from the universalism of its current built form to a spatial romanticism. This is often described as the revulsion against uniformity, generality, calculated simplicity and the reduction of living phenomena to a common denomination; and as the

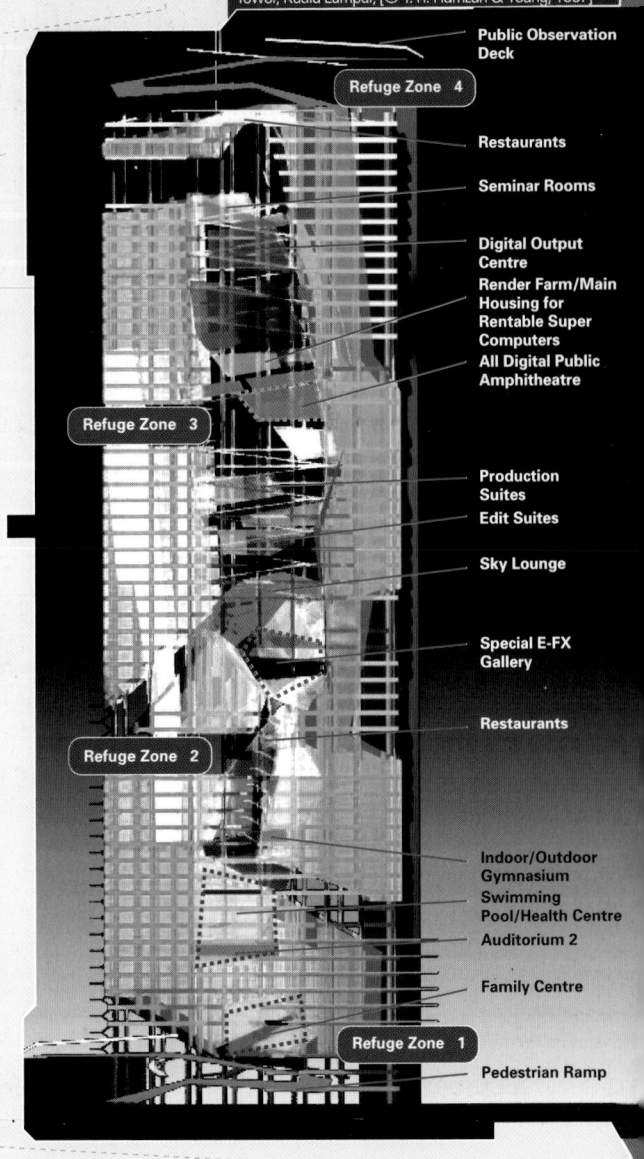

Public Observation Deck

Refuge Zone 4

Restaurants

Seminar Rooms

Digital Output Centre

Render Farm/Main Housing for Rentable Super Computers

All Digital Public Amphitheatre

Refuge Zone 3

Production Suites

Edit Suites

Sky Lounge

Special E-FX Gallery

Restaurants

Refuge Zone 2

Indoor/Outdoor Gymnasium

Swimming Pool/Health Centre

Auditorium 2

Family Centre

Refuge Zone 1

Pedestrian Ramp

aesthetic antipathy to standardisation and the abhorrence of platitudinous mediocrity. However, as population intensity in tall buildings today gets greater and greater it is obvious that there is increasing diversity in the needs of its users. The intensive skyscraper is no longer a conventional building. As argued earlier, its sheer internal intensity of built-up space and user population makes it into an urban precinct-in-the-sky. The articulation of the skyscraper's range of spatial programmes becomes one of concern to the designer, where all the issues of urbanism must come into play as a form of vertical urbanism.

004

006

008

033

056

072

090|091

101

126

138

148

173

180

193

212

218

220

Multiple circulation systems should also be provided in addition to the primary circulation system [1] that serves all floors [main banks of elevators, staircase and escape staircase]. A secondary circulation system [2] serves 10 - 12 floors [secondary elevators, escalators, staircases, ramps, etc]. A tertiary circulation system [3] serves 2 - 3 floors [hydraulic elevators, escalators, ramps, stairs, etc].

In the same way that the suburb or city precinct, has a variety of parks and open spaces, we need to have a similar range of green open spaces at the upper levels of the high-rise.

Circulation 3

Circulation 2

Circulation 1

Main Park 3

Main Park 2

Main Park 1

Ramping Park

In many cities today the traditional use of zoning ordinances by some planners has destroyed the integrity of urbanism by separating land-use functions that had traditionally been integrated into a total urban way of life. There is a strong justification for multiplicity in land use in the skyscraper's built form with higher levels of mixed use. This could mean the provision of a rich array of urban amenities and recreational and green environments within the high-rise that would be within easy reach and which could contribute greatly to the quality of life in the sky.

Diversification of Vertical Land Uses

Observation deck

L 60
L 59
L 58
L 57
L 56
L 55
L 54
L 53
L 52
L 51
L 50
L 49
L 48
L 47
L 46
L 45
L 44
L 43
L 42
L 41
L 40
L 39
L 38
L 37
L 36
L 35
L 34
L 33
L 32
L 31
L 20
L 29
L 28
L 27
L 26
L 25
L 24
L 23
L 22
L 21
L 20
L 19
L 18
L 17
L 16
L 15
L 14
L 13
L 12
L 11
L 10
L 9
L 8
L 7
L 6
L 3
L 2
B 1
B 2
B 3

restaurants
Continous vertical garden
Digital output centre
Outdoor public space
Interzone public elevator
Internal voids/ terraces
Special E-FX gallery
Sky plaza
Restaurants
LRT
Operable plaza roof

Entrance atrium

Mounded parks

Service entrance

Main retail levels
IRTS
Traffic circulation level
Basement parking levels
Public ev
Public ev

In today's key global cities millions of people once trooped from one building (their home) to another (their office) every morning, only to reverse the procedure every evening. Commuting requires a transport network built to cope with these two peak daily migrations. Roads must accommodate the weight of rush-hour traffic, and commuter railways and buses must carry the mass of peak-load passengers. Commuting wastes time and building capacity. One building – the home – often stands empty all day; another – the office, often in another part of town – usually stands empty all night. To

004

006

008

033

056

072

▷ 092|093

101

126

138

148

173

180

193

212

218

220

▽ We must design high-rise communities that have a diverse population, provide a full mix of uses, maintain walkable streets and positive public spaces, integrate civic and community centres, are transit-oriented, offer accessible open spaces and honour the unique qualities of space.

avoid making similar errors in the urban design of the skyscraper, the high-rise built form should not have one single function (eg, office usage) but instead have multiple internal programmes. Instead of the traditional functional zoning of its internal uses, it should have a diversity of uses.

In practice, the blending of leisure and work may well mean that work increasingly intrudes into leisure; not every downtown development, if deprived of office tenants, can be quickly transformed into an

aza

Office tower

Apartment tower

Main entrance to the exhibition gallery

za   IRTS   Main retail block   Service entrance

Traffic circulation level

entertainment centre. On balance, the direction of change might be to restore the communities by design, to improve the quality of dense areas within cities and to give people more control over their working lives. We need to re-envision the purpose, structure and range of amenities within the high-rise, with increased participation in local user requirements. We need to provide essential facilities for residents within walking distance in the sky at an acceptable travel time of about 10 minutes. The politics of universal or abstract space must yield to the politics of differentiation or recognition.

Diversification of Vertical Land Uses

The denser parts of today's cities and their centres must now readjust to a sustainable diverse role based on the economic and cultural functions that have been performed in the core since the beginning of civilisation. These diverse core areas need to rediscover their pre-industrial role as centres for the arts, entertainment and face-to-face trading, and the provision of specialised artisanal goods and services. An

urban environment's habitability has to do with fulfilling the need for health, employment, income, education, housing, leisure activities, accessibility, design quality and community.

A colony of skyscrapers can be like stems with pads at the upper most floors for aerial access. Example: Access of the building by helicopters.

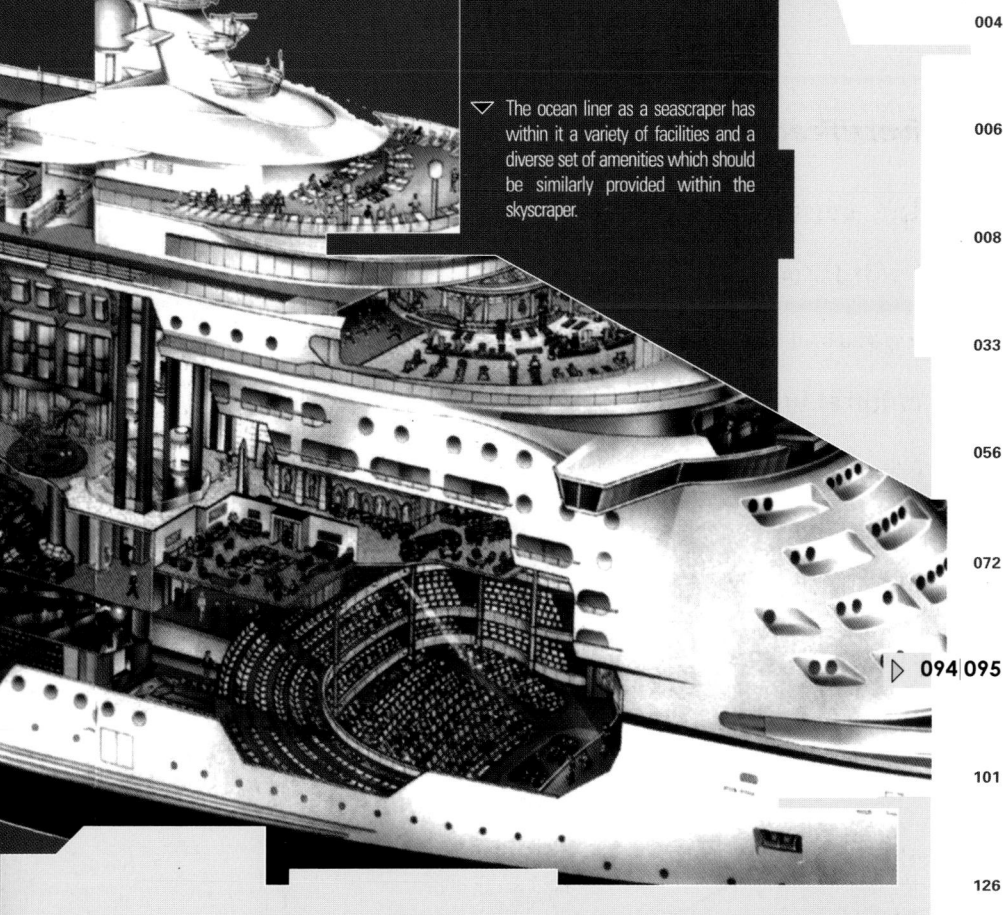

The ocean liner as a seascraper has within it a variety of facilities and a diverse set of amenities which should be similarly provided within the skyscraper.

004
006
008
033
056
072
094|095
101
126
138
148
173
180
193
212
218
220

In a similar way, the diversity of uses within the high-rise must be spatially distributed over the upper levels of the built form and not be concentrated on the lower floors of the built configuration. Other components of urban life that make it tenable, such as leisure, entertainment, shopping, banking and government services, must all be factored into the mix of uses within the skyscraper built form and placed in relation to the intensity within it.

One way to approach this (in suitable locations) is to recreate the urban high street in the skyscraper with the integration of a linear, ramped, leisure shopping environment within the upper floors of the built form. This will also contribute to the retention of retail facilities within the city as opposed to their agglomeration of shopping malls at the city's fringes.

Diversification of Vertical Land Uses

This greater spatial diversity will provide new meanings, innocence, origins, roots, certainties, leadership and heroes within its high-rise spatial environments.

In addition, residential neighbourhoods need to comprise a mix of uses that can work together to encourage formal and informal transactions, sustaining activity throughout the day. Studies have shown that people's satisfaction with housing has little connection with height and density. It is the other features of the housing environment, that result in different degrees of satisfaction. The mixing of different activities within the high-rise should also serve to strengthen social integration and civic life. Achieving this requires concentrating a range of public and commercial facilities in neighbourhoods. In any habitable suburban setting the community or cluster of residences will have within walking distance the local pub, the launderette, the newsagent, the chemist, the DIY shop, the stationer, etc, all of which should be incorporated in the new high-rise.

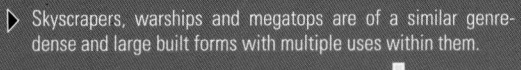

▷ Skyscrapers, warships and megatops are of a similar genre-
dense and large built forms with multiple uses within them.

004

006

008

033

056

072

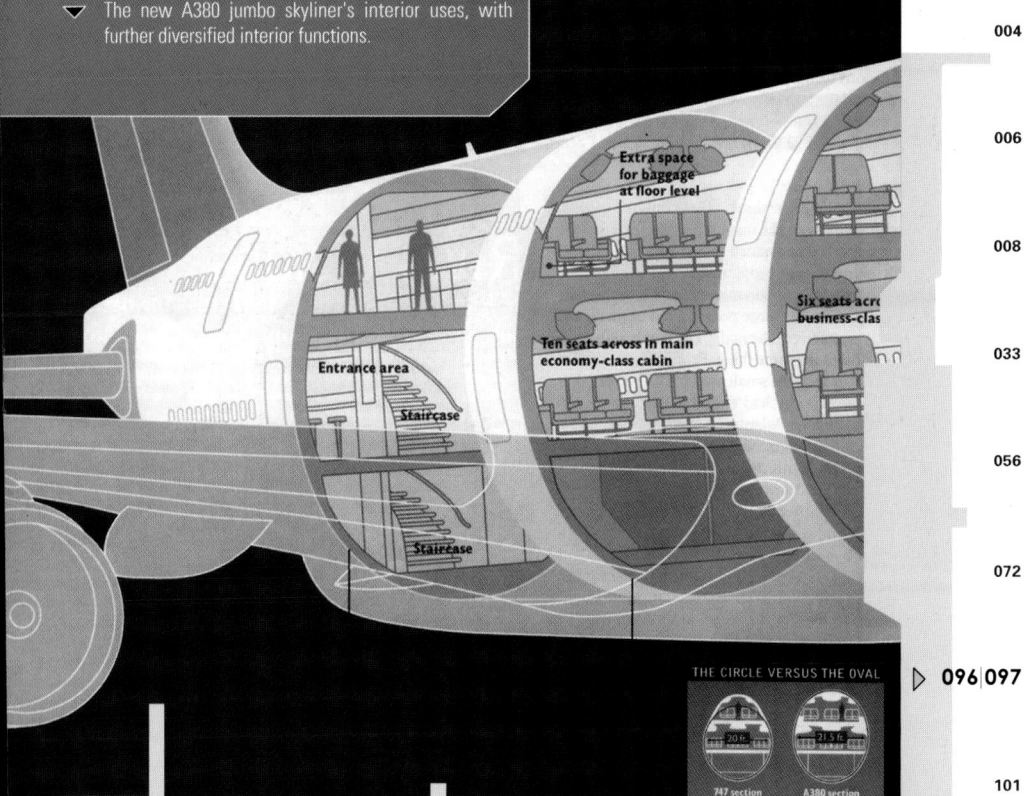

Extra space
for baggage
at floor level

Six seats acro
business-clas

Ten seats across in main
economy-class cabin

Entrance area

Staircase

Staircase

THE CIRCLE VERSUS THE OVAL

20.06

21.57

747 section

A380 section

▷ 096|097

101

126

138

148

173

180

193

212

218

220

In most high-rise developments all these amenities tend to be located at the ground plane or at the lower podium floors. The inhabitants of the high-rise must get to the ground floor or to the lower levels in order to have access to them. Why should this be the case? What is needed is to consider the spaces and units in the high-rise as neighbourhoods and to disperse the amenities in the upper parts of the high-rise built form, much as they would be located at critical locations and high-activity areas at the ground plane. In this way the skyscraper's built form is no longer one of homogeneous spaces stacked in the tower with the amenities located at the lower floors, but is more of an integrated mix aided by multiple access and secondary/tertiary circulation systems that enable the articulation of the spatial differentiation in the high-rise built form.

Diversification of Vertical Land Uses

▽

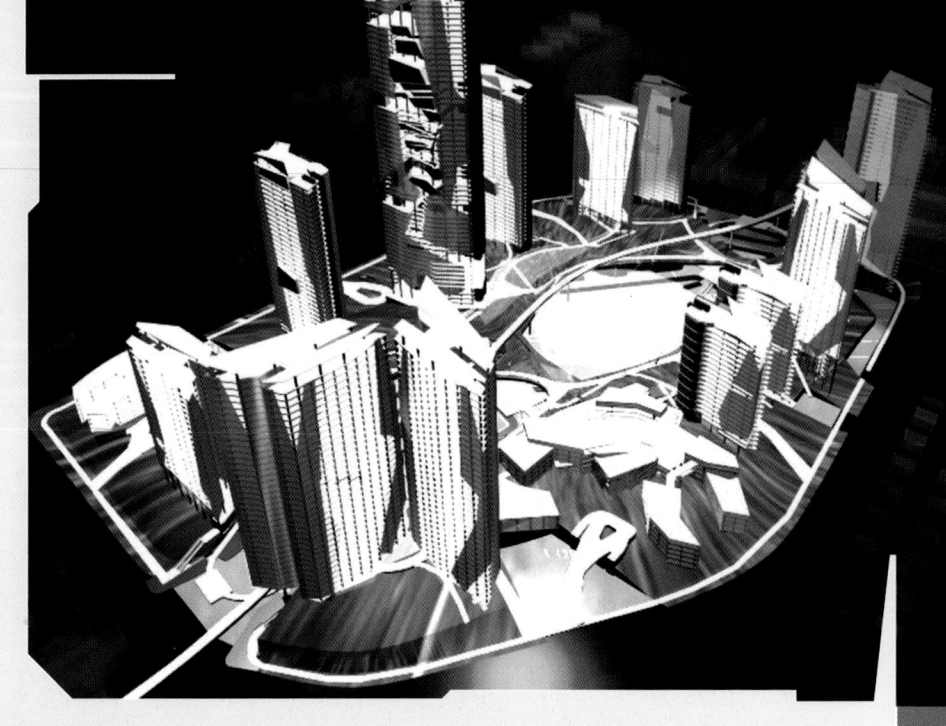

Provisions should also be made for shopping, entertainment, education and low-intensity manufacturing in the upper parts of the skyscraper. As shopping becomes a leisure activity in itself an entertainment context can be added to help generate traffic. The average family can do its weekly grocery shopping in less than 50 minutes, and the addition of entertainment to enhance the buying experience is likely to keep them at the shops' locations and increase the opportunities for further sales.

Ideally, the diversity of land use within the skyscraper will lead to the enabling of a life style where home, work and leisure are vertically interwoven within a single neighbourhood. Then, through diversification of land uses in the high-rise, new closer links can be forged between the different components of city life

◁ The skyscraper with a series of linked spaces within its built form.

within one single high-rise precinct. Residential, commercial, leisure and educational uses can be combined or placed in close proximity within a given area, allowing a new synergy to develop between users and uses.

The city itself must also gradually become more oriented towards leisure pursuits and recreational use. Another special aspect is the number of young people who now use the city. It is only in recent decades that they have had the opportunity and money to spend time there. However, the city centre is used widely by all age groups. Even though there are more young people today, there is still a reasonable balance between the various user groups of the city.

▲ Accessibility means immediacy and not only proximity. A person may live within a one-minute walk of a grocery store, but because his purely accidental neighbourhood is separated from the commercial district by a barrier [eg, a fence or a six - eight - lane highway] he cannot walk to it directly.

Diversification of Vertical Land Uses

The city's special character and charm are closely linked to the existence of several important balances. Whereas some city centres might feature specific user groups – business people or smartly dressed shoppers or young people – the public life in most city centres is highly diverse. There are people from all age groups, income groups and educational backgrounds whose needs must be taken into account. This wide variety must be reflected in the dense inner-core design. There are residents, students, customers and visitors. People live, work, shop and enjoy themselves in the city. This mix is decisive for the city's vitality because activities are constantly blended and woven together. The balance, mixture and integration of various user groups and activities are key to making the city attractive and must be designed into the new high-rise built form.

Landscaped bridge

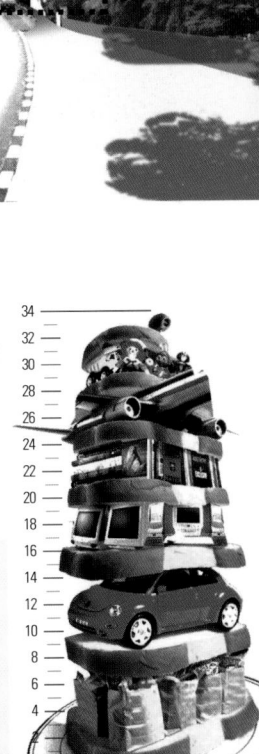

Designing the skyscraper as analogous to a stack of goodies and treats.

34
32
30
28
26
24
22
20
18
16
14
12
10
8
6
4
Ground

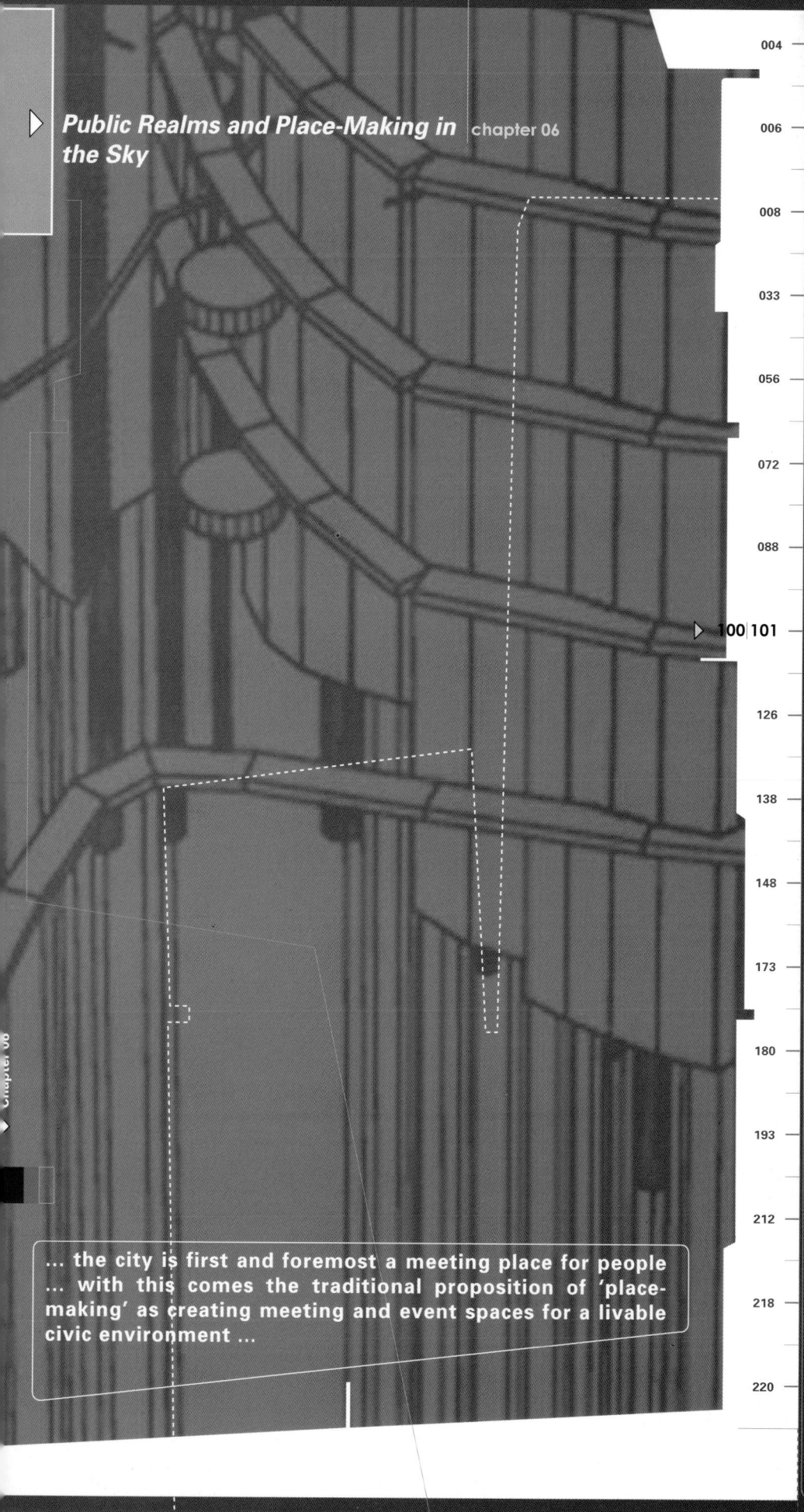

Public Realms and Place-Making in the Sky   chapter 06

... the city is first and foremost a meeting place for people ... with this comes the traditional proposition of 'place-making' as creating meeting and event spaces for a livable civic environment ...

Public Realms and 'Place-Making' in the Sky

Cafés are the type of social interactive places that we need to provide at the upper levels of the skyscraper to make it more livable.

Cafés are the type of social interactive places that we need to provide at the upper levels of the skyscraper to make it more livable.

The city is first and foremost a meeting place for people. This is the fundamental premise and framework that holds together the many institutions, schools, hospitals and work places that form part of our everyday lives. With this comes the traditional proposition of 'place-making' as creating meeting and event spaces for a livable civic environment. Urban design involves provision of public realm spaces such as plazas, boulevards and avenues that respect the city's unique cultural differences. The shifting nature of these public spaces is the nexus that links the divergent interests of the city, giving people the qualitative experience that they are somewhere. It is the equivalents of these that we need to design into the high-rise.

The 'Rambla' in Barcelona is a lively people-zone that gives a unique and distinctive urban character to the city. We need to recreate similar event places in the high-rise built form.

They may be in the form of sky courts, plazas and streets-in-the-sky. They are the essential spaces in the city for the social discourse that must now be recreated in the new skyscraper. In the city, even the streets themselves are important places the needs they meet are different to those met by public spaces and outdoor rooms. The challenge to the designer is how to create such streets-in-the-sky in the upper parts of the new high-rise, and planning them as linked spaces in its three-dimensional matrix. In contemporary cities the importance of 'place' has diminished in the face of accelerated flows of people, ideas, capital, mass media and other products, and the reinvention of these spaces provides the opportunity to reconstruct the city as new high-rise precincts.

004

006

008

033

056

072 —

088

▷ 102|103 —

126

138

148

173

180 —

193 —

212 —

218 —

220

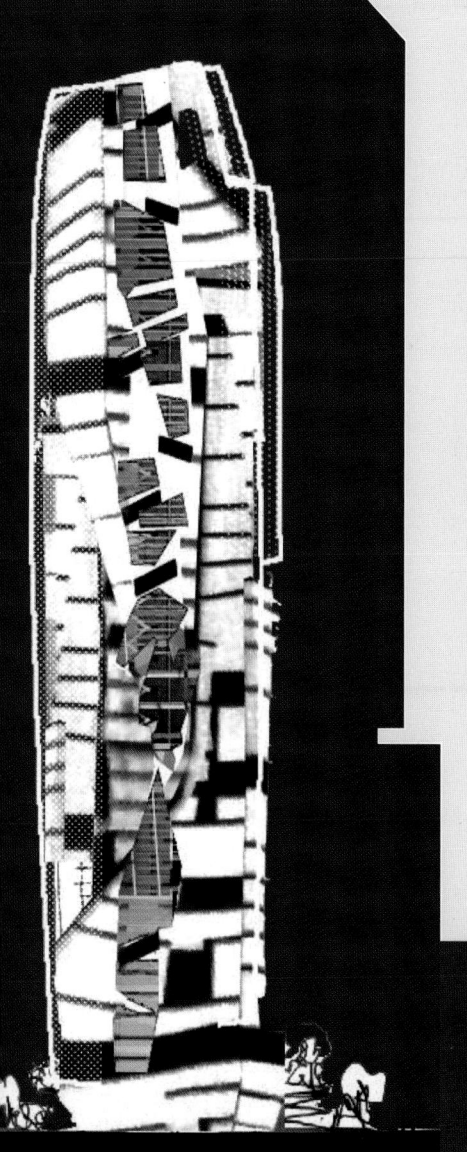

◁ The high-rise built form designed as a sequence of connected public realms that flow from the uppermost floor down to the ground plane.

Traditional walkable cities have evolved into global cities with a less legible urbanised landscape where the erstwhile distinctions between city, suburb and countryside no longer apply. This is both a geographical and perceptual shift that leads to deterritorialisation and placelessness in today's city. In the case of the high-rise not only are these aspects prevalent, there is also an evidently profound sense of loss in the users because of their separation from life at the ground plane. The consequence is a corresponding nostalgia in the inhabitants of high-rises for life at the horizontal level at the ground. The design response is to make the high-rise accessibly walkable (eg, with the use of ramps, bridges and secondary circulation systems) and link it directly to the ground plane.

Site/building solar sky courts

Site/building adjustments

Transitional spaces

Curtain wall at North and South faces

Environmentally interactive wall

Recessed sun-spaces

△ Opportunities to articulate the skyscraper built form.

We need to provide informal spaces like this one in the high-rise built form, that can contract and expand depending on the spontaneous social needs of the community.

Informal Expansion & Contraction

004

006

008

033

056

072

088

104|105

126

138

148

173

180

193

212

218

220

In urban design the exterior spaces become the force that gives definition to the urban form and its borders, establishing the walls of the outdoor room. The main requirement for a plaza (as for a room) is the enclosed character of its space. We need to form a whole within the high-rise built form, with the surrounding buildings or structures as a wall or implied wall. People's image of, and reaction to, a space is largely determined by the way it is enclosed. Generally stated, people like rooms. They relate to these daily in their homes and at work. In this regard, these outdoor rooms have to be designed in a three-dimensional relationship between the unenclosed and enclosed spaces within the skyscraper. The opening up of urban spaces within the high-rise (eg, as sky courts and green parks) allows for free-flowing landscape elements that provide daylight and natural ventilation. These places must also be designed with an understanding of human behaviour. The spaces should not be uncritically huge or vast or formless but should be designed with properties of shape and scale and be connected to other spaces in the high-rise. The integration of these, both physically and visually, with the internal spaces of the skyscraper will also help in the decompartmentalising of its built form.

Public Realms and 'Place-Making' in the Sky

In designing these outdoor rooms in the skyscraper as we would design them for ground conditions, the emphasis should be on their groups and sequences and their relationships with the precincts-in-the-sky, rather than focusing on an individual space as an isolated entity. Special attention should be given to the residual spaces between the precincts-in-the-sky. By consciously creating public realms in the skyscraper we would avoid the resultant leftover spaces that we find in existing cities, which are ill-shaped and ill-planned for public use. These places-in-the-sky should be designed as part of the skyscraper's fabric of streets, squares and viable open spaces within its built form.

Ants design better and more complex skyscrapers than we do. They can also build ones that are many times their own heights proportionately much higher than the skyscrapers we build.

Public realms in temperate zones need to be solar-access spaces.
Reference : Eco Towers, Elephant and Castle, London; latitude 52 with a southerly low solar path.
[© T. R. Hamzah & Yeang, 2000]

With regard to the high intensity of inhabitants in the high-rise, what is needed is a respect for the diversity of the urban subcultures within this intensity. This means that users can read many meanings (multivalency) rather than only one 'truth' and it is necessary to express this through the symbolic new and much-needed multidimension of the skyscraper's built form.

004

006

008

033

056

072

088

106|107

126

138

148

173

180

193

212

218

220

The skyscraper as a 'vertical city'. Reference: Bishopsgate Tower, London [© T. R. Hamzah & Yeang, 1999]

Rain collection pan as rain-screens

M & E
Roof
Level 60

Photovoltaic Panels as rain-screens

Pub

Multilayered Environmental Moderator

Creche

Photovoltaic Panels as rain-screens

Level 41

Secondary Programmed Places in the Sky

Level 40

Pub

IT Knowledge Centre

Intermediate Garden "Squares"

Level 29

Level 28

Electronics Shop

Level 25

Library/Bookshop

Intermediate Garden "Squares"

Level 20

Café on the Ramp

Pub

Retail, General

Urban Agriculture

Research Laboratory

Bird Sanctuary

Carpark Level 03
Carpark Level 02

Ground Level
Basement 01
Basement 02
Basement 03

Sandwich Shop

Intermediate Garden "Squares"

Restaurant

Pub

Intermediate Garden Squares

Launderette

Mini-Market

Secondary Circulation Systems.

Bank

Retail, General

Pub

Hardware Store

Sandwich Shop

Oxfam

Academia

Restaurant

Pub

Launderette

Creche

Public Realms and 'Place-Making' in the Sky

Another way to reconceive the high-rise built form as vertical urban design is to regard it as urban space similar to urban space at the horizontal ground plane. For in a similar way place-making in the high-rise, as in urban design, must involve designing places as destinations, so that there is a 'there' when we arrive (in the temporal realities of the design). They must become evocative places (as against 'non-places') that remind us of who we are (our sense of identity), where we are (our sense of genius loci) and when we are (our sense of reality). These aspects are the essential settings for the public and cultural activities that make a place memorable so that users return to revisit.

In fact, the vertical urban space in the high-rise can become the primary organising urban morphology within its framework

The stacked deck can be as monotonous and demeaning as the rigidly gridded city streetscape.

(with perhaps typological and morphological models taken from existing cities as the bases), to revive a new spatial configuration or internal architectural discipline within the skyscraper's built form. The historical typologies of traditional cities such as the street, the square, and quarters can be critically reinterpreted and thus reconstructed in the high-rise built form to provide a new internal life, thereby creating a new architecture. They can provide ▶

004
006
008
033
056
072
088
108|109
126
138
148
173
180
193
212
218
220

△ The articulated tower is
◁ analogous to the city's fabric
of spaces and places.

the basis for reconstructing the high-rise built form, and restructuring of it into complex parts for a new 'vertical city' as 'cities within the city', and into high-rise quarters that integrate all the functions of urban life within the tower or slab built form. Generally stated, any new architecture must create a new form of internal life for its inhabitants, and in the process of reconstructing the new skyscraper this new form of architecture is emerging.

Public Realms and 'Place-Making' in the Sky

The earlier ideas of the 'neorationalist' urbanists used the European city's pre-industrial past as inspiration and legitimisation for urban design. These ideas can similarly be adapted here, but interpreted as 21st century spaces, to assist in creating a vertical urbanity in terms of a new form of high-rise typology and morphology.

These new places within the high-rise become new theatres of memory within a previously bland and aesthetically inconsequential stacking of floors. They enable a new vertical sense of place, established by the memories associated with it. A new strategic design approachto investigate is the inventive recreation within the high-rise built form of the traditional fundamental forms of the city's existing typology and morphology: the street, the arcade, the square, the yard, the quarter, the colonnade, the avenue, the boulevard, the centre, the nucleus, the crown, the radius, the knot.

▷ The spiral playground chute as a metaphor for spatial continuity and access with linked landscaping.

▷ The skyscraper design can provide a gradual spatial colonisation within its framework over time. Reference: MCA Tower renovation, Kuala Lumpur.
[© T. R. Hamzah & Yeang, 2001]

These become the key design challenges for creating the new high-rise for the city. All of them need to be reinterpreted in the new high-rise's built form. The design explorations in this endeavour can provide an exciting journey towards creating a new high-rise built form, where its vertical urbanism can be walked through in its entirety.

The high-rise as a city-in-the-sky can now have its public and domestic spaces articulated within its formal urban fabric, with high-rise squares and streets-in-the-sky, but reinvented without the classical baggage and affectations of the neorationalists which come with these morphologies. These design features can be spatially reinterpreted in the high-rise built form, not just as incremental action within it but through extensive restructuring of the built form at the onset.

▽ Conceptual diagram of the tower as a series of green platforms.

◁ Green platforms at the upper levels of the tower.

004
006
008
033
056
072
088
▷ 110|111
126
138
148
173
180
193
212
218
220

Public Realms and 'Place-Making' in the Sky

In urban design the organisation of traditional cities tends to be along the following patterns: the pre-industrial patterns of the Baroque or Neoclassical ceremonial city, the essentially British residential form or the colonial chequerboard grid. The Baroque urban form predicates monuments, broad avenues lined with uniform buildings, parks, vistas and geometrical dispositions. The British townscape pattern is designed around 'squares' with limited population densities, the streets broadly designed around these squares with a high standardisation of dwellings. The colonial chequerboard is the gridiron plan found in many North American cities. While these organisational concepts may be considered to be essentially dated, they remain unexplored areas in their reinterpretation, vertically in the high-rise, to create contemporary spaces in the three-dimensional matrix.

The tower as a digital media armature. ▷

004
006
008
033
056
072
088

◁ The agora above contrasts with electronic media space-age indeterminate public realms that enable dense public activities to take place.

▷ 112|113
126
138
148
173
180
193
212
218
220

In today's urban design we need also to take into consideration such issues as gender, designing for comfort, accessibility, privacy, territory and defence. In addition, we need also to design for the digital community as our cities become by nature antispatial. The worldwide computer network and the digital revolution subvert, displace and radically redefine our notions of community life and urban life and the concept of the gathering place (see Chapter 12). Our new place-in-the-sky may in effect be an electronic agora.

◁ Multi-level interlinked 'Places-in-the-Sky'.
[Source: Manmachine Interface, Shirow Masamune]

Public Realms and 'Place-Making' in the Sky

Contrary to the expected increase of a spirit of 'placelessness', the digital economy may have precisely the opposite effect on place. In principle people, companies or industries can truly live anywhere, or at least choose from a multiplicity of places. The question of where to locate becomes increasingly contingent on, with even more dependency upon, the peculiar attributes of a given location. Contrary to expectations, place-making in the digital economy becomes even more crucial because the importance of differentiating between locations and the variables governing their success has become, if anything, even more vital. For instance, decisions on where to locate will depend more on 'quality of life' and the environment of that locality than on any traditional factors such as taxes, regulations or land costs.

In the same way that place-making is a key component of urban design, the fundamental bases for place-making in horizontal urban design are also applicable to the high-rise built form. In every design for a skyscraper we need to consider the creation and provision of these places at the upper parts of the skyscraper's built form.

▷ Aggregate of towers with floors that are fragmented to accommodate public realms within their skyscraper built form. Reference: BATC Tower, Kuala Lumpur. [© T. R. Hamzah & Yeang, 1997]

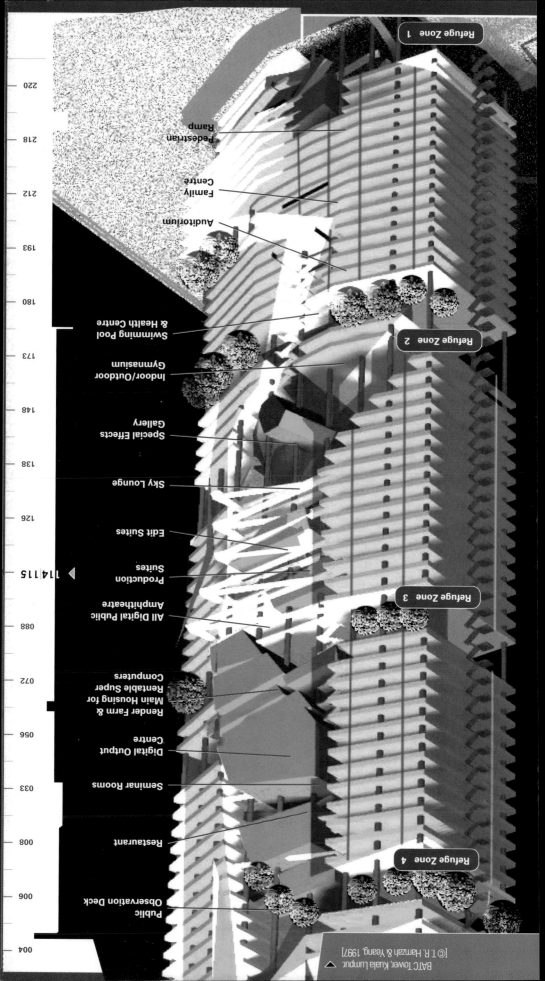

Refuge Zone 1

220
218   Pedestrian Ramp
212   Family Centre
193   Auditorium
180
173   Swimming Pool & Health Centre   Refuge Zone 2
148   Indoor/Outdoor Gymnasium
138   Special Effects Gallery
126   Sky Lounge
        Edit Suites
114|115 ◄ Production Suites
088   All Digital Public Amphitheatre   Refuge Zone 3
072   Render Farm & Main Housing for Rentable Super Computers
056   Digital Output Centre
033   Seminar Rooms
008   Restaurant   Refuge Zone 4
006   Public Observation Deck
004

Public Realms and 'Place-Making' in the Sky

Generally stated, public spaces can help nurture a sense of cultural belonging and at the same time acknowledge and respect diversity. Even ordinary urban landscapes have the power to nurture the public's memory and this power remains untapped for most people's working neighbourhoods in the traditional cities. These urban landscapes are potential storehouses for individual and collective social memories.

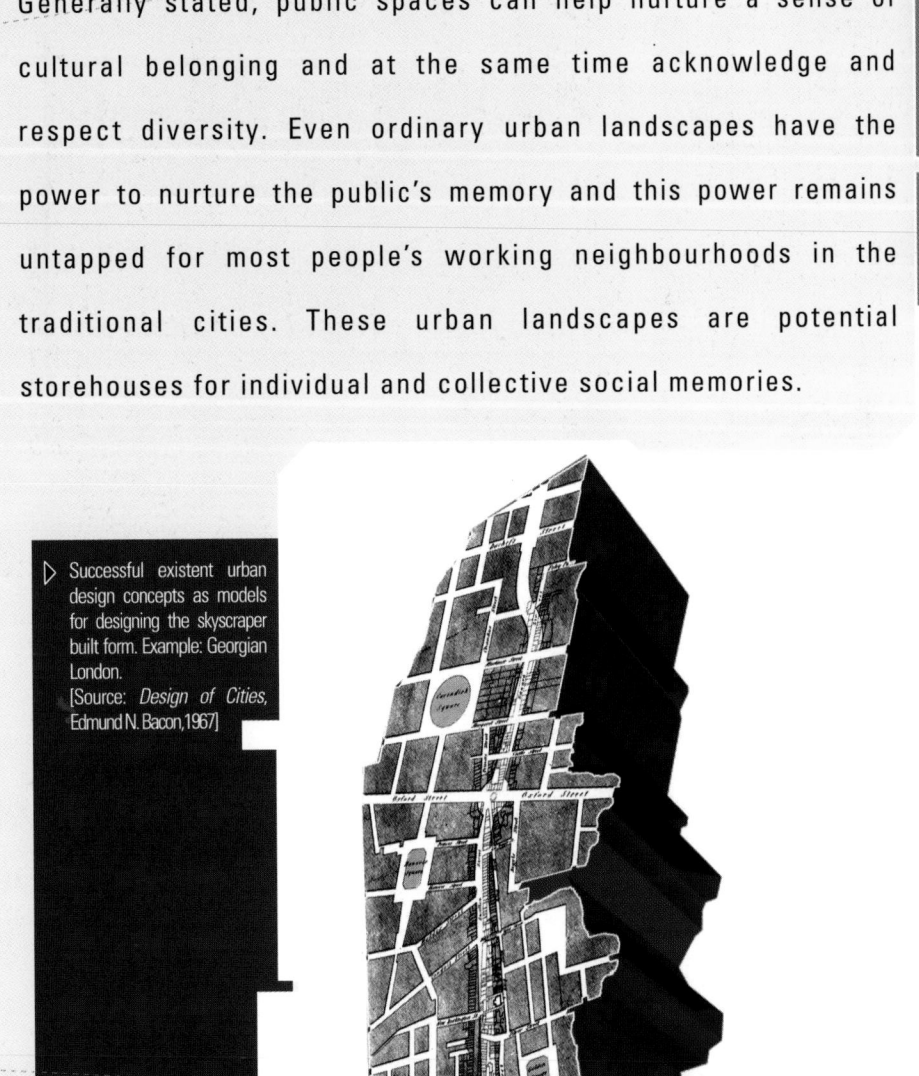

▷ Successful existent urban design concepts as models for designing the skyscraper built form. Example: Georgian London.
[Source: *Design of Cities*, Edmund N. Bacon, 1967]

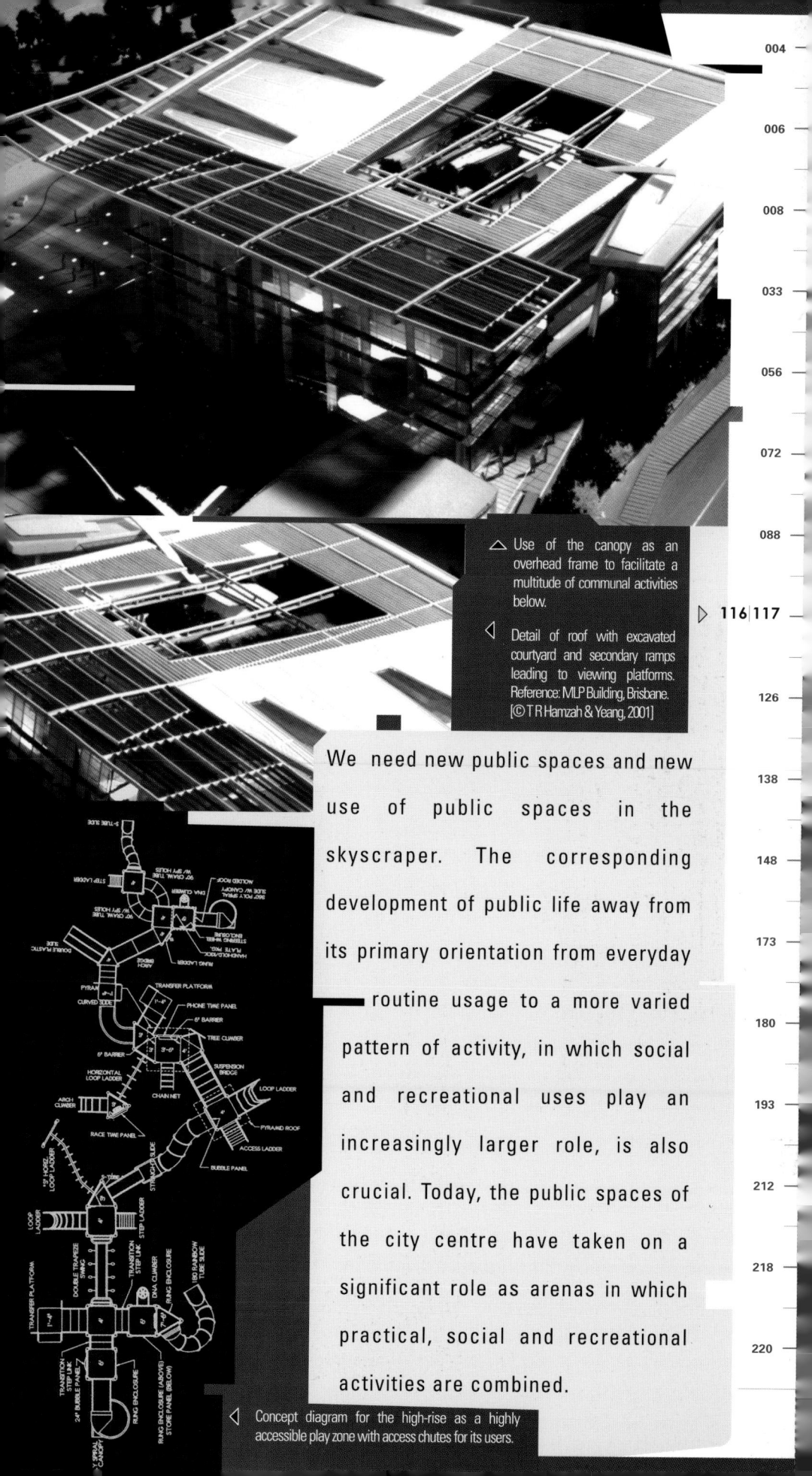

004
006
008
033
056
072
088
116 117
126
138
148
173
180
193
212
218
220

△ Use of the canopy as an overhead frame to facilitate a multitude of communal activities below.

◁ Detail of roof with excavated courtyard and secondary ramps leading to viewing platforms. Reference: MLP Building, Brisbane. [© T R Hamzah & Yeang, 2001]

We need new public spaces and new use of public spaces in the skyscraper. The corresponding development of public life away from its primary orientation from everyday routine usage to a more varied pattern of activity, in which social and recreational uses play an increasingly larger role, is also crucial. Today, the public spaces of the city centre have taken on a significant role as arenas in which practical, social and recreational activities are combined.

◁ Concept diagram for the high-rise as a highly accessible play zone with access chutes for its users.

Public Realms and 'Place-Making' in the Sky

▷ The approach to place-making is not unilaterally at the upper levels of the tower or only at the ground plane. There must be a continuum from the ground to the upper levels of the skyscraper.

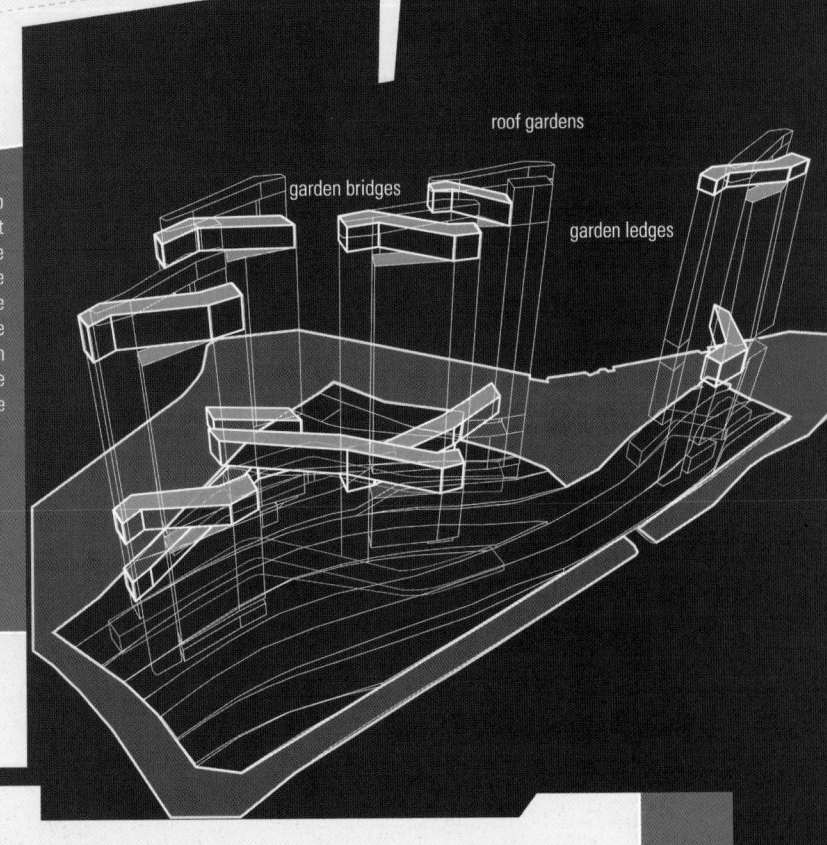

roof gardens

garden bridges

garden ledges

In designing these places-in-the-sky (in high- and mid-latitude locations in the biosphere), the space should maximise: first, shelter from the wind for user comfort; second, dispersion of air pollutants; and third, urban warmth to reduce the need for space heating and give the inhabitants solar access (in the autumn and winter months). For warm-climate locations, the third is to reduce the need for space cooling. At the same time, these places should enable the provision of a variety of relationships between the interior and the exterior.

stranded ground: that is, combed in the direction of linkages

△ Horizontal integration of
◁ skyscraper slabs.

rooftop extensions of the ground plane

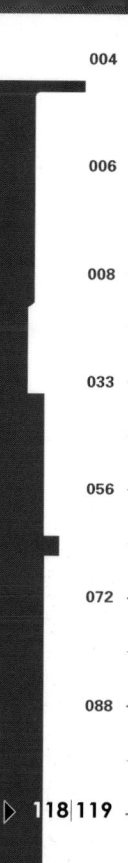

These new endeavours in the spatial articulation of the high-rise must also seek new urban and architectural morphologies within the skyscraper built form. We need to identify the elements of townscape morphologies- typologies- within the skyscraper's new urban scales and the aesthetic dimensions for the new skyscraper's built environment.

Public Realms and 'Place-Making' in the Sky

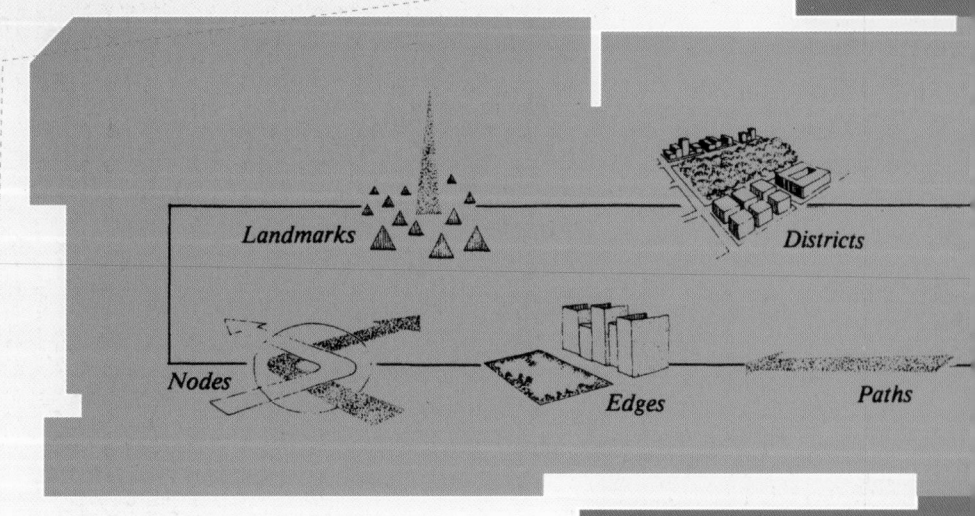

Landmarks

Districts

Nodes

Edges

Paths

Traditional urban design regards the location's context as the determinant of the design. Urban design involves rediscovering the urban realm from the context and can be the result not of the simple addition or superimposition of private spaces but, in most instances, of the definition of public spaces. We need to produce a secondary architecture within the high-rise's overall architecture which would no longer be isolated objects ordering overall residual spaces within, but become part of an aggregate ensemble forming urban realms within the skyscraper's built form.

△ The use of urban design techniques for skyscraper design (Kevin Lynch). Design must re-examine the issues of districts, paths, edges, nodes and landmarks in the upper levels of the skyscraper.
[Source: *Finding Lost Space*, Roger Trancik, 1986]

△ The provision of large communal sun-deck spaces in the skyscraper.

004

006

008

033

056

072

088

▷ **120|121**

126

138

148

173

180

193

212

218

220

▽ The provision of impromptu performance spaces in the skyscraper.

In today's practice, urban design must endeavour to give back to the inhabitants (in this case, to the inhabitants of the high-rise) the right to the high-rise building's public spaces through, for instance, the provision of open lobbies, large sky courts, well-vegetated sky gardens, accessible communal areas, usable in-between spaces, etc.

◁ The provision of multiple-level accessibility in the skyscraper.
[Source: *Benkei in New York*, Jinpachi Mori and Jiro Taniguchi, 1996]

Public Realms and 'Place-Making' in the Sky

Kevin Lynch found that people come to understand places through five major features of the physical landscape: paths (to direct movement), edges (boundaries to limit one's world), districts (zones for each activity),

△ The provision of communal solar-access spaces in the sky.

nodes (points of intense activity) and landmarks (points of reference). Creating the equivalence of these components within the skyscraper's built form provides new means for the articulation, humanising and deconstruction of its homogeneity. Strategically it enables us to delineate internal routes as meaningful pathways between destinations. The edges between the compartmentalised spaces need to be further articulated. Within the built form we might designate definable precincts as neighbourhoods and districts. At crucial points and locations across the high-rise's height there would be nodes and points of intense activity to differentiate these spaces from the others. The vertical spaces must also have definable

004

006

008

033

056

072

088

122|123

126

138

148

173

180

193

212

218

220

The articulated penthouse as a tropical garden.
Reference: Waterfront House, Kuala Lumpur.
[© T. R. Hamzah & Yeang, 2001]

Lower floors with an ampitheatre and conference
facilities. Reference: Waterfront House
[© T. R. Hamzah & Yeang, 2001]

markers or landmarks within them as
points of reference in this new vertical
townscape. All these aspects become
meaningful when the circulation systems
achieve the multiplicity of having not just one main
access or circulation system as in the conventional high-
rise, but a series of secondary, tertiary and quarternary
access routes and systems as would be found at the
ground.

Public Realms and 'Place-Making' in the Sky

We can also apply a townscape approach to the urban design of the skyscraper. This approach seeks the creation of the experience of place as a result of 'serial vision'; or, in this instance, through designing the skyscraper's internal environment as an unfolding sequence of street (in-the-sky) scenes, and as a compendium of optimal qualities in a vertical townscape that includes the architectural, the painterly, the poetic and the practical (G Cullen). By design, we can then spatially emphasise the relationships between secondary built forms within the skyscraper's built form and all that surrounds them, and seek to enclose such secondary spaces around public realms rather than site the secondary built forms haphazardly within the skyscraper's prime built form. As with horizontal urban design, vertical urban design must further deal with the sense of desolation of its inhabitants and recover its lost community and centre.

Joined at the ground plane

Raised above the ground plane

Mounded at the ground

Submerged below ground

▷ The tower with a deep facade containing vegetation.

004

006

008

033

056

072

088

▷ **124|125**

126

138

148

173

180

193

212

218

220

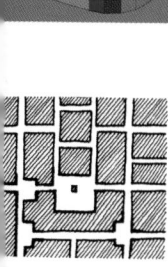

A further aspect of conventional urban design is the figure-ground relationships between built forms within the townscape. In the case of the high-rise we need to map the in-between spaces found in figure-ground analysis not just in plan but also sectionally. In urban design, such spaces between buildings need to be designed. Similarly, then, in the case of the high-rise we need to create these transitional spaces between the net usable areas within each floor. These spaces need to be configured to work for the people who inhabit them. In designing the new high-rise our design becomes a generator of contexts and of new internal spaces within its built form that redefine the in-between spaces between floors rather than seeking to displace or eliminate them.

The design of the new high-rise therefore requires a radical departure from the conventional design of this building type. By relooking at the internal spaces in the skyscraper using an approach that requires the creation of a vertical townscape, the floors of the built form can be further destratified and be reconfigured with greater blurring of spaces and merging of spatial programmes.

◁ Plan diagram of streets and squares and the park in the city grid. Parks and open gardens are urban spaces that provide contrast to the hard urban environment and opportunities for relaxation and recreation. Skyscrapers should be designed as mimetic cities. [Source: *Finding Lost Space*, Trancik, 1986]

Vertical Landscaping and Open Spaces
chapter 07

... Urban parks serve a respiratory function in cities but, in addition, provide spaces for public recreation, relaxation and health. They are also important for environmentally sustainable and ecological reasons ...

004
006
008
033
056
072
088
101
▷ **126** 127
138
148
173
180
193
212
218
220

... Landscaping also has aesthetic benefits that soften and make less artificial the intensity of the high-rise built form. In aggregate, the introduction of vertical landscaping can serve to produce- ecologically, socially and aesthetically- a fusion of rural and urban existence in a life-in-the-sky, as well as the fusion of outdoor and indoor space ...

Vertical Landscaping and Open Spaces

Landscaping is a key aspect of any city's urban design and the provision of open spaces in the city is similarly important. Urban parks serve a respiratory function in cities but, in addition, provide spaces for public recreation, relaxation and health. They are also important for environmentally sustainable and ecological reasons. Landscaping serves to balance the inorganic hard quality of the man-made built environment with greenery and the full complement of ecosystem components.

▷ Greening could also mean the provision of social parks for public recreational use within the high-rise's upper levels.

◁ View of Central Park.

004
006
008
033
056
072
088
101
128|129 ▷
138
148
173
180
193
212
218
220

◁ Central Park in New York is a large mat of green external landscape that can be recreated as a large park within the mega high-rise built form.

◁ The park-in-the-sky should also have a water feature.

Landscaping also has aesthetic benefits that soften and make less artificial the intensity of the high-rise built form. In aggregate, the introduction of vertical landscaping can serve to produce ecologically, socially and aesthetically – a fusion of rural and urban existence in a life-in-the-sky, as well as the fusion of outdoor and indoor space.

Vertical Landscaping and Open Spaces

Ecologically, macro landscape design must maintain a continuity of vegetation as vertical ecological corridors flowing upwards to all levels in the high-rise built form from the landscaping at the ground plane (as in the city's horizontal ecological corridors). New techniques of constructing and maintaining vertical landscaping need to be developed (ie, irrigation and drainage). There are a number of ways to locate landscaping vertically in the high-rise built form by juxtaposing, intermixing and integrating the organic components with the inorganic.

Horizontal strategy . The park should preferably be linked to the ecosystems at the ground plane.

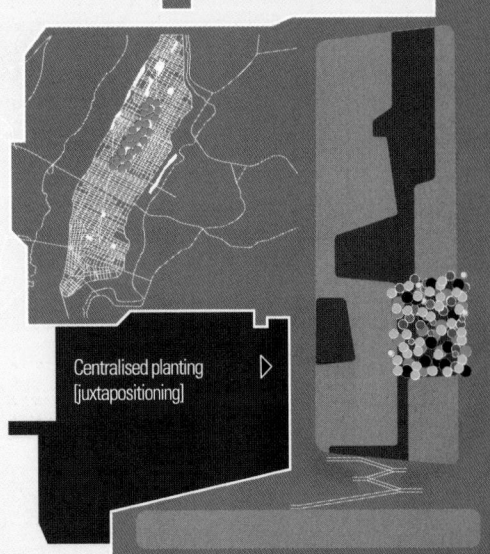

Centralised planting [juxtapositioning]

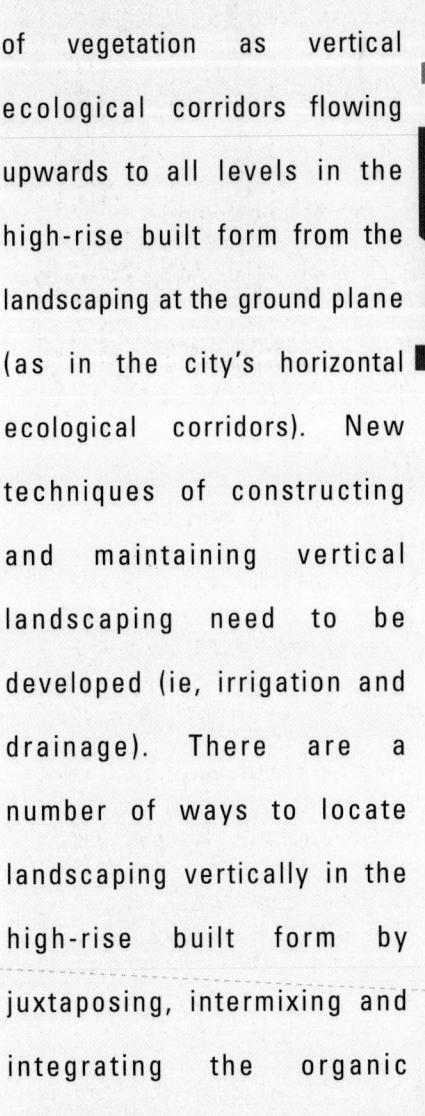

Dispersed/ intermixing planting strategy.

Basic strategies for incorporating green mass into the skyscraper built form.

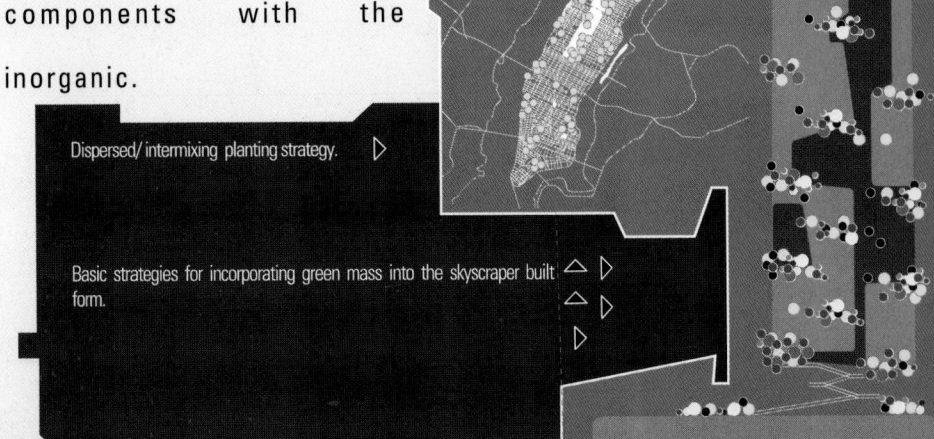

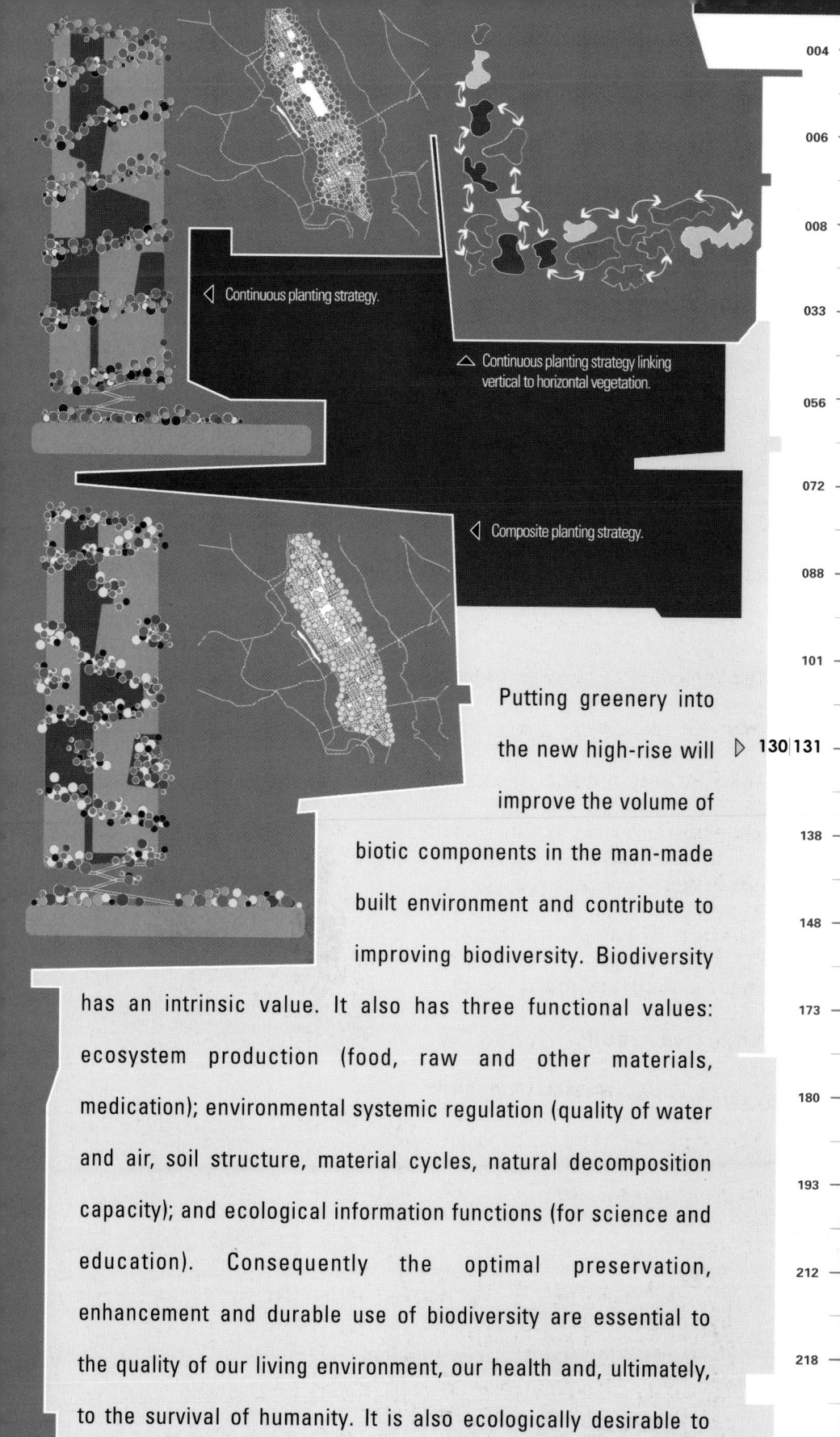

Continuous planting strategy.

△ Continuous planting strategy linking vertical to horizontal vegetation.

◁ Composite planting strategy.

004

006

008

033

056

072

088

101

130|131

138

148

173

180

193

212

218

220

Putting greenery into the new high-rise will ▷ improve the volume of biotic components in the man-made built environment and contribute to improving biodiversity. Biodiversity has an intrinsic value. It also has three functional values: ecosystem production (food, raw and other materials, medication); environmental systemic regulation (quality of water and air, soil structure, material cycles, natural decomposition capacity); and ecological information functions (for science and education). Consequently the optimal preservation, enhancement and durable use of biodiversity are essential to the quality of our living environment, our health and, ultimately, to the survival of humanity. It is also ecologically desirable to design the systemic aspects of the high-rise as a man-made intensive mimetic ecosystem (see Chapter 11).

Vertical Landscaping and Open Spaces

Ebenezer Howard's garden city concept envisions a city encircled by an inalienable green belt. His ideal city is projected as 6000 acres with 1000 acres for city use, a ratio of city to green at 1:6. The WHO (World Health Organization), however, recommends the provision of 25 square metres of greenery per resident in urban development. This same standard (or higher) must be applied to the high-rise with provisions of greenery located not only at the ground plane but distributed throughout the tower's built form. Using a standard of 130 square metres (gross area) per occupant to calculate the population in an office tower, the consequence of providing of 25 square metres of greenery per resident, is that 20 per cent total gross floor area should be added to any office tower for landscaped sky courts. This is commensurate with the general town planning standards for master

Integrating the city's ecological corridor with building as a mega-sandwich landscape. Reference: Kowloon waterfront, Hong Kong. [© T. R. Hamzah & Yeang, 2001]

◁ Greening the tower need not diminish the form of the building.

004

in the provision of 10–15 per cent of gross planning area for parks. However, as built systems are mostly inorganic, it is preferred that the organic mass be equivalent to, or more than, the inorganic, and a more desirable ratio of between inorganic areas to organic landscaped areas might be 1:1 .

In the way that landscape design is a crucial component of any urban design plan, vertical landscaping must be an essential aspect of the new high-rise. Vegetation in the high-rise can also directly mitigate urban heat islands, both by shading heat-absorbing surfaces and through evapotranspiration cooling. Studies have shown that vegetation consistently lowers wall surface temperatures by about 17°C and can reduce air-conditioning costs by 25–80 per cent.

006
008
033
056
072
088
101
▷ 132|133
138
148
173
180
193
212
218
220

Vertical Landscaping and Open Spaces

Horizontal and vertical landscaping strategy. Reference: Bishopsgate Towers, London.
[© T. R. Hamzah & Yeang, 1997]

The extent to which measured reductions in surface temperature and savings in cooling costs can be attributed to direct building shade rather than evaporation cooling is not currently clear. In most circumstances, the impact of one or several large plants and trees on ambient temperatures and cooling load is small compared to the shading effect. Cool air produced in the tree crown is dissipated by the much larger volume of air moving through the tree. However, large numbers of trees and expansive green spaces can reduce local air temperatures by 1–5°C, and the advection of this cool air can lower the demand for air conditioning in hot climates at lower latitudes.

Overlay of vertical landscaping concept. Reference: Bishopsgate Towers, London.
[© T. R. Hamzah & Yeang, 1997]

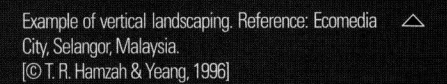

Example of vertical landscaping. Reference: Ecomedia City, Selangor, Malaysia.
[© T. R. Hamzah & Yeang, 1996]

Landscaping costs are offset by benefits to users who enjoy a healthier environment,

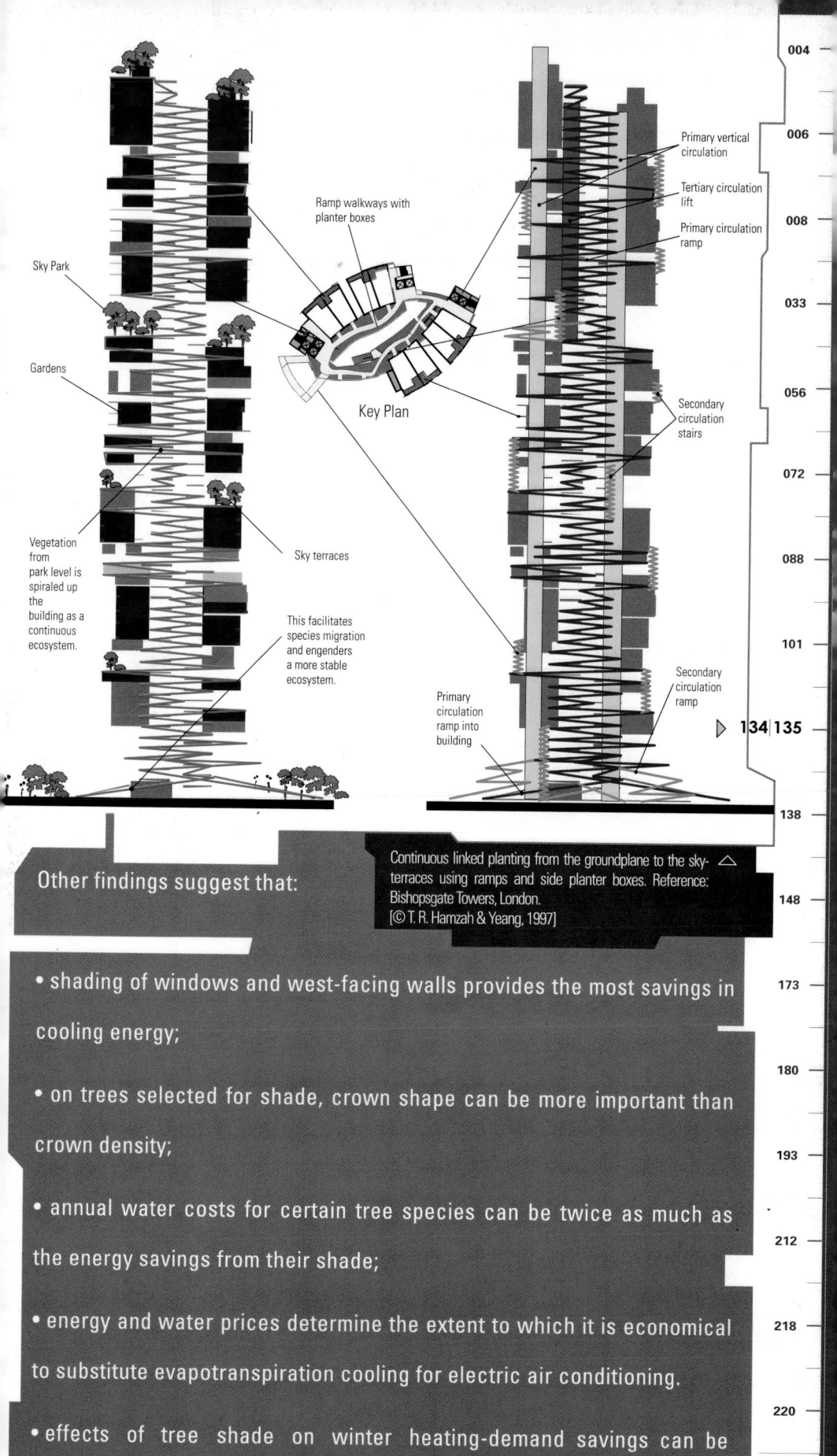

Sky Park

Gardens

Vegetation from park level is spiraled up the building as a continuous ecosystem.

Ramp walkways with planter boxes

Key Plan

Sky terraces

This facilitates species migration and engenders a more stable ecosystem.

Primary vertical circulation

Tertiary circulation lift

Primary circulation ramp

Secondary circulation stairs

Secondary circulation ramp

Primary circulation ramp into building

Continuous linked planting from the groundplane to the sky-terraces using ramps and side planter boxes. Reference: Bishopsgate Towers, London.
[© T. R. Hamzah & Yeang, 1997]

Other findings suggest that:

- shading of windows and west-facing walls provides the most savings in cooling energy;

- on trees selected for shade, crown shape can be more important than crown density;

- annual water costs for certain tree species can be twice as much as the energy savings from their shade;

- energy and water prices determine the extent to which it is economical to substitute evapotranspiration cooling for electric air conditioning.

- effects of tree shade on winter heating-demand savings can be substantial.

004
006
008
033
056
072
088
101
▷ 134|135
138
148
173
180
193
212
218
220

Vertical Landscaping and Open Spaces

Parks in the high-rise can be important sources of fresh cool air in the city as a whole. They can be designed to increase nocturnal cooling and the advection of cool air into the warmer surroundings. Much of the park can be well-irrigated turf without trees. Transpiring turf shades the horizontal ground surfaces and cools the air. Although trees in turf can increase the evapotranspiration cooling effect, they can also reduce radiant heat loss to the sky and convection/advection. Multilayered plantings of drought-tolerant species can create a buffer along the perimeter of the green areas.

The provision of ecological corridors to ▷
the city and up the built form.
Source: *Finding Lost Space*, Trancik,
1986]

More specifically, vertical landscaping can be carried out at both the micro and macro levels in the high-rise. At the macro level, the provision of landscaping is similar to the provision of green open spaces, green corridors, green parks, green avenues and promenades at the ground plane. In the skyscraper, large spaces equivalent to parks may be in the form of larger trays that can be vegetated or as a series of stepped

Elements can be △
greened using
proprietary roof-
garden systems.

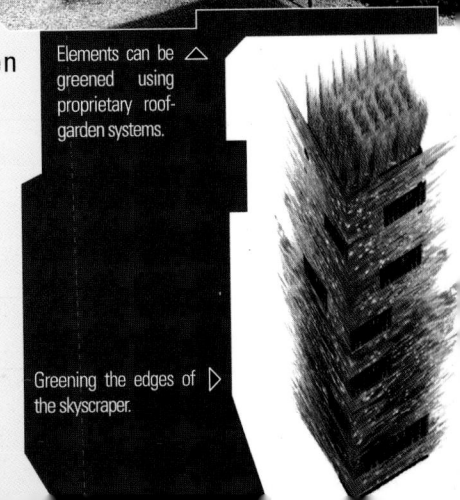

Greening the edges of ▷
the skyscraper.

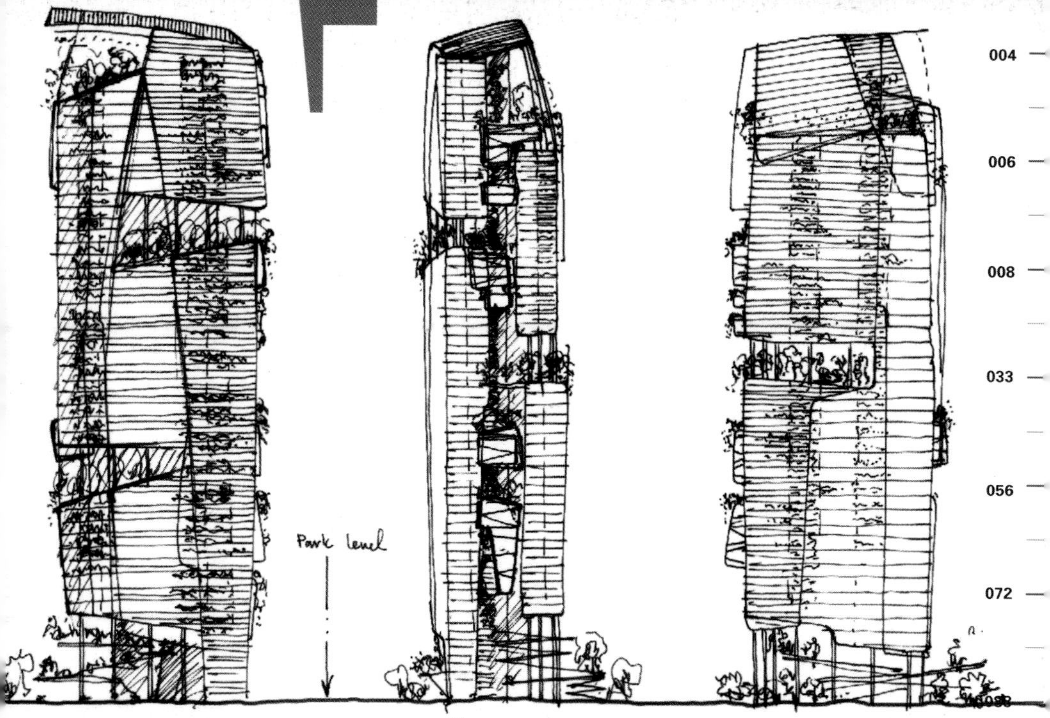

004

006

008

033

056

072

Park level

Reference: Sketches of Eco Tower, Elephant and Castle , London by Ridzwa Fathan . [© T R Hamzah & Yeang, 2000]

△

▽ Greening opportunities within the high-rise.

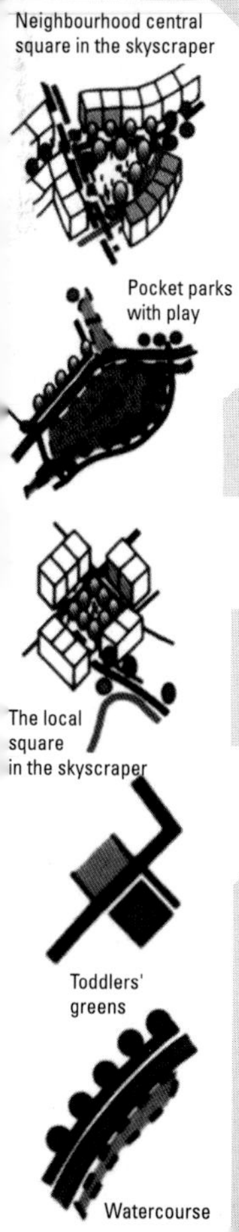

101

136|137

138

148

173

180

193

212

218

220

Neighbourhood central square in the skyscraper

Pocket parks with play

The local square in the skyscraper

Toddlers' greens

Watercourse

gardens. Large ramps can be vegetated to act as continuing vertical ecological corridors. Residences can have 'front garden' terraces and 'back garden' balconies. The predominant factor limiting the provision of greenery in the high-rise is access to daylight. In temperate climatic zones, for instance, the sun path is generally southwards and it is at the southerly aspects of the skyscraper facade that greenery is best located in order for it to survive. Conversely, in the tropics the greenery would be on the east and west facades and on the roof.

In the same way that landscaping and green spaces are vital to the traditional city, it is crucial to incorporate these as vertical landscaping and as parks-in-the-sky in the new high-rise.

... As with the design of residential developments at the ground plane, the design of the residential high-rise must seek to create communities as neighbourhoods in the towers ...

004
006
008
033
056
072
088
101
126

▷ **138|139**

148
173
180
193
212
218
220

... The biggest social problems in the case of the high-rise are isolation and the increasing alienation of inhabitants from each other...

Creating Neighbourhoods in the Sky

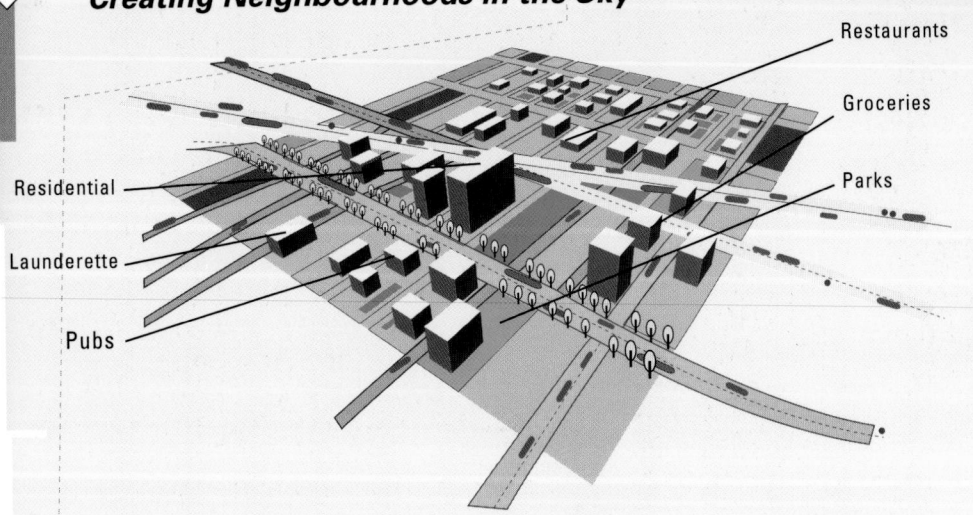

Restaurants

Groceries

Parks

Residential

Launderette

Pubs

As with the design of residential developments at the ground plane, the design of the residential high-rise must seek to create communities as neighbourhoods in the towers. Within its built form the new high-rise must provide opportunities to create a sense of community, of neighborhood and, eventually the development of an internalised local townscape. The design of the relationship between these and the building's circulation systems should enable inhabitants of a high-rise community to move and circulate within the boundaries of their neighbourhood realms.

The biggest social problems in the case of the high-rise are isolation and the increasing alienation of inhabitants from each other. The layouts of the individual floors and the relationship between floors must provide adequate opportunities for inhabitants to interact socially. In ameliorating the quality of residential life in the high-rise, the design must seek to recreate (as far as possible) the ideal neighbourhood residential unity that we find effective at the ground plane.

△ We need to avoid the stacked deck and the monotonous tower.

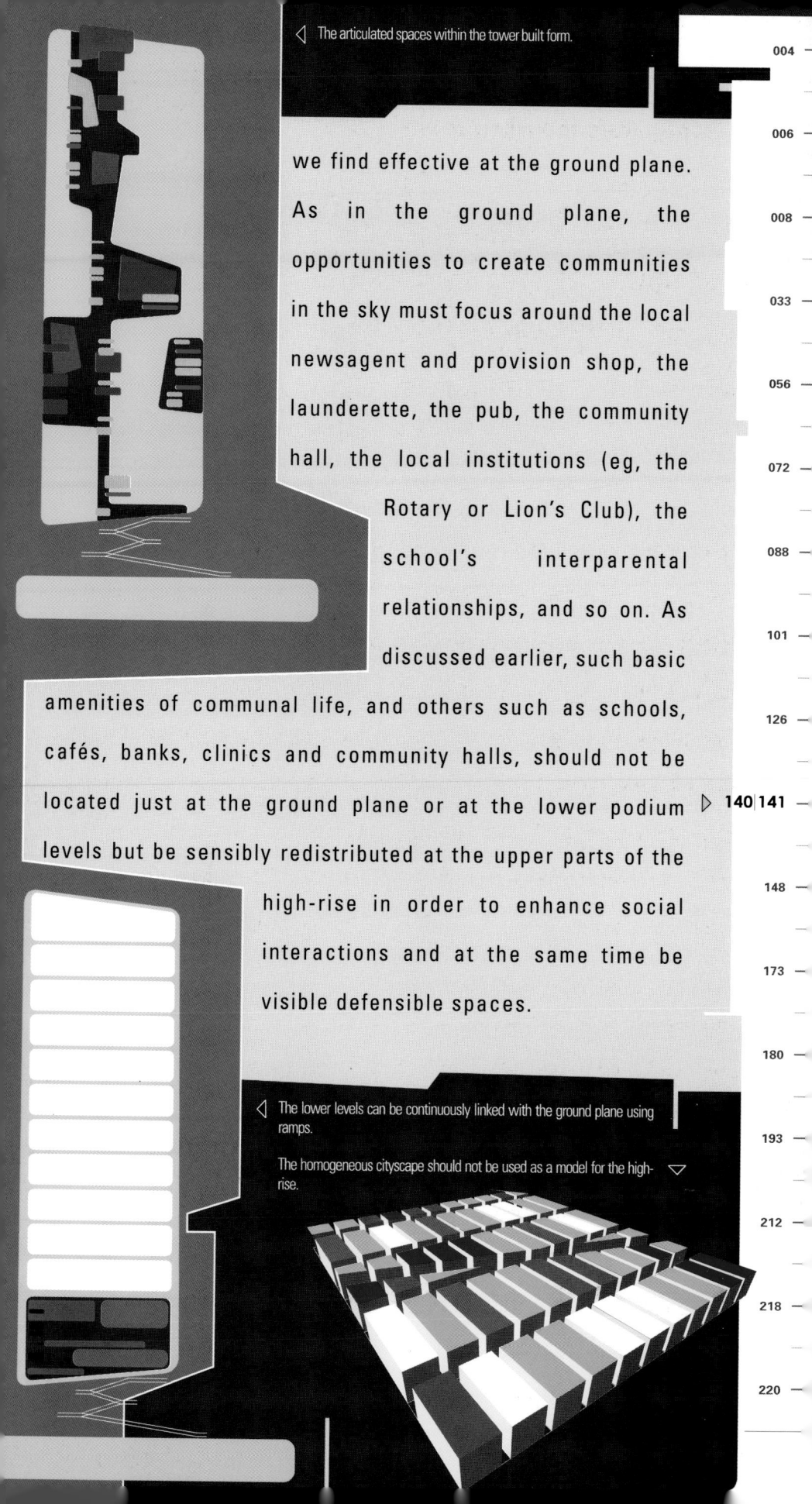

we find effective at the ground plane. As in the ground plane, the opportunities to create communities in the sky must focus around the local newsagent and provision shop, the launderette, the pub, the community hall, the local institutions (eg, the Rotary or Lion's Club), the school's interparental relationships, and so on. As discussed earlier, such basic amenities of communal life, and others such as schools, cafés, banks, clinics and community halls, should not be located just at the ground plane or at the lower podium levels but be sensibly redistributed at the upper parts of the high-rise in order to enhance social interactions and at the same time be visible defensible spaces.

◁ The lower levels can be continuously linked with the ground plane using ramps.

The homogeneous cityscape should not be used as a model for the high-rise. ▽

Creating Neighbourhoods in the Sky

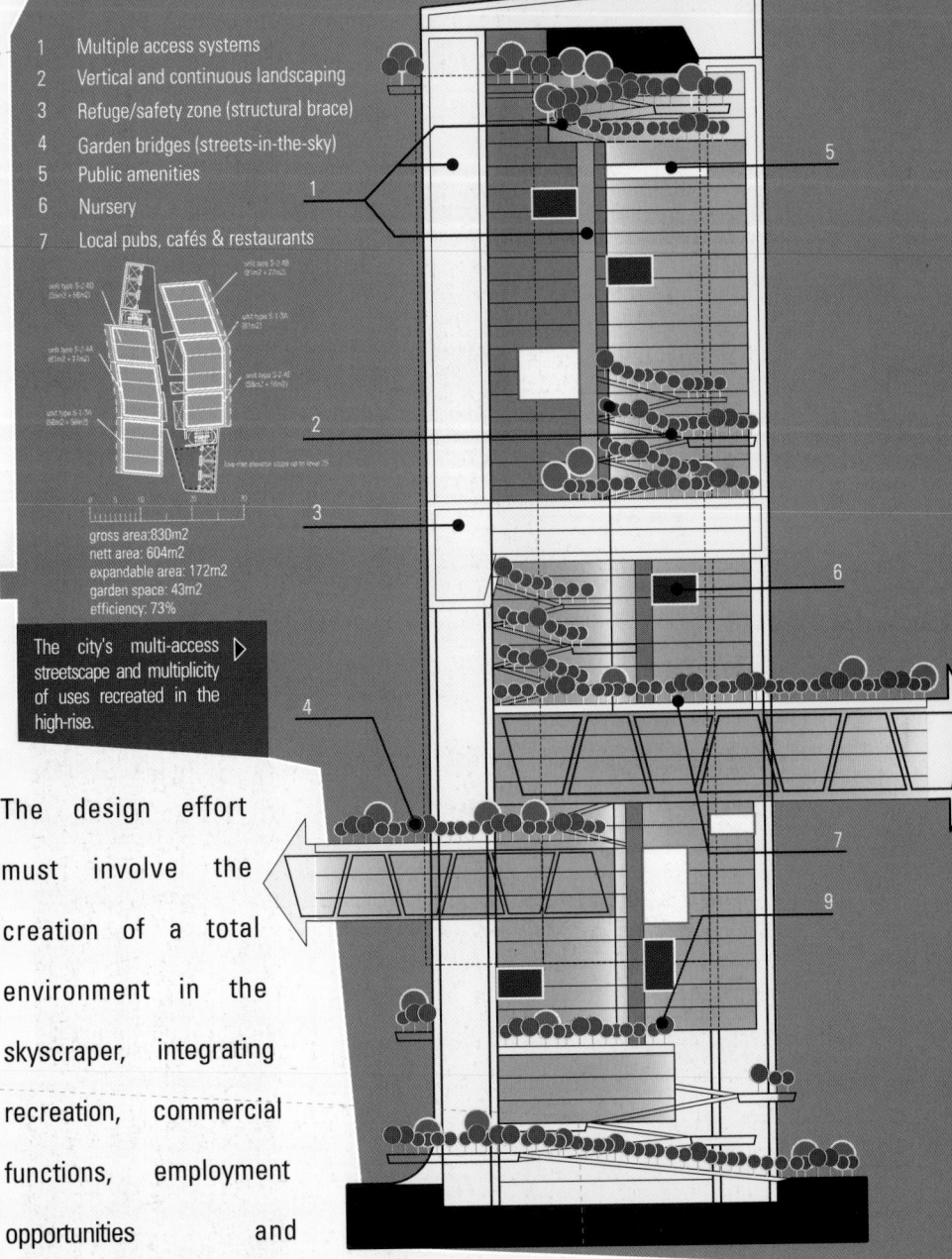

1   Multiple access systems
2   Vertical and continuous landscaping
3   Refuge/safety zone (structural brace)
4   Garden bridges (streets-in-the-sky)
5   Public amenities
6   Nursery
7   Local pubs, cafés & restaurants

gross area:830m2
nett area: 604m2
expandable area: 172m2
garden space: 43m2
efficiency: 73%

▷ The city's multi-access streetscape and multiplicity of uses recreated in the high-rise.

The design effort must involve the creation of a total environment in the skyscraper, integrating recreation, commercial functions, employment opportunities and educational facilities with the housing provision. Well-designed urban districts and neighbourhoods succeed because they recognise the primary importance of the public realm – the network of spaces between buildings that determines the layout, form of the area and, eventually, of the city. As with conditions at the ground, the shape of public spaces in the high-rise and the way they link together are essential to the cohesion of urban neighbourhoods and communities. Design should also permit a multiplicity of different forms of

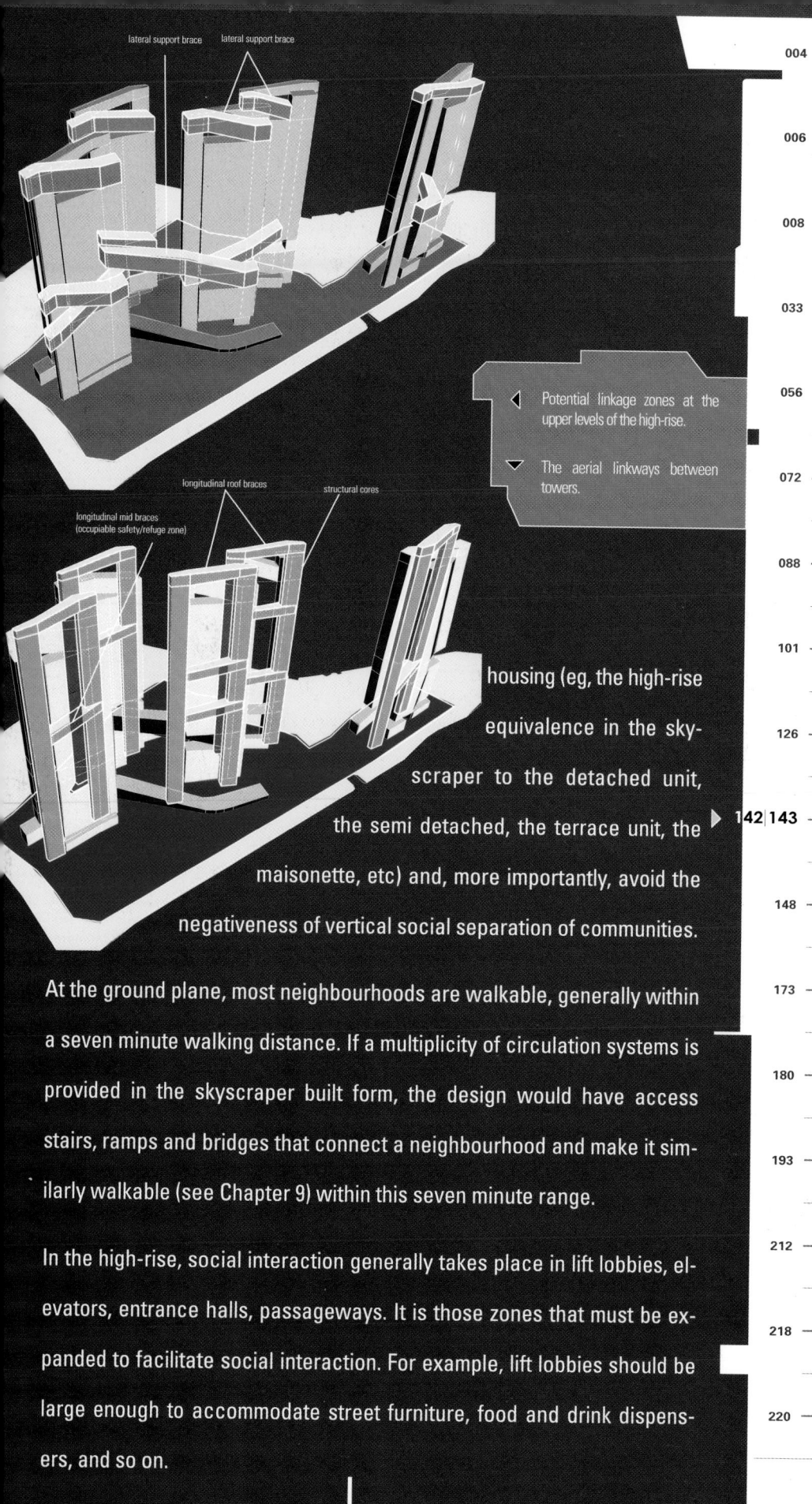

lateral support brace   lateral support brace

longitudinal roof braces   structural cores

longitudinal mid braces
(occupiable safety/refuge zone)

004

006

008

033

056

072

088

101

126

142|143

148

173

180

193

212

218

220

◄ Potential linkage zones at the upper levels of the high-rise.

▽ The aerial linkways between towers.

housing (eg, the high-rise equivalence in the sky-scraper to the detached unit, the semi detached, the terrace unit, the maisonette, etc) and, more importantly, avoid the negativeness of vertical social separation of communities.

At the ground plane, most neighbourhoods are walkable, generally within a seven minute walking distance. If a multiplicity of circulation systems is provided in the skyscraper built form, the design would have access stairs, ramps and bridges that connect a neighbourhood and make it similarly walkable (see Chapter 9) within this seven minute range.

In the high-rise, social interaction generally takes place in lift lobbies, elevators, entrance halls, passageways. It is those zones that must be expanded to facilitate social interaction. For example, lift lobbies should be large enough to accommodate street furniture, food and drink dispensers, and so on.

Creating Neighbourhoods in the Sky

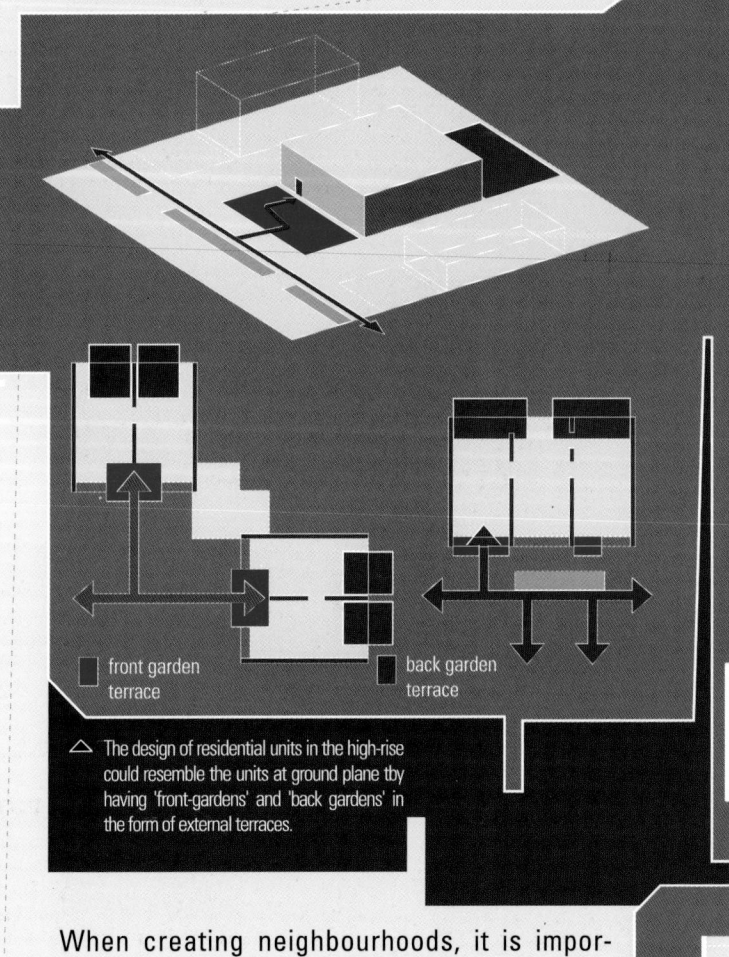

front garden terrace

back garden terrace

△ The design of residential units in the high-rise could resemble the units at ground plane tby having 'front-gardens' and 'back gardens' in the form of external terraces.

When creating neighbourhoods, it is important to have mixed and inclusive communities that offer a choice of housing and lifestyles. Different types of housing and tenures do not make bad neighbours. The creation of successful residential communities is about much more than visually attractive design. It is in essence about providing opportunities for dwelling units that respond to people's needs, and providing a framework within which communities can become established and grow.

0 1   5   10

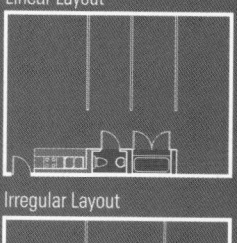

Dispersed Layout

Compact Layout

Linear Layout

Irregular Layout

004
006
008
033
056
072
088
101
126

144|145

148
173
180
193
212
218
220

△ Internal floor plans can vary to produce a range of options for residential occupants.

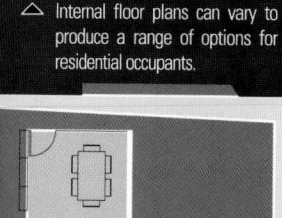

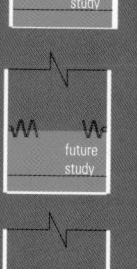

future study

future study

future study

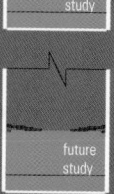

future study

The provision of mixed neighbourhoods in the high-rise, with people of different ages and economic status, different lifestyles and different levels of mobility and independence can have a number of important community benefits. For example, they can:

• lead to a better balance of demand for community services and facilities such as schools, recreation facilities and care for elderly people;

• provide opportunities for 'lifetime communities' where people can change dwellings without leaving a neighbourhood;

• make neighbourhoods more robust by avoiding large concentrations of dwelling units of the same type;

• enable community self-help such as arrangements for child care, help with shopping, the garden or during the winter freeze;

• assist community surveillance with people coming and going throughout the day and evening, compared to the dormitory suburb which becomes deserted during the working day making opportunities for crime easier.

◁ Rooms can be designed to facilitate their being subdivided to provide

Creating Neighbourhoods in the Sky

The provision of a mix of dwelling types and uses in the high-rise can also contribute to the creation of more attractive residential precincts by enabling a greater diversity of built forms and scales. For example:

• dwelling units can give scale to local centres;

• the larger units (multiple-level, equivalent to town houses on the horizontal plane) can contribute to more formal compositions of avenues, circuses and squares-in-the-sky and help frame the open spaces;

• community user spaces such as schools and health centres can be designed to give status to civic spaces and provide a focus for thecommunity in the new high-rises.

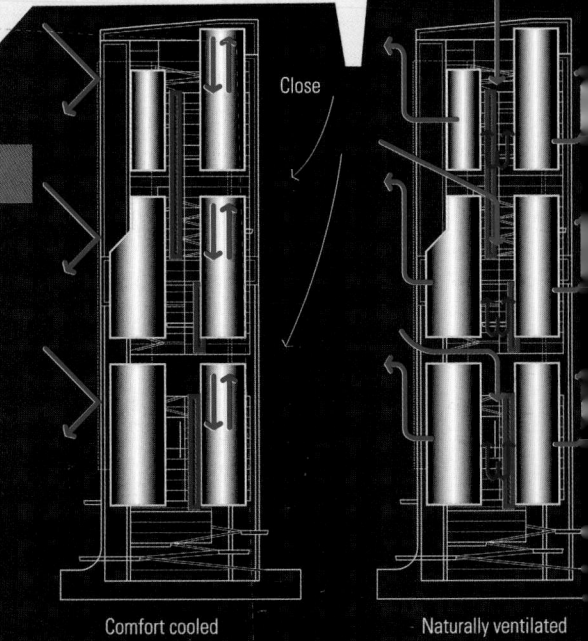

Naturally ventilated

Minimum mechanical air

Close

Comfort cooled

Naturally ventilated

The internal voids in the skyscraper built form can be designed to provide comfortable conditions over the various seasons of the year, particularly in temperate zones.

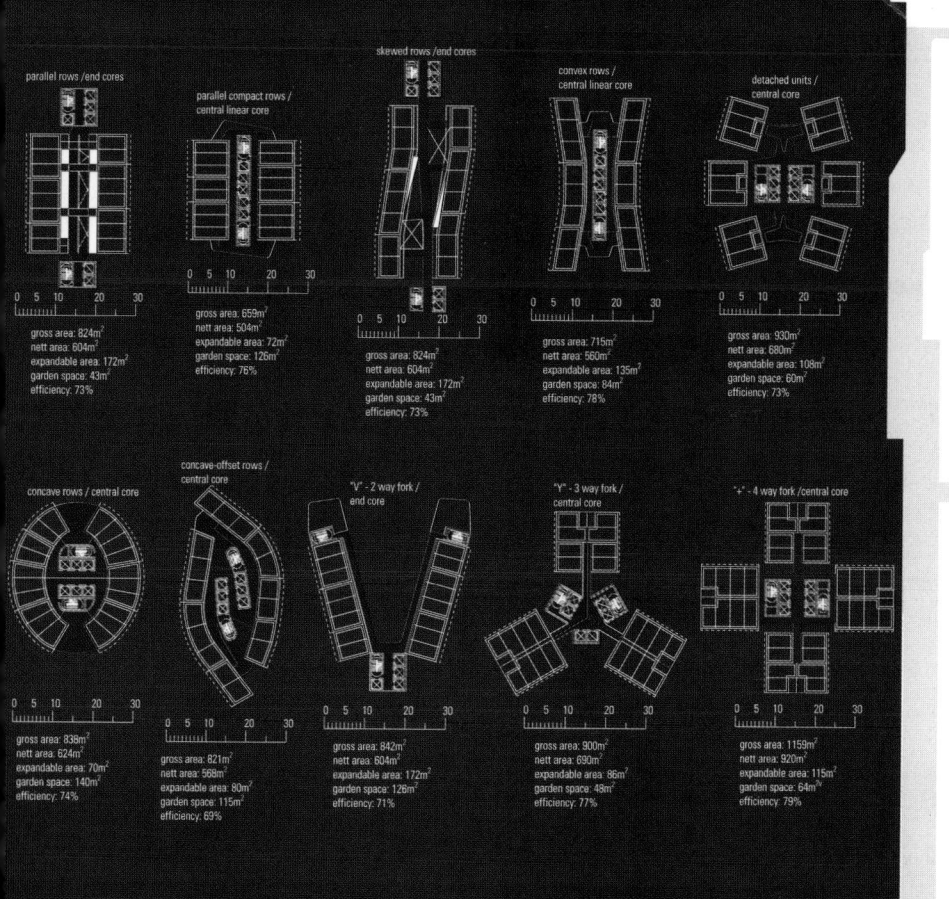

parallel rows /end cores

gross area: 824m²
nett area: 604m²
expandable area: 172m²
garden space: 43m²
efficiency: 73%

0 5 10 20 30

parallel compact rows /
central linear core

gross area: 659m²
nett area: 504m²
expandable area: 72m²
garden space: 126m²
efficiency: 76%

0 5 10 20 30

skewed rows /end cores

gross area: 824m²
nett area: 604m²
expandable area: 172m²
garden space: 43m²
efficiency: 73%

0 5 10 20 30

convex rows /
central linear core

gross area: 715m²
nett area: 560m²
expandable area: 135m²
garden space: 84m²
efficiency: 78%

0 5 10 20 30

detached units /
central core

gross area: 930m²
nett area: 680m²
expandable area: 108m²
garden space: 60m²
efficiency: 73%

0 5 10 20 30

concave rows / central core

gross area: 838m²
nett area: 624m²
expandable area: 70m²
garden space: 140m²
efficiency: 74%

0 5 10 20 30

concave-offset rows /
central core

gross area: 821m²
nett area: 568m²
expandable area: 80m²
garden space: 115m²
efficiency: 69%

0 5 10 20 30

"V" - 2 way fork /
end core

gross area: 842m²
nett area: 604m²
expandable area: 172m²
garden space: 126m²
efficiency: 71%

0 5 10 20 30

"Y" - 3 way fork /
central core

gross area: 900m²
nett area: 690m²
expandable area: 86m²
garden space: 48m²
efficiency: 77%

0 5 10 20 30

"+" - 4 way fork /central core

gross area: 1159m²
nett area: 920m²
expandable area: 115m²
garden space: 64m²
efficiency: 79%

0 5 10 20 30

△ Options in the configuring of the floor plate for a variety of residential types.

A good mix of housing types and sizes is important in creating the basis for a balanced community in the new high-rise. Case studies show that even comparatively small developments can embrace a wide mix of dwelling types. In aggregate, the new high-rise must create neighbourhoods-in-the-sky with the appropriate provision of a range of housing in terms of dwelling size, type and affordability as well as appropriate community facilities and services such as open spaces, crèches, day-care and health services. All these are important in creating the framework within which communities can grow.

... Accessibility has to include an integrated transport system that prioritises the needs of the building's occupants, providing a multiple circulation system with secondary, tertiary and even quarternary systems which may include using vertical light rail, elevators, moving travelators, escalators, ramps and stairs ...

... There are obvious correlations between movement patterns and modes of transport and land use and density...

▷ **148** | **149**

004
006
008
033
056
072
088
101
126
138
173
180
193
212
218
220

Movement, Accessibility and Streets-in-the-Sky

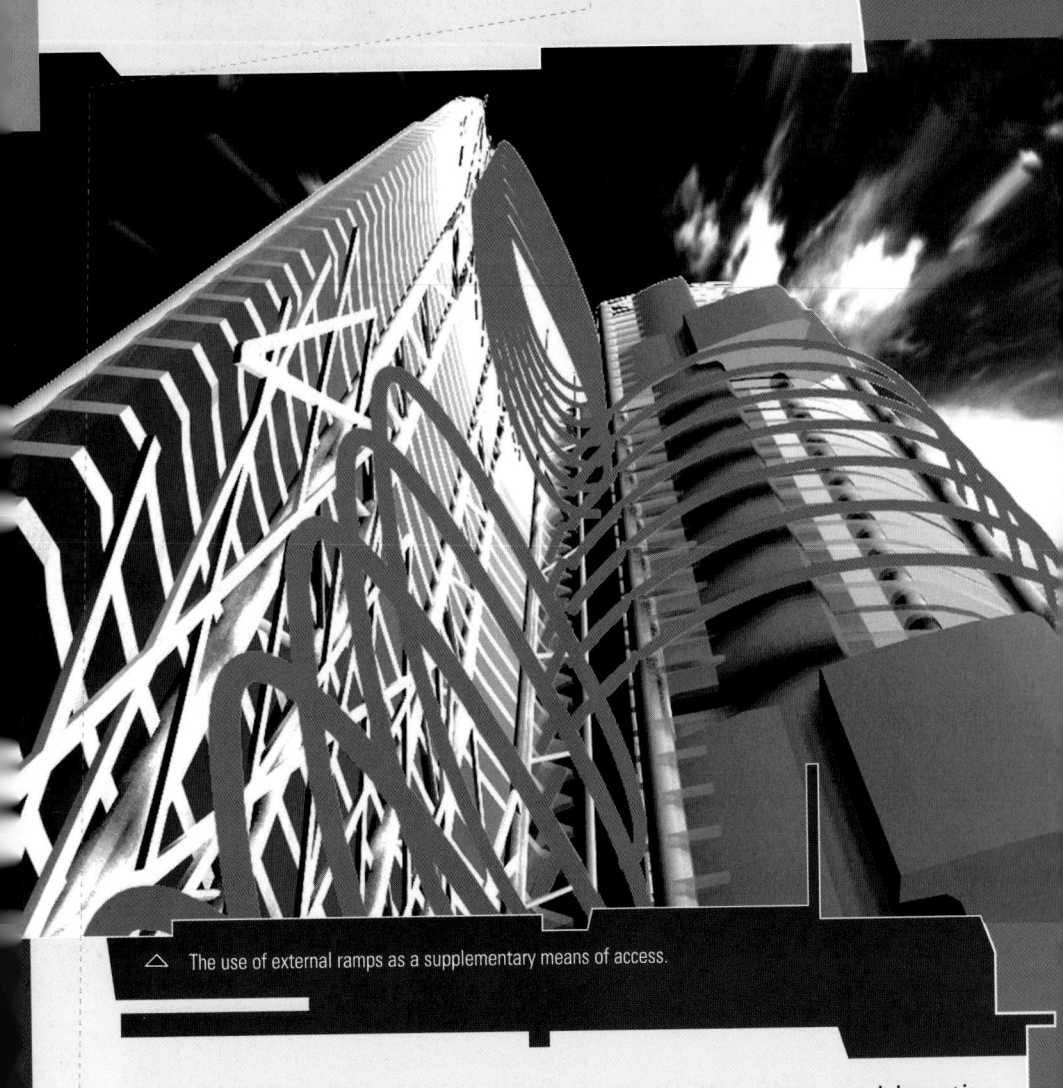

△ The use of external ramps as a supplementary means of access.

Accessibility within the high-rise affects the range and location of activities. Accessibility has to include an integrated transport system that prioritises the needs of the building's occupants, providing a multiple circulation system with secondary, tertiary and even quarternary systems which may include using vertical light rail, elevators, moving travelators, escalators, ramps and stairs. In city planning and urban redevelopment the design of transportation systems is a critical issue as mobility and communication become increasingly difficult.

Existing skyscrapers in cities do not facilitate intertower circulation.

004
006
008
033
056
072
088
101
126
138
150|151
173
180
193
212
218
220

These systems have traditionally dominated public space and planning and contribute significantly to the structuring of the city. There are obvious correlations between movement patterns and modes of transport and land use and density. The dominant forces that have shaped cities are their transportation priorities, socioeconomic priorities and cultural priorities. Transportation priorities include the extent of automobile infrastructure compared to transit. Economic priorities deal with how, for instance, a new suburban infrastructure enables greenfield growth rather than redevelopment and renewal of present urban areas. In a similar way such relationships also affect the transportation systems of the skyscraper. With the creation of streets-in-the-sky, we can consider the use of communal microelectric buses and an external light-rail rapid transit attached to the periphery of the skyscraper's built form.

▷ Staircases and mezzanine levels can be opportunities to create social meeting and interaction places.

As in the case of city planning, the transportation problem in the new high-rise is essentially one of moving people over short distances. However, the transportation problem in the high-rise is different from that in the city, in that in the latter the problem is one of restraining vehicular traffic, whereas the high-rise is conventionally an essentially car-free environment (although we should not preclude the future use of electric carts and buses). Designing a successful high-rise urban neighbourhood means thinking about journeys in a way that not only considers desired destinations and modes of transport but, importantly, acknowledges the role of such journeys in responding to social, economic and environmental objectives. It requires the definition of movement frameworks which improve accessibility while reducing the need for mechanical travel, and takes full account of the movement demands that a development will generate and

004 —
006 —
008 —
033 —
056 —
072 —
088 —
101 —
126 —
138 —
▷ 152|153 —
173 —
180 —
193 —
212 —
218 —
220 —

◁ The spaces in the skyscraper can be placed around the main circulation routes within the tower, analogous to highways in cities.

of the need to connect new areas to existing networks, for travel by foot, cycle, communal transport and electric vehicles. To ensure that a neighbourhood is well integrated with its context it must be well connected to its immediate neighbours and, within the neighbourhood itself, provide a clear structure of accessible routes that lead from one destination point to another.

△ Multilevel ramps can be used to link spaces within the high-rise built form.

Movement, Accessibility and Streets-in-the-Sky

△ The mobile population needs to be accomodated with greater interfloor accessibility.

The amount of time people devote to leisure, culture and education is increasing. This points to more mobile populations, able to move freely between residences with reduced ties to family or work.

The types of routes and streets that form a movement framework in the high-rise are crucial in determining the character of its built form. Conventionally, size and layout have been based on estimates of population (for elevators) rather than on their overall, multifunctional role. There are also other potential high-level street users, such as cyclists, which may result in the segregation of uses.

A traditional street hierarchy in the high-rise is a reminder that to have main routes passing through, rather than around, the edge of a precinct helps to sustain a variety of uses and connections. It enhances the viability of public transport provision and the mutual support between public transport and other facilities. Only when traffic levels on the principal route threaten to sever an area is it necessary to consider the need for alternative routes.

Crucial to the new skyscraper is the creation of pedestrian links, especially between important destinations. If people are to be persuaded not to use elevators, pedestrian routes demand particular attention. Because walking is a simple, low-key mode of travel requiring no complex infrastructure, pedestrians can be too easily neglected. Walking within the skyscraper must not be a disjointed and disorientating experience. We need to avoid gaps in spatial continuity.

▽ Segregation of pedestrian and vehicular traffic within the high-rise.

004
006
008
033
056
072
088
101
126
138
▷ 154 | 155
173
180
193
212
218
220

Movement, Accessibility and Streets-in-the-Sky

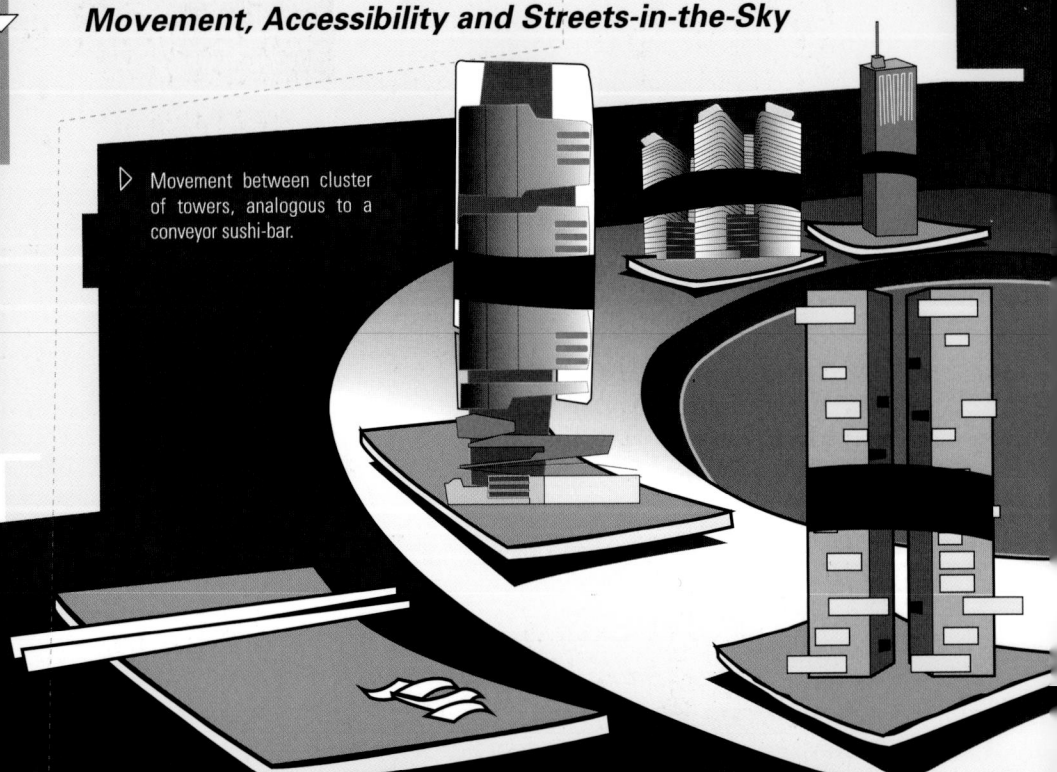

▷ Movement between cluster of towers, analogous to a conveyor sushi-bar.

Pedestrians need routes which are positive, safe, direct, accessible and free from barriers. Genzerally, routes designed for vehicles with low traffic speeds (eg, electric carts) are safe for walking, especially when the detailed layout design of, for example, junctions, crossings and surfacing have their users' needs in mind. People feel safer on access ways where there is activity, where they can be seen by drivers and other users.

▽ The hypothetical game of golf between towers.

Routes in the high-rise should lead where people want to go. Providing for the optimum variety of journeys means creating open-ended, well-connected layouts. Introverted, dead-end layouts limit people's choice of how to travel.

004

006

008

033

056

072

088

101

126

138

Secondary local access within floors enhances internal connectivity.

They also limit the adaptation or extension of the ▷ **156|157**

development. By contrast, a well-connected layout should

have the following characteristics:

- frequent points of access into and through the precincts;
- more convenient and direct routes;
- better opportunities for the provision of communal transport services through the precincts;
- clear views, easy orientations and way-finding;
- a form of traffic dispersal within the high-rise built form;
- flexibility to permit long-term adaptation and change.

173

180

193

212

218

220

Movement, Accessibility and Streets-in-the-Sky

▷ The elevatoring system should not determine the shape and layout of the tower.

The success or failure of a new high-rise development depends significantly on how well its internal precincts are connected, especially in terms of access to local services. In the contextual analysis of a site, the question of how its complexity will link to established routes and facilities is important. Generally, communities of every shape and size have always relied on effective movement as their lifeblood, both within their area and in linking them to the wider world.

It is all too easy, however, for the design of movement systems to be an end in itself, shaping the high-rise built form to the exclusion of other factors. This is particularly detrimental when one form of

△ The primary circulation system within the high-rise, consisting of elevators and stairs, is analogous to the main highway and transportation system of the city.

movement is given priority above others, as happens when a route layout designed largely for the requirements of one form of traffic [eg, elevators] is allowed to dictate the whole character of a development. Routes have a multitude of functions in addition to carrying traffic. Generally stated, places which have stood the test of time are those where traffic and other activities have been successfully integrated and where the enclosed and unenclosed spaces, and the needs of the people, not just of their vehicles, shape the area. Successful environments are those designed at the human scale with the needs of pedestrians in mind.

A secondary circulation system in the tower is analogous to the secondary network of roads in the city. These could be provided to serve 5 to 10 floors.

Large volumes within the tower built form enable subspace linkages to be made.

004
006
008
033
056
072
088
101
126
138
158 159
173
180
193
212
218
220

Movement, Accessibility and Streets-in-the-Sky

The rigidity and standardisation of floor layouts are partly the result of the dominance of the primary circulation systems of elevators and staircases in the skyscraper. Layouts in high-rises have been based on the geometry of vertical vehicle movement, with the natural result that inhabitants find it easier to use the elevators than any other form of travel. But there should be many other journeys within the skyscraper and between skyscrapers which, with better planning and multiple circulation systems, could be made by walking, cycling or mini public transport. The layout of residential components in the high-rise can also have a significant influence on which movement system is chosen.

△ The multiple-deck mobile tower.

▷ The tower as a network of primary, secondary and tertiary circulation systems.

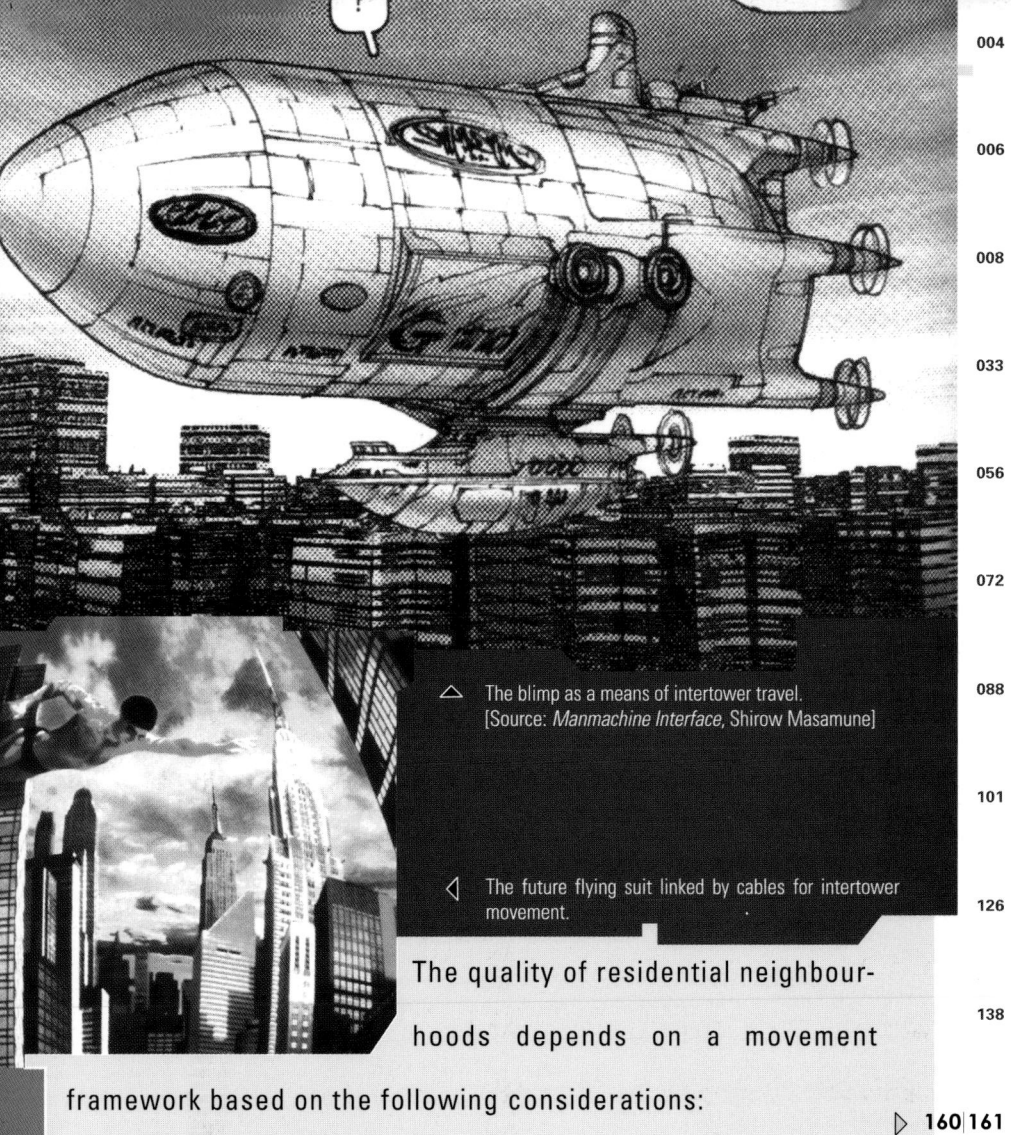

004
006
008
033
056
072
088
101
126
138

△ The blimp as a means of intertower travel.
[Source: *Manmachine Interface*, Shirow Masamune]

◁ The future flying suit linked by cables for intertower movement.

The quality of residential neighbour-

hoods depends on a movement

framework based on the following considerations:

▷ **160|161**

• the integration of new precincts into existing routes;

• providing for the maximum choice in how people make their

journey;

• the control of vehicle movement and speed;

• the design of routes that reinforce the character of the place;

• the location of shops and services near the new neighbour-

hoods.

160|161
173
180
193
212
218
220

◁ Multilevel access ways in the 3D matrix.
[Source: *Manmachine Interface*, Shirow Masamune]

Movement, Accessibility and Streets-in-the-Sky

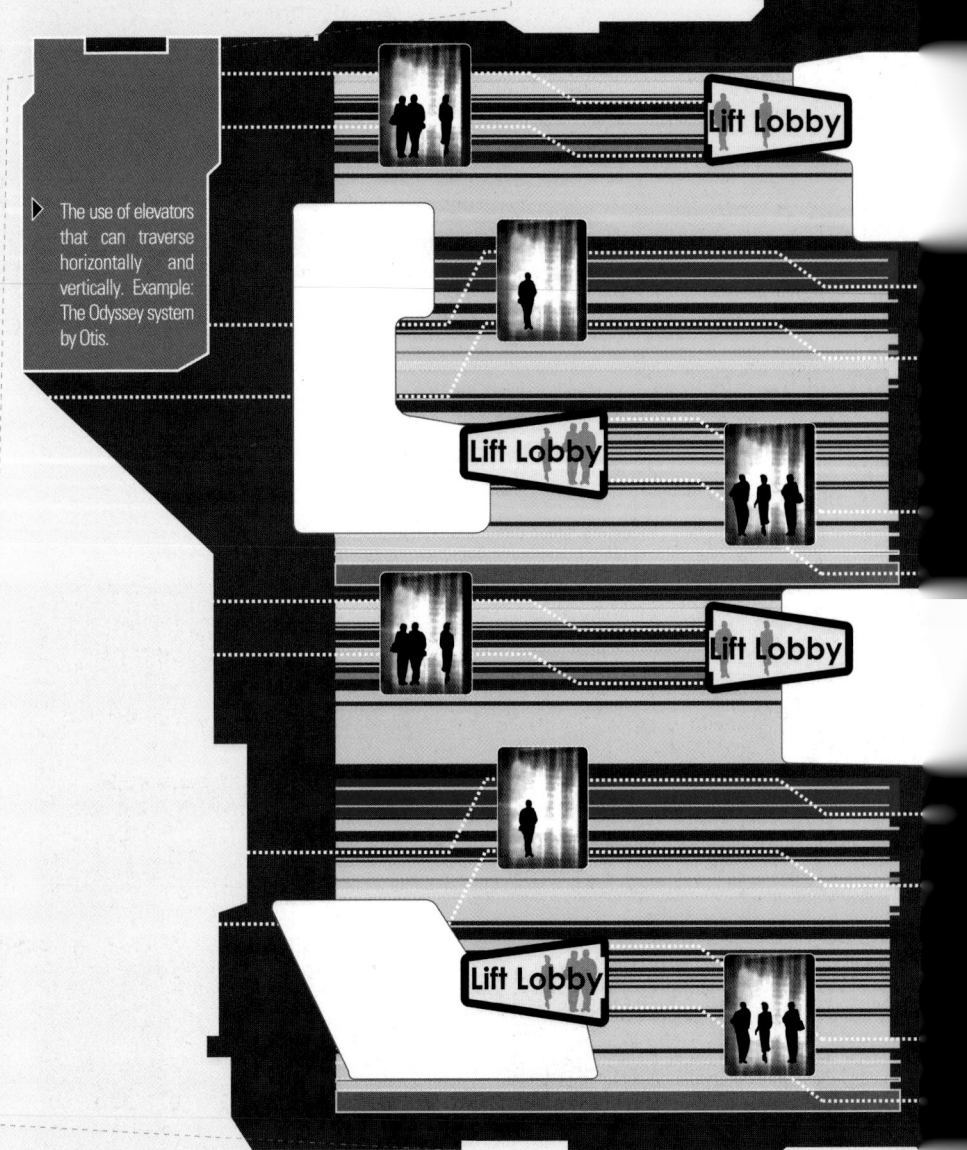

▷ The use of elevators that can traverse horizontally and vertically. Example: The Odyssey system by Otis.

Lift Lobby

Lift Lobby

Lift Lobby

Lift Lobby

The way each form of public transport is provided for in the three-dimensional matrix in the new high-rise city- namely the location of stops, walking distance to facilities and the design of routes- is fundamental to the shaping of the vertical urban design concept.

Whatever the size of the development, when designing the movement systems provision should always be made for the mobility of disabled and visually impaired people, especially in the design of footways, crossings, parking and access to front doors.

In making the high-rise walkable, pedestrian distances beyond 500 metres may be too great to walk without an alternative mode of movement. The analogy of the horizontal elevator could be made here. Multi-level buildings rely on lifts, with around 4–5 per cent of the building costs set aside for their provision. Similarly, for the new high-rise, secondary systems of transport need to be considered at the planning stage for large areas which have to be crossed on foot, for example from the main generators of movement. Here will be an opportunity to use systems such as moving pavements or travelators. Moving pavements help to alleviate the tedium of walking to remote places and are useful where walking distances in excess of 500 metres are the norm. They have a major advantage over other systems as they can be built incrementally in lengths of 100 metres and longer, with breaks between each to give access to places and lobbies as well as to allow the pavements themselves to be crossed.

The multi-media workstation tower △
for space optimisation.

004
006
008
033
056
072
088
101
126
138
▷ 162|163
173
180
193
212
218
220

Movement, Accessibility and Streets-in-the-Sky

△ Intertower linkages using a light-rapid-transit [LRT] system.

The considerations a designer would give to the movement systems when carrying out an urban design masterplan (eg, circulation systems such as roads, railways, mass transit systems, public trains, subways, pedestrian walkways, etc), need to be vertically rethought in the case of the high-rise's built form, particularly where there might be several linked high-rises in the three-dimensional matrix of spaces (eg, linkages and circulation, elevator systems, vertical LRT systems, staircases, ramps, secondary and tertiary systems, etc). In the same way that multi-accessibility at the ground plane contributes to a more comfortable and usable urban environment, there should be similar multiple accessibility in the high-rise.

We need to design the new high-rise with secondary and even tertiary and quarternary circulation systems. For instance, the main elevatoring system must not become the dictatorial system in the high-rise. There might be a set of secondary

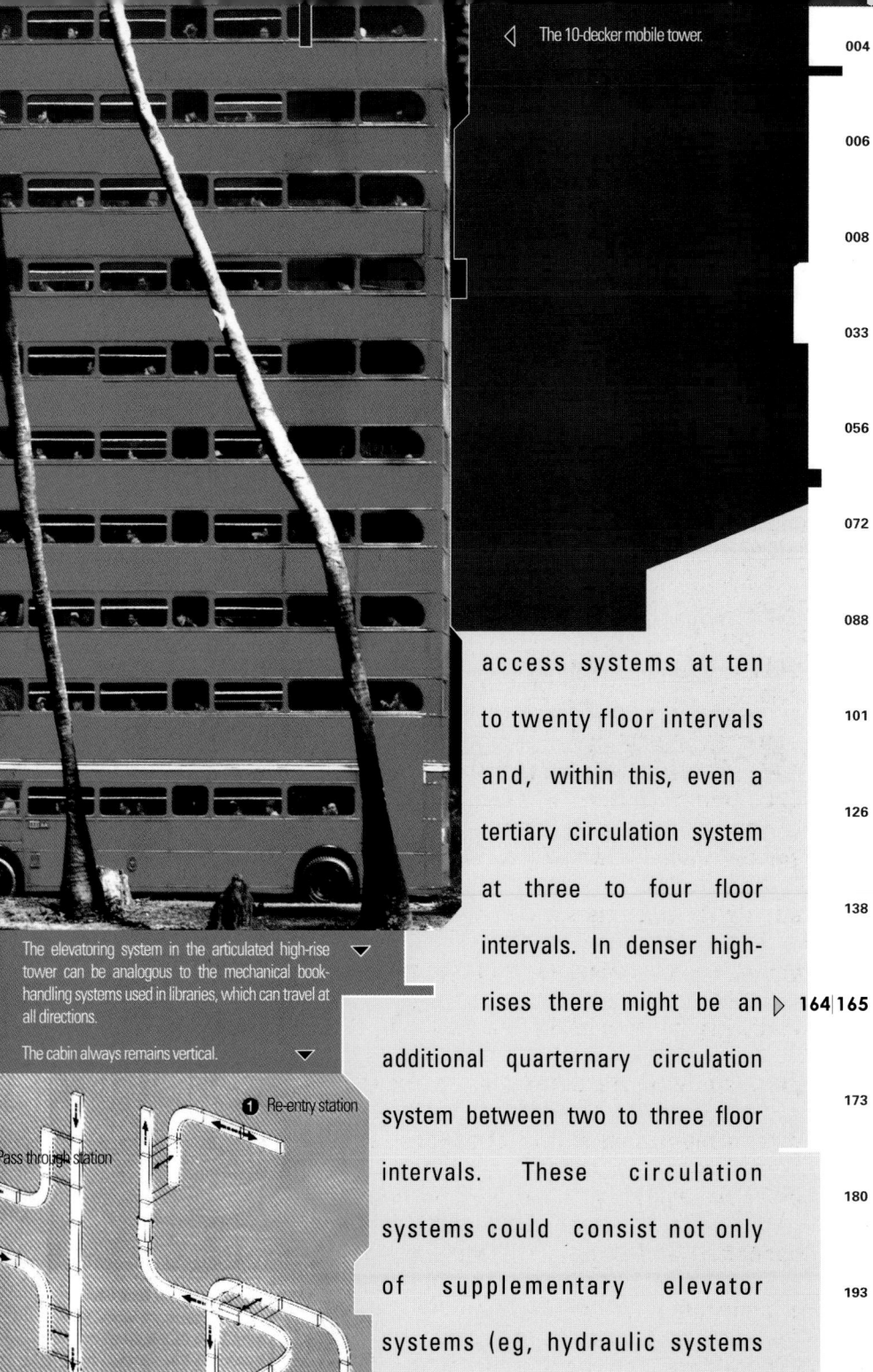

004
006
008
033
056
072
088
101
126
138
173
180
193
212
218
220

The 10-decker mobile tower.

The elevatoring system in the articulated high-rise tower can be analogous to the mechanical book-handling systems used in libraries, which can travel at all directions.

The cabin always remains vertical.

❶ Re-entry station

Pass through station

Looping station ❸

access systems at ten to twenty floor intervals and, within this, even a tertiary circulation system at three to four floor intervals. In denser high-rises there might be an ▷ **164|165** additional quarternary circulation system between two to three floor intervals. These circulation systems could consist not only of supplementary elevator systems (eg, hydraulic systems for short travel distances) but could also be pedestrian ramps, stairs, etc. All these will complement the inclusion of a multiplicity of uses in the high-rise and add to an increased internal diversification of environments.

Movement, Accessibility and Streets-in-the-Sky

> The possible provision of antigravity spaces within the tower.

With these secondary and other sublevels of accessibility, the new residential neighbourhoods-in-the-sky can be designed within acceptable walking distances between communities (ie, within 10 minutes). With this approach we need to put the pedestrian first, to ensure that walking is the preferred option in accessing different facilities within a neighbourhood or precinct in the new high-rise. This does not negate elevators as a means of vertical transport - they offer improved personal mobility and freedom of movement - but provided that these key primary vertical transport systems are in place between the different precincts in the high-rise, walking can become the easiest and quickest way to get within precincts.

Walking is an essential part of movement in cities and, in a similar way, it must become a viable alternative and pleasurable means of access in the high-rise. It has been found that within city centres walking is done largely by choice as being the easiest and quickest or most pleasant means of moving over short distances. In walkable cities a destination can be reached on foot in 30 minutes on average, and thus these cities are rarely more than 5 kilometres across (an average trip is 2–5 kilometres).

Walking is slow, depending on the kind of trip and the age and number of other people in a group. Estimated walking speeds can be around 4.7 kph for a shopping trip, rising to a speed of 7.3 metres/hr. for a journey

◁ Escape and access can be up the facade using a cable and harness system.

▷ **166|167**

to work in mixed traffic. An acceptable shopping trip would be about 300–500 metres or, if walking on ramps at 1:20, the equivalent of moving between six to seven floors in the high-rise.

004

006

008

033

056

072

088

101

126

138

173

180

193

212

218

220

Comparative Plans of Transport Systems		Comparative Sections Two-Way Operation	Turning Radii	Economic Distance Between Stops	Passenger or Vehicle Capacity Per Hour One Way	Average Speed
					1 015 000	4.8 km/hr 3 mph
					2-5 000	16 km/hr 10 mph
			Straight	100-400m	6000	2.5 km/hr 1.5 mph
			Straight & curved	100-400m	6000	7.5 km/hr 4.5 mph
					700-900 v.p.hr	13-24 km/hr 8-15 mph
			24 m 80'	600 m 5 mile	4-5 000	50 km/hr 30 mph

△ The different public modes used at the ground plane can be transposed vertically in the skyscraper.
[Source: *Future Transport in Cities*, Brian Richards, 2001]

The high-rise's elevatoring system is equivalent to the subway system in a city and can be mapped in a similar way (see Chapter 4). However, it is inadequate as the only means of mass transport in the vertical city. We need to supplement it with not just other multi-accessibility systems but with novel adaptations of light-rail systems. These could be located at the periphery of the high-rise with stations (at about every 10 to 20 floors) to provide rapid mass-transit access up and down the building, especially in the case of the supertall or superdense high-rise (eg, over 100,000 square metres skyscraper per tower). Such light-rail vehicles are generally articulated, capable of high acceleration and run at average speeds of 17–20 kph with top speeds of 30–40 kph. Potentially they can carry 20 to 30 passengers depending on their length. In as far as possible, the design should reduce the number of interchanges because the public dislikes them; an ideal transport network avoids the need for excessive interchanges in a movement system that gives a seamless transition from one mode to another.

During the past century people have tended to live further and further from their place of employment. They have moved from city centres to suburbs and from suburbs to commuter towns. In some cities almost all the reduction in working hours have been used up in increased commuting time. One of the main reasons for this is the concentration of people and employment in large units (in buildings) which led to high growth in CBDs and city centres. However, the nature of working life is starting to change again in the digital economy. A primary shift in the location of work will affect people in three main ways: routine teleworking jobs, vehicle-based jobs; and jobs involving top-level personal contacts.

▽ The management of crowds at high-density zones within the skyscraper needs to be addressed.

004
006
008
033
056
072
088
101
126
138
173
180
193
212
218
220

Movement, Accessibility and Streets-in-the-Sky

To make the skyscraper walkable there can be greater provision of walkways and ramps between floors so that inhabitants have an alternative walkable circulation system in addition to the main stairs and the escape stairs. The design of other movement routes such as passageways, bridges and ramps can be expanded at critical places to provide small open spaces and mini-parks within the high-rise built form. These become rest spaces as the skyscraper becomes a walkable realm.

The DNA molecule as a model for linkages in the high-rise.
[Source: *Nature- Concise Encyclopedia*, David Burnie,1998]

SRT systems

Ramp promenade

Fire stairs

Helipads

Evacuation zones

District lifts

Service cranes

Local lifts

Skin crawlers

Local stairs

Gondolas

Travelators

Primary Circulation

Function: Links all major program-matic zones in hypertower with the entrance and its environs
Features: Continuous SRT system with fully automated monorail twin tracks, integrated SRT stations @ every 3 segments [36m], high speed lifts - entrance to major pavilions.

Secondary Circulation

Function: Circulation between hy-perzones [15 segments separated by refuge zones]
Features: District lifts that connect refuge zone, evacuation routes within each hyperzone that terminates in the refuge zones

Tertiary Circulation

Function: Circulation within each hyperzone
Features: Local lifts that serve every segment, skin crawlers that link @ every 3-5 segments

Quarternary Circulation

Function: Inter-segment circulation
Features: Continuous gondola system that runs between 3 segments, contin-uous ramp and travelator system that run through every segment.

◁ Four levels of circulation systems.

006
008
033
056
072
088
101
126
138
▷ 170|171
173
180
193
212
218
220

City life-support systems include water supply, drainage, sewerage, waste disposal, power supply, telecommunications and transport systems. These systems and networks have impacts on the urban structure as well as on the formal perception, and activities of the city. Similar to urban infrastructures, the internal services systems are the high-rises infrastructure and they must be designed to enable change and growth in the three-dimensional planning matrix, with thresholds to its internal expansion and growth.

Movement, Accessibility and Streets-in-the-Sky

In the same way that urban design at ground conditions results in multiple access systems, from the start the design of the skyscraper should not be dependent on one single circulation system, for instance a control bank of elevators (although in taller buildings there may be transfer floors). Design must, at the onset, provide secondary, tertiary and, where applicable, even quarternary circulation systems. These are not just elevatoring systems but include ramps, stairs, combination stair and ramps, skybridges, LRT systems and others.

Programmed Places-in-the-Sky.

Private Front and Back Gardens.

Public Parks-(Commons) in-the-Sky.

Tertiery Circulation Systems

Secondary Circulation Systems

Primary Circulation Systems

Primary Circulation Systems

Tertiery Circulation Systems

Continuous Landscaped Ramp Up the Tower

▷ Multiple circulation systems within the skyscraper as found at the ground plane.

004
006
008
033
056
072
088
101
126
138
148

▷ **Artificial Land in the Sky : Flexibility** chapter 10
and Change

▷ **172|173** —

180

193

212

218

220

... The early stages in the production of a skyscraper involve conventional land and property development which can be traced through a process involving land assembly, servicing, construction, marketing and management to the finished property ...

Artificial Land in the Sky: Flexibility and Change

In its generic state the skyscraper is artificial land as real estate. The complex management process of the skyscraper's built-up space is essentially real estate development and includes other considerations such as logistics, legal matters, real estate marketing and related planning aspects. The early stages in the production of a skyscraper involve conventional land and property development which can be traced through a process involving land assembly, servicing, construction, marketing and management to the finished property.

The urban design of the new high-rise cannot be done in isolation from the socioeconomic-political realities of the development. The development process, impact assessment,building economics, development, planning techniques, legislation, real estate marketing strategy and

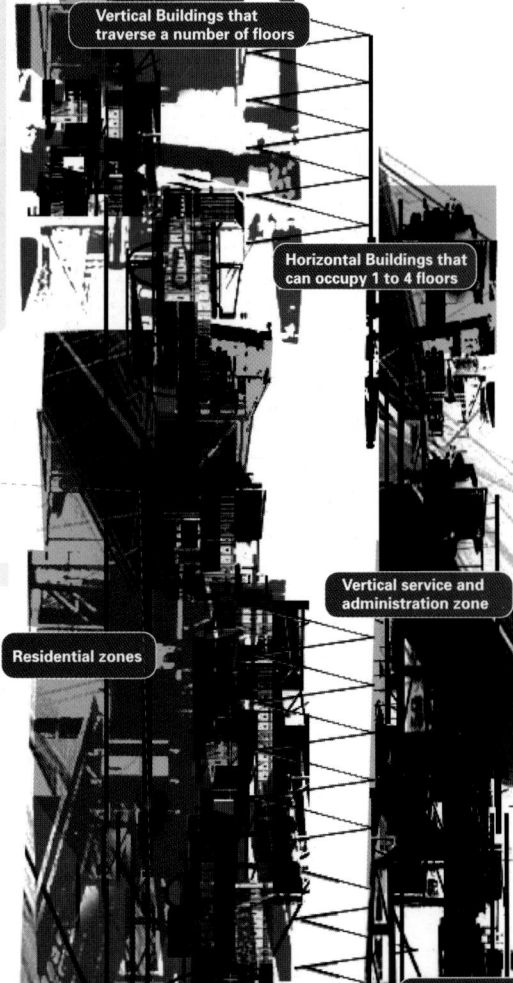

Vertical Buildings that traverse a number of floors

Horizontal Buildings that can occupy 1 to 4 floors

Vertical service and administration zone

Residential zones

Entrance Zone

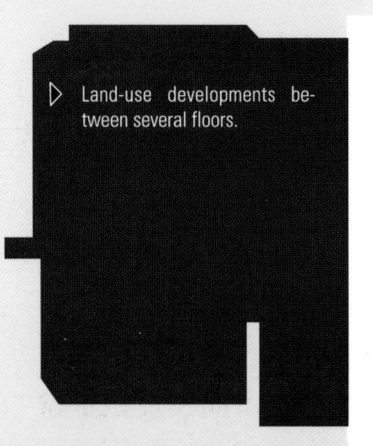

▷ Land-use developments be-tween several floors.

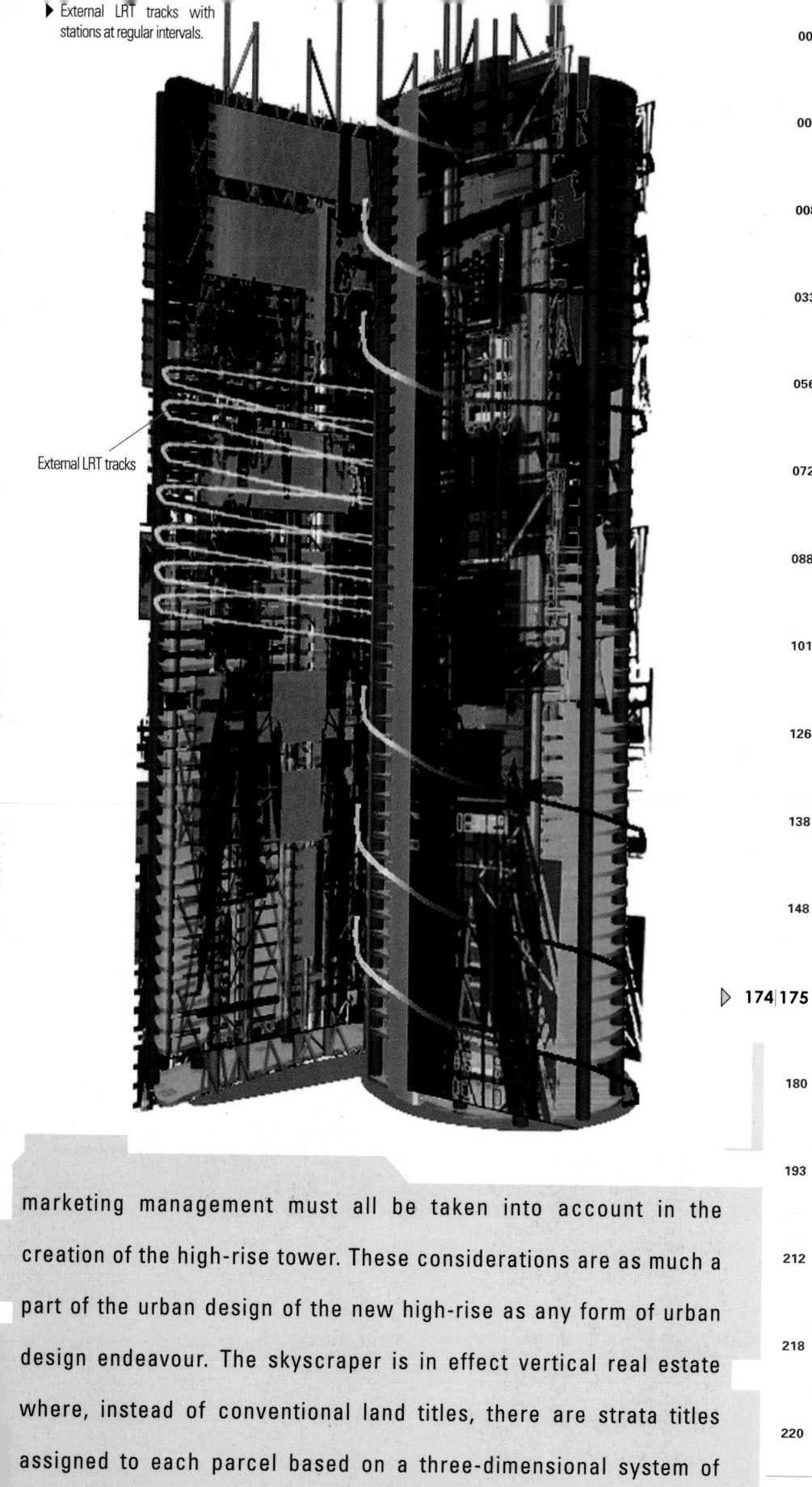

External LRT tracks

004 —
006 —
008 —
033 —
056 —
072 —
088 —
101 —
126 —
138 —
148 —
▷ **174|175** —
180 —
193 —
212 —
218 —
220 —

marketing management must all be taken into account in the
creation of the high-rise tower. These considerations are as much a
part of the urban design of the new high-rise as any form of urban
design endeavour. The skyscraper is in effect vertical real estate
where, instead of conventional land titles, there are strata titles
assigned to each parcel based on a three-dimensional system of
spatial parcellation.

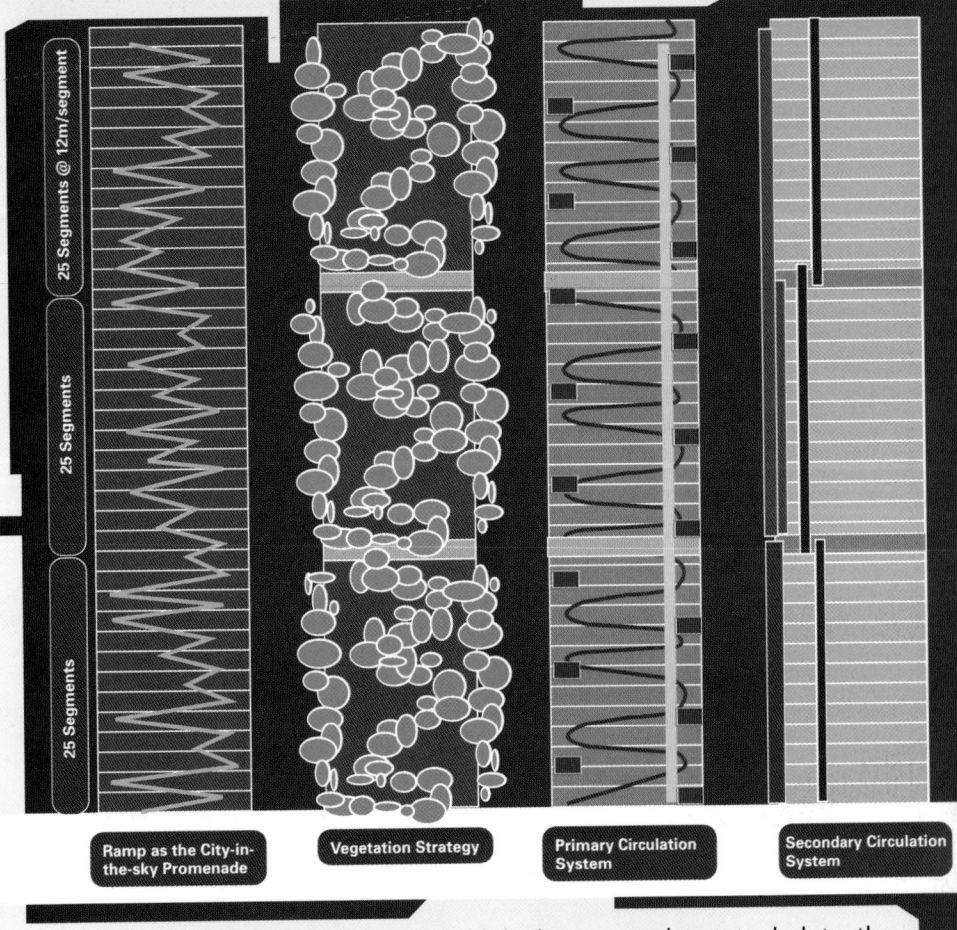

25 Segments @ 12m/segment | 25 Segments | 25 Segments

Ramp as the City-in-the-sky Promenade **Vegetation Strategy** **Primary Circulation System** **Secondary Circulation System**

The conventional approach to the high-rise as real estate led to the delineation of spatial zones in a three-dimensional format, as 'strata titles' that determine the extent of ownership. Conceptually the high-rise is in effect the creation of new land in the sky and now becomes embedded as part of a three-dimensional matrix of critical space that is placed over the land area at the ground plane. Based on the three-dimensional matrix land-use mapping of the vertical urban design for a locality, the real estate correlation would be a similar matrix of parcellation of strata titles. Then in the same way that a city has limits and boundaries, the tower could only permit a limited extent of expansion and change. Over time, issues such as interior renovations, repair, repair versus restoration, new buildings in conservation areas within the high-rise built-form, values and ethics in conservation and authenticity would need to be accommodated.

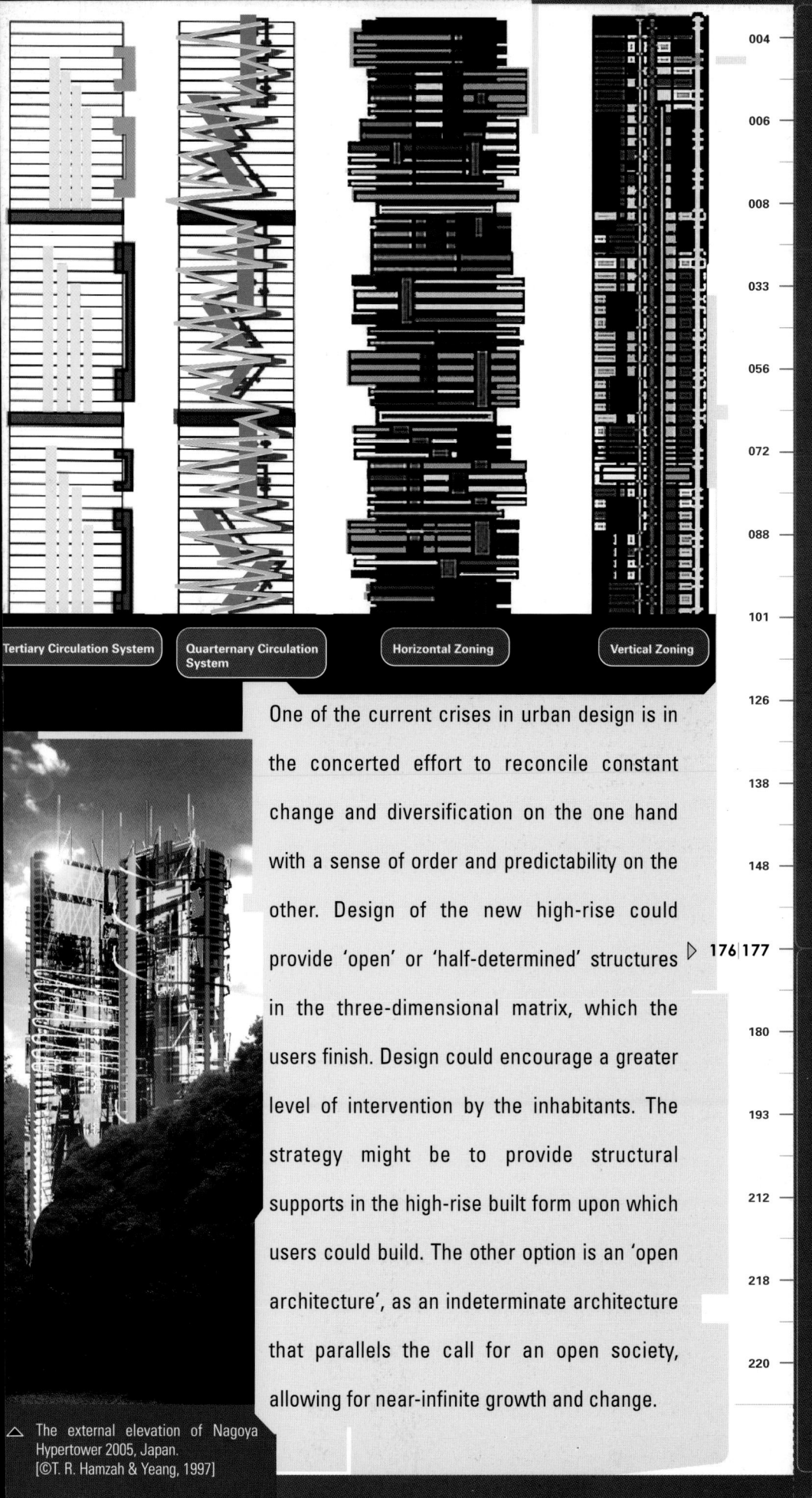

Tertiary Circulation System

Quarternary Circulation System

Horizontal Zoning

Vertical Zoning

004
006
008
033
056
072
088
101
126
138
148
180
193
212
218
220

One of the current crises in urban design is in the concerted effort to reconcile constant change and diversification on the one hand with a sense of order and predictability on the other. Design of the new high-rise could provide 'open' or 'half-determined' structures ▷ **176|177** in the three-dimensional matrix, which the users finish. Design could encourage a greater level of intervention by the inhabitants. The strategy might be to provide structural supports in the high-rise built form upon which users could build. The other option is an 'open architecture', as an indeterminate architecture that parallels the call for an open society, allowing for near-infinite growth and change.

△ The external elevation of Nagoya Hypertower 2005, Japan. [©T. R. Hamzah & Yeang, 1997]

12m floor to ceiling segment height will allow up to 3 storey construction of small buildings with independent quarternary circulation system.

Artificial Land in the Sky: Flexibility and Change

The extension of the high-rise as artificial land means that other comparative developmental concepts can be applied to it. For instance, the high-rise can be developed as a science park (eg, Silicon Valley), a leisure park or megamall (eg, Bluewater, UK). Examples already exist in New York and Tokyo of large department stores that have multiple (ie, seven or more) levels – such as Tokyo Hands which contains DIY products – and high-rise buildings such as Roppongi in Tokyo that contain, almost exclusively, cafés, bars and nightclubs.

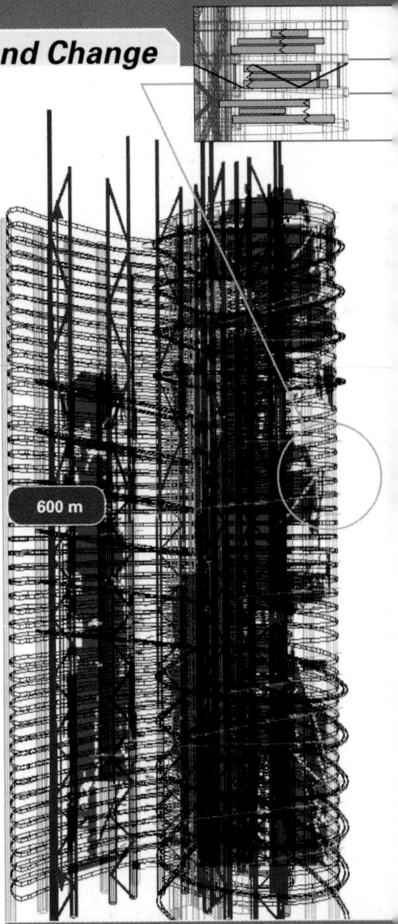

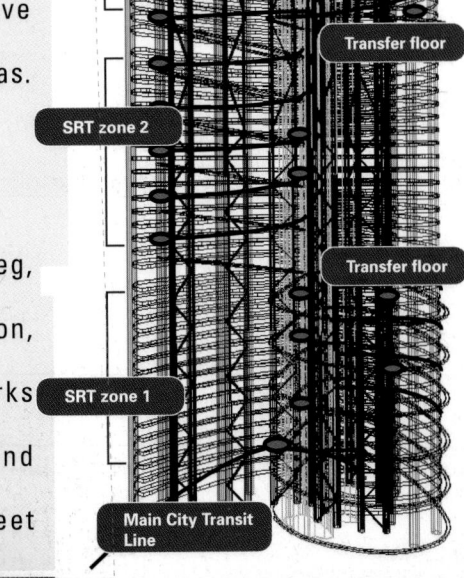

600 m

▲ Secondary circulations within builtform.

▼ External LRT track.

SRT zone 3
Transfer floor
SRT zone 2
Transfer floor
SRT zone 1
Main City Transit Line

Some considerations in urban design for the new high-rise involve services for managing urban areas. These include:

- local environmental services: eg, street cleaning, refuse collection, grounds maintenance, parks management, regulation and enforcement of traders, street

management, regulation and enforcement of traders, street lighting;

• security services: eg, policing, enforcement, guarding;

• housing management and maintenance: eg, tenancy relationships, repairs;

• other property: eg, estates management, repairs of all publicly and privately-owned property;

• local transport and utilities: eg, buses, trains, gas, electricity, water;

• local amenities: eg, water features, shopping malls;

• local personal services: eg, health, social care, providings advice and information ;

• education and leisure: eg, schools, colleges, adult education, youth clubs, leisure centres.

The creation of the high-rise – in effect the creation of artificial land – and all the conventional aspects of real estate premises and management are applicable to spaces-in-the-sky.

◁ Seaworld the ocean liner seeking to be an apartment skyscraper or a floating real estate.

004
006
008
033
056
072
088
101
126
138
148
▷ 178|179
180
193
212
218
220

Artificial Land in the Sky: Flexibility and Change

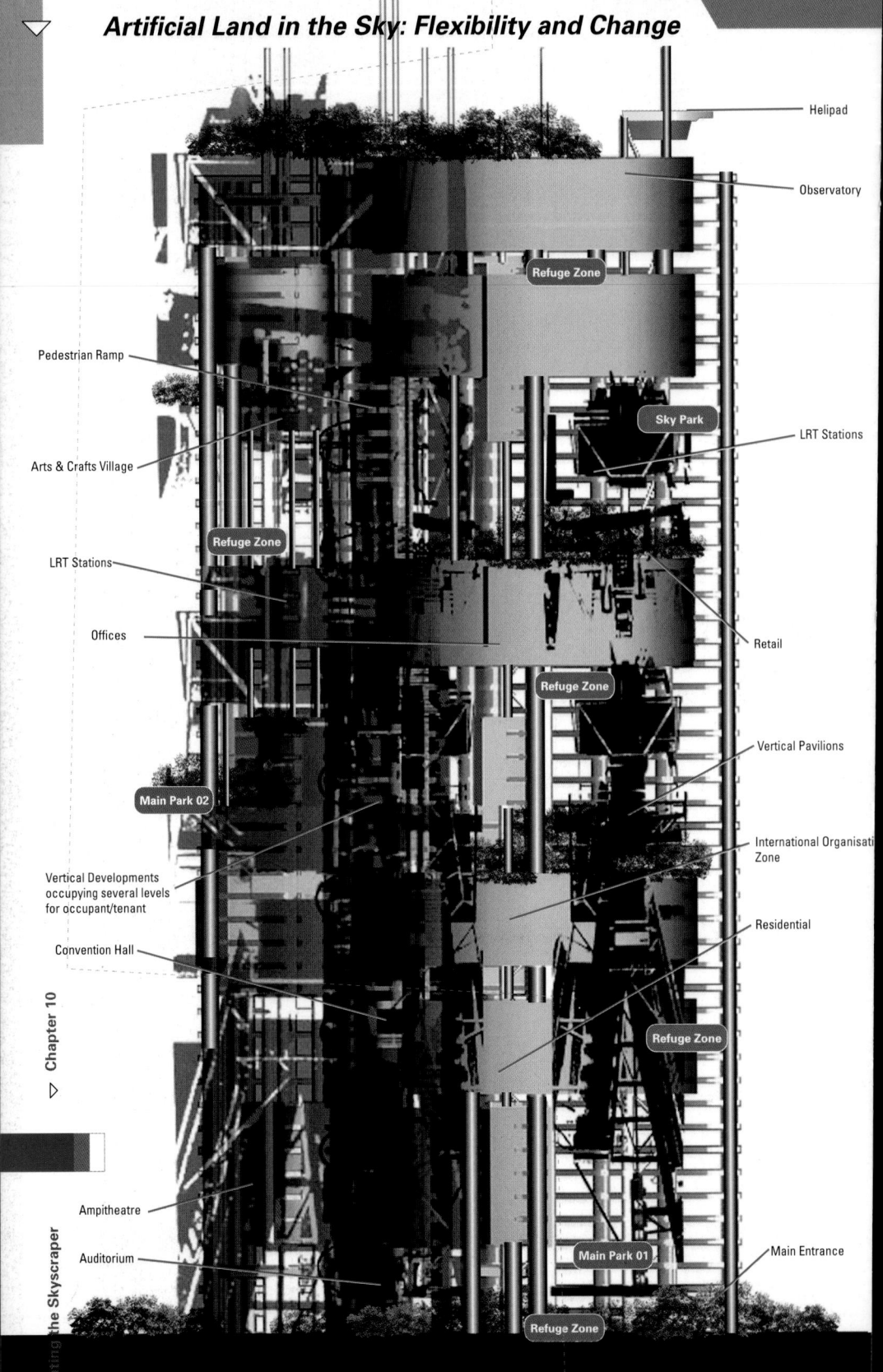

Helipad

Observatory

Refuge Zone

Pedestrian Ramp

Sky Park

LRT Stations

Arts & Crafts Village

Refuge Zone

LRT Stations

Offices

Retail

Refuge Zone

Vertical Pavilions

Main Park 02

International Organisation Zone

Vertical Developments occupying several levels for occupant/tenant

Residential

Convention Hall

Refuge Zone

Ampitheatre

Auditorium

Main Park 01

Main Entrance

Refuge Zone

Parking Facilities

... Buildings will need to be designed not as high-energy polluting open systems but as mimetic urban ecosystems that relate their inputs, outputs and operations within the context and carrying capacities of the ecosystems in the biosphere ...

The Skyscraper as an Urban Ecosystem

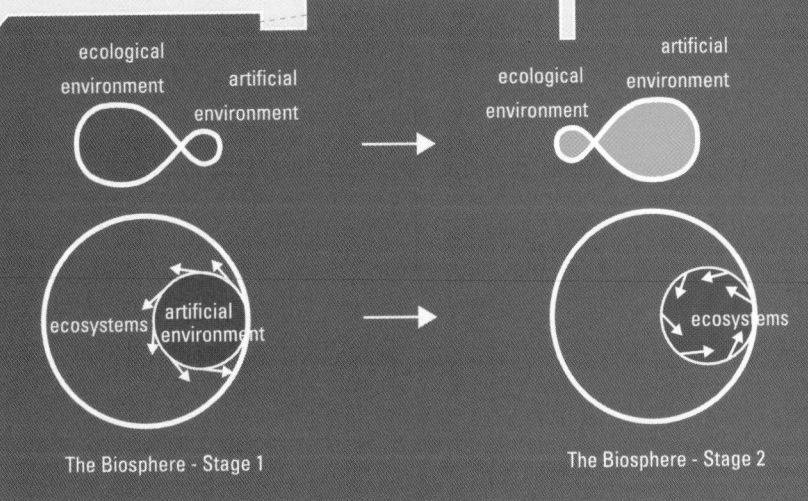

ecological environment · artificial environment

ecological environment · artificial environment

ecosystems · artificial environment

ecosystems

The Biosphere - Stage 1

The Biosphere - Stage 2

△ Increasing urbanisation as a consequence of population growth is making the biosphere more and more inorganic and artificial.

▷ To balance the increasing inorganic aspect of our built envrironment, we need to green and re-vegetate the surfaces of the man-made built environment.

In response to the need for a sustainable future, the urban design for the new high-rise must address the limitation and constraints of our ecological environment. Buildings will need to be designed not as high-energy polluting open systems but as mimetic urban ecosystems that relate their inputs, outputs and operations within the context and carrying capacities of the ecosystems in the biosphere.

▷ The balancing of the abiotic with the biotic can be done vertically on the facade.

Greening the high-rise means going beyond the conventional 'set-asides' of open space in the urban area, beyond the provision of sky parks. Applying the ideas of sustainability requires that we demonstrate and manage the regenerative capacity of the renewable elements in the new high-rise and in the city. This, ultimately, will mean utilising the discharges or residuals from the urban system, converting them through recycling to inputs that sustain local subsystems useful to the city as a whole.

Cities exist on the basis of surplus products, whether food supplies, which were of critical significance in antiquity, or manufactured goods and services, which are the principal items of modern economic exchange. The ways in which such flows focus upon individual centres are primary determinants of the structure and organisation of national hierarchies and the arrangement of centres in a world system of cities.

004
006
008
033
056
072
088
101
126
138
148
173
▷ **182|183**
193
212
218
220

$$LP = \begin{array}{c|c} L_{11} & L_{12} \\ \hline L_{21} & L_{22} \end{array}$$

◁ The system's view of the set of ecological interactions in the built environment.

1   System
2   Environment to the system
L_{11} Processes + activities within the system [internal interdependencies]
L_{22} Processes + activities in the environment of the system [external interdependencies]
L_{12} Exchanges of the system with its environment [transactional interdependencies of the system/environment]
L_{21} Exchanges of the environment with the system [transactional interdependencies of the environment/system]
LP   Ecological design

The Skyscraper as an Urban Ecosystem

Our human settlements consume resources from near and far on a massive scale. The process of urbanisation has dramatically changed the character of natural landscapes, disgorged huge amounts of residuals from both production and consumption and rendered much of the natural environment unfit for further use as well as destroying the habitats of many species of nonhuman nature. This transformation of nature is now one of the most basic and critical processes shaping the urban habitat and one for which we must make allowances.

It is estimated that some 25 per cent of the world's population lives in the highly urbanised countries of the developed world but they account for 70 per cent of the world's energy consumption, 75 per cent of metals and 85 per cent of wood.

△ The mixed-mode ventilated suit as metaphor for the tower.

▽ The umbrella as a canopy.

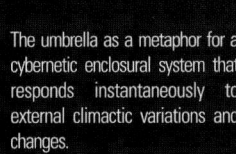

▷ The umbrella as a metaphor for a cybernetic enclosural system that responds instantaneously to external climactic variations and changes.

The major cities of the developed world draw upon the ecological capital of all other nations to provide food for their economies and land, air and water in which to discharge their waste products. Urban residents in developed countries generate an average of 0.7–1.8 kilograms of domestic waste daily, compared to 0.4–0.9 kilograms daily in developing countries. Measured in per capita terms urban residents, for instance in the USA and Australia are estimated to generate carbon dioxide emissions that are up to 25 times the levels in Dhaka, Bangladesh.

◁ The tower as a stack of self-sufficient pods.

004
006
008
033
056
072
088
101
126
138
148
173
▷ 184|185
193
212
218
220

Physical Constituents

Biological Constituents

climate

geology

soils

hydrologic processes

human communities

animal communities

plant communities

◁ The systemic model of the ecosystem.

The Skyscraper as an Urban Ecosystem

The concern for the sustainability of our urban environment can be expressed at two levels. The first is global and involves a wide range of issues surrounding the long-term stability of the earth's resources and environment and the implication for cities. It is clear that the world's cities cannot remain prosperous if the aggregate impact of their economies' production and their inhabitants' consumption draws on global resources at unsustainable rates, and their wastes are deposited in global sinks at levels which lead to the destruction of the biospheric processes and climatic change. The second is local and involves the possibility that urban life could be undermined from within because of congestion, pollution and waste generation and their accompanying social and economic consequences.

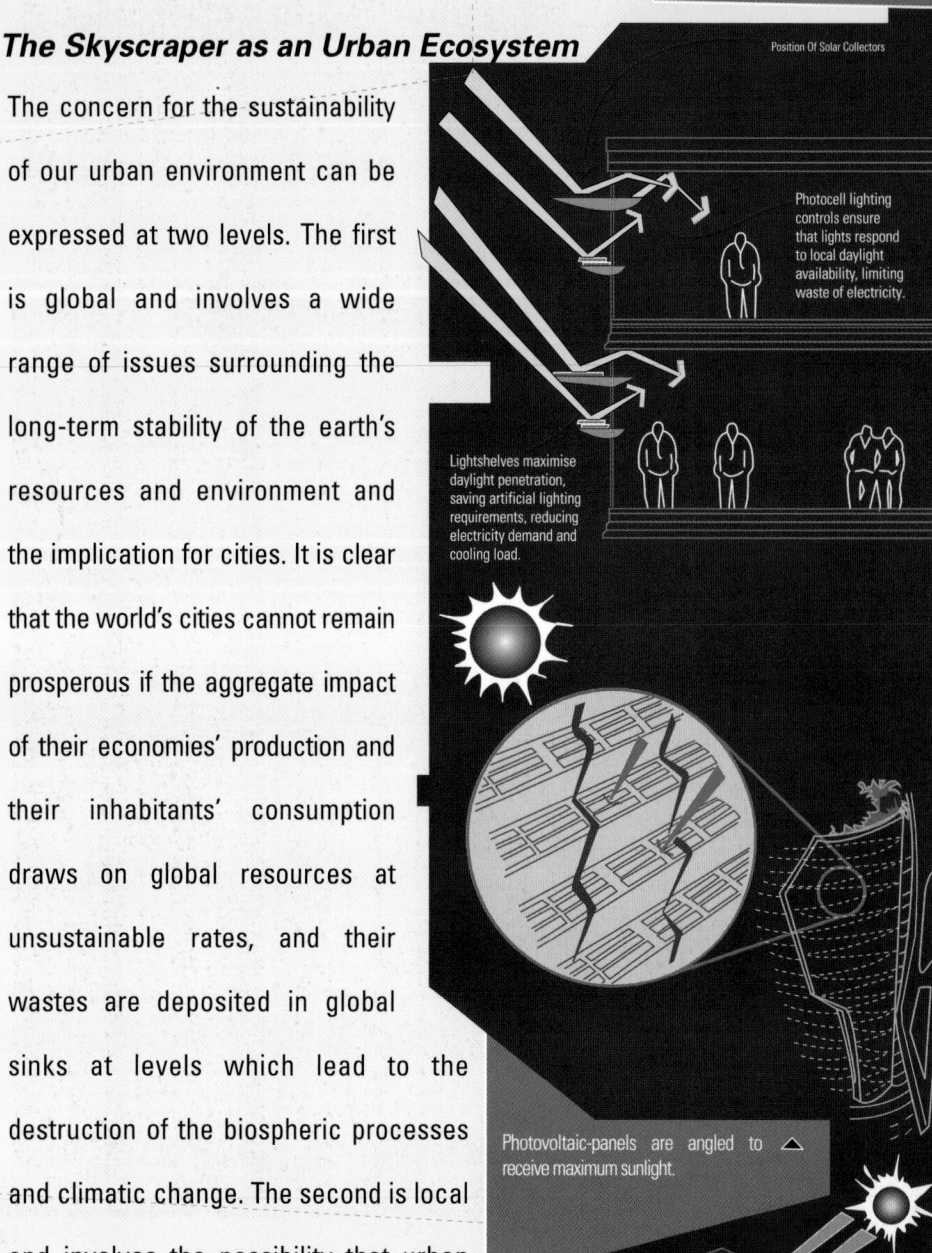

Photocell lighting controls ensure that lights respond to local daylight availability, limiting waste of electricity.

Lightshelves maximise daylight penetration, saving artificial lighting requirements, reducing electricity demand and cooling load.

Photovoltaic-panels are angled to △ receive maximum sunlight.

Array Meter
Array Energy

SMA 5 kW
Inverter

Inverter

To The Utility
Connection

REC Meters
Energy Import
Energy Export

Demand
Switch

Load Demand
Office Energy
Power Current

The use of PV cells in the tower as ▷
a productive mode.

Distribution Board

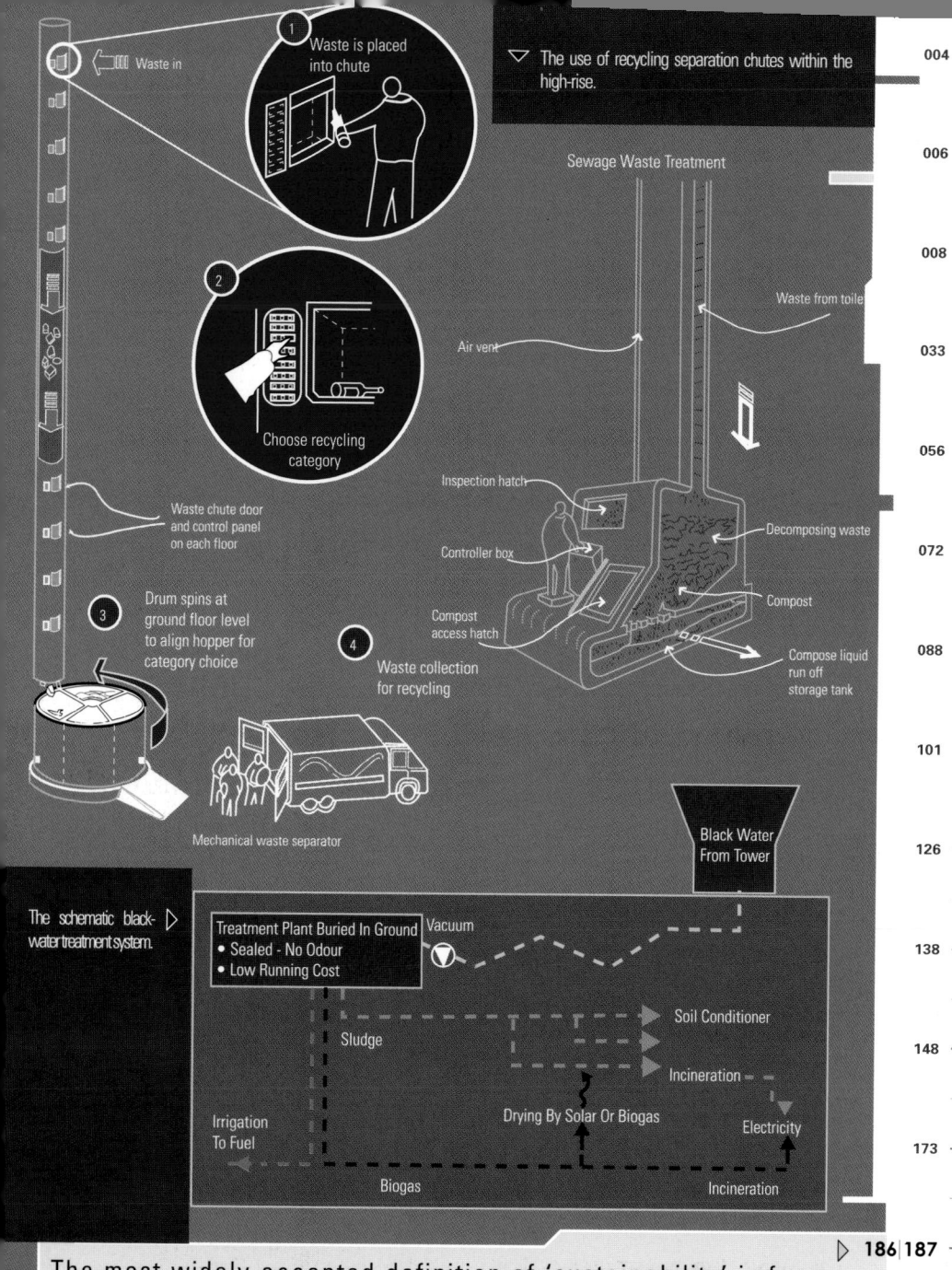

004

006

008

033

056

072

088

101

126

138

148

173

① Waste is placed into chute

Waste in

② Choose recycling category

Waste chute door and control panel on each floor

③ Drum spins at ground floor level to align hopper for category choice

④ Waste collection for recycling

Mechanical waste separator

▽ The use of recycling separation chutes within the high-rise.

Sewage Waste Treatment

Air vent

Waste from toilet

Inspection hatch

Controller box

Compost access hatch

Decomposing waste

Compost

Compose liquid run off storage tank

Black Water From Tower

The schematic black-water treatment system. ▷

Treatment Plant Buried In Ground
• Sealed - No Odour
• Low Running Cost

Vacuum

Sludge

Soil Conditioner

Incineration

Irrigation To Fuel

Drying By Solar Or Biogas

Electricity

Biogas

Incineration

The most widely accepted definition of 'sustainability' is from the report of the World Commission on Environment and Development (WCED, 1987), also known as the Brundtland Commission, which defined sustainable development as 'development which meets the needs of the present without compromising the ability of future generations to meet their own needs'. Emphasis was placed on the need for action today so as to provide for economic and ecological viability tomorrow.

The Skyscraper as an Urban Ecosystem

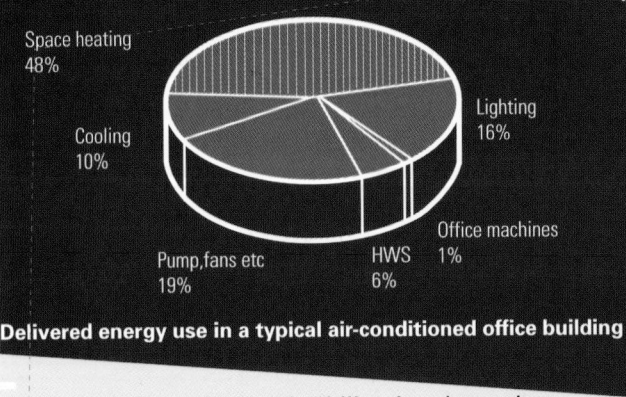

Space heating
48%

Cooling
10%

Lighting
16%

Office machines
1%

Pump,fans etc
19%

HWS
6%

Delivered energy use in a typical air-conditioned office building

Mwh/sq.m.

35
30
25
20
15
10
5
0

0 10 20 30 40 50 60 70 80 90

% glazing ratio

Single glazing

▲ The high-rise to be designed as a low-energy-consumption structure.

▽ Service decks within the tower for M&E plants.

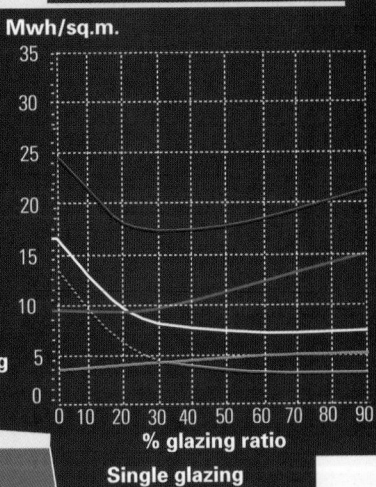

This concept of sustainability involves three major principles. The first is about generational equity and concerns the legacy that is left to future generations. It argues that the success of cities in the future depends to a large extent upon the assets and resources which are available and that it is therefore incumbent upon the current generation not to indulge in indiscriminate and wasteful consumption. A sustainable future requires that national capital assets of at least equal value to those of the present are passed on to succeeding generations.

The second is that a fair and equitable use of present resources is clearly necessary and this is enshrined in the principle of 'social justice'. Some form of central control over access to, and use of, resources is implied. The fact that both resources and consumption are widely distributed and are interdependent means that such management must be on a broad scale.

Energy Consumption (kWh/m2/yr)

Passive Mode   Mixed Mode   Full Mode

△ Indicative operational energy indexes.

▽ Vertical landscaping to be integrated with land uses to help cool the facade and reduce the heat-island effect in the precinct.

A third precondition for sustainable development is that of 'transfrontier responsibility' insofar as key issues such as pollution, waste disposal and climatic warming are not constrained by national or regional boundaries but are essentially global in cause and consequence. In the design of the new high-rise we need to take into account the five fundamental goals that should guide its design and planning so as to ensure sustainability.

• The first concerns conservation and involves the need to ensure the supply of natural resources for present and future generations through the efficient use of land, less wasteful use of nonrenewable resources, their replacement by renewable resources wherever possible and the maintenance of biological diversity.

• The second concerns the use of physical resources and their impact on the land. It seeks to ensure that the development and use of the built environment, is in harmony with the natural environment and that the relationship between the two is one of balance and mutual enhancement.

• A third goal is to prevent or reduce the processes that downgrade or pollute the environment and to promote the regenerative capacity of ecosystems.

004
006
008
033
056
072
088
101
126
138
148
173
▷ 188|189
193
212
218
220

The Skyscraper as an Urban Ecosystem

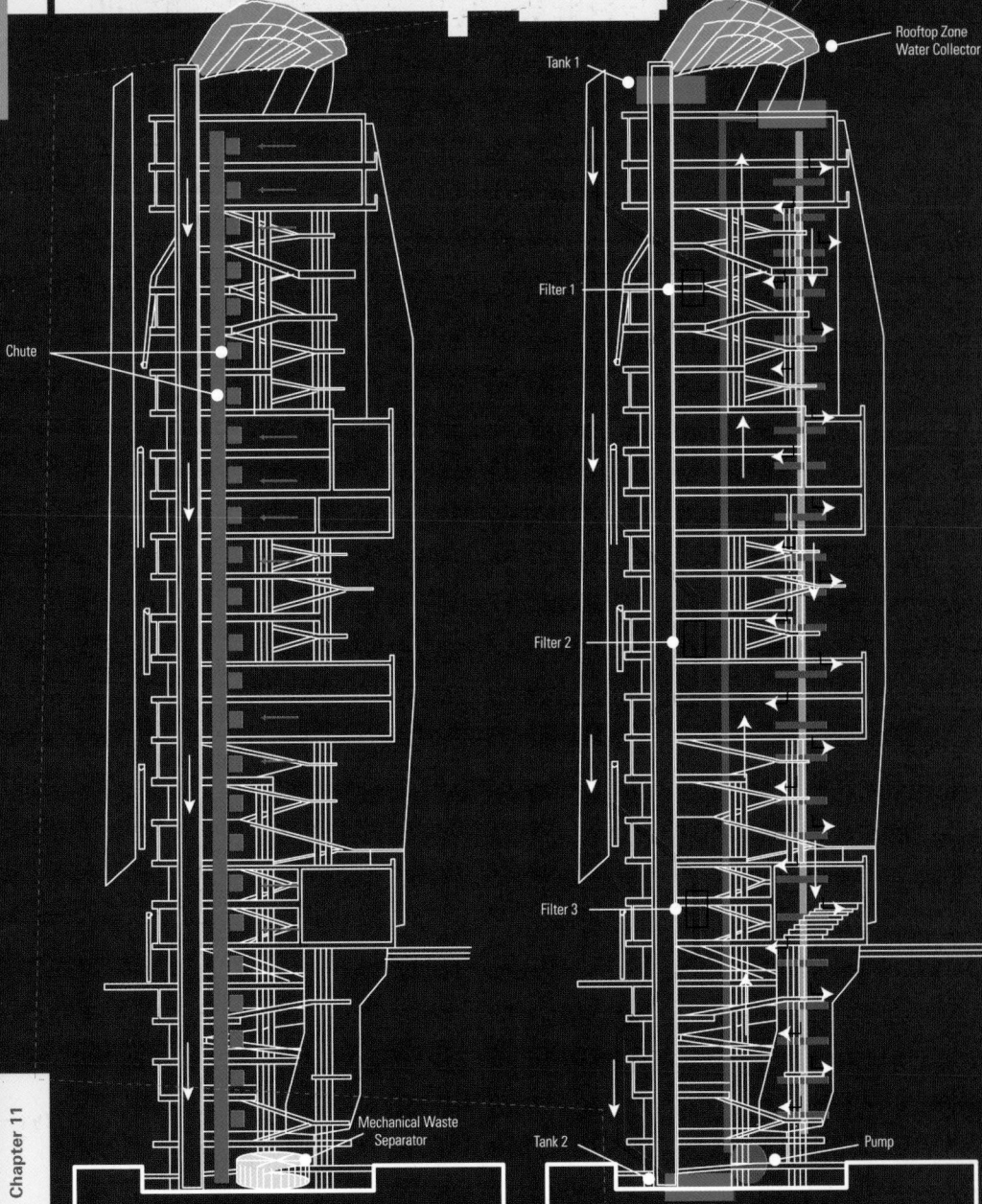

Rain

Rooftop Zone
Water Collector

Tank 1

Filter 1

Chute

Filter 2

Filter 3

Mechanical Waste
Separator

Tank 2

Pump

The final two goals are social and political in character.

• The aim of goal four is to prevent any development that increases the gap between rich and poor and to encourage development that reduces social inequality.

• The final goal is to change attitudes, values and behaviour by encouraging increased participation in political decision-making and in initiating environmental improvements at all levels from the

Rain

Rooftop Zone
Water Collector

Rainwater
catchment
Scallops

Sunlight

Solid waste, water recycling and energy management.

local community upwards.

A specific focus upon the sustainability of our urban environments
and cities arises because the urban level is where many
environmental problems begin and where they are experienced
with greatest intensity. Our urban environments are both great
consumers and degraders of the natural environment. They extract
far more from the environment than they return.

004

006

008

033

056

072

088

101

126

138

148

173

193

212

218

220

The Skyscraper as an Urban Ecosystem

The new high-rise should be designed to imitate nature and be

mimetic of its uses:

	Natural Ecosystem	Man-made Ecosystem
Energy and Materials	• Reduced gross photosynthetic activity, high efficiency	• Reduced energy, high efficiency
	• Recycling of nutrients	• Recycling of nutrients and materials
Economic Diversity	• Balance of producers, consumers, decomposers and integrative species	• Balance of producers, manufacturers and services
	• Many functional niches – specialists	• High functional diversity
Spatial Efficiency	• High spatial efficiency – compact	• High spatial efficiency – compact
	• High structural diversity – small and large, lateral and vertical, large variety	• High structural diversity – small and large, lateral and vertical, large variety
Information and Organisation	• High species and community diversity	• High community diversity
	• High community organisation – much interconnection	• High community organisation – many networks
Environmental Control	• High environmental control – resources availability controlled within biotic system, climate buffered	• Strong protection from environmental perturbations – resources tightly managed, more able to buffer and cope with changes
	• System stability	• System stability

▷ EDITT Tower, Singapore
[© T. R. Hamzah & Yeang, 1997]

The New Skyscraper chapter 12

... It is contended that with the digital revolution 'place' has never been more important. Today people can search the whole world to find the places most desirable to them ... People will still occupy physical space although their work may become increasingly electronic, and they will continue to be gregarious and seek communities ...

004
006
008
033
056
072
088
101
126
138
148
173
180
192 193
212
218
220

The New Skyscraper

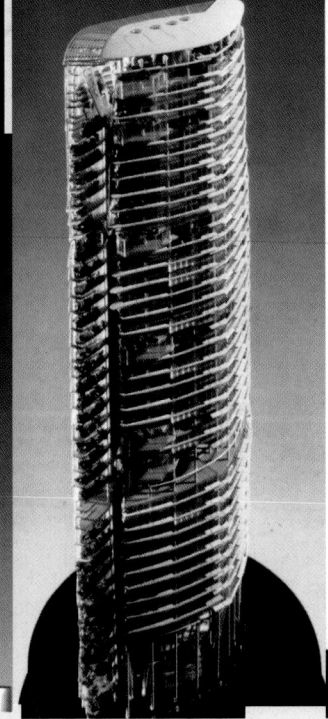

What will be the impact of the digital revolution on the skyscraper? Will it make the high-rise obsolete? What will happen when all places and cultures are in a continuous time–place fusion with the simultaneous uprising of local cultures and expression of place?

It is a well-accepted fact that the digital economy's rise has turned the established economic and social geography of many of the developed countries on its head in a manner not seen since the Industrial Revolution. The focus of IT has started to reshape our urban physical, economic and social environments.

Many people are led to believe that with the explosion of the Internet and the new communications technologies, and our growing freedom to work from anywhere, place no longer matters and that we shall see the demise of the office building as a building type. The digital revolution not only accelerates the speed with which information is processed and disseminated, it also relates

004

006

008

033

056

072

088

101

126

138

148

173

180

212

218

220

Eco-Tower, Elephant and Castle.
[© T. R. Hamzah & Yeang, 2000]

the relationship of space and time ▷ **194|195**

within our communities. Work will be

globally time-driven as distance will no

longer determine the cost of

communicating electronically. Companies will organise certain

types of work in three shifts according to the world's three main

time zones: the Americas, East Asia/Australia and Europe.

The New Skyscraper

Decisions on where to locate business, for example, once dependent upon the question of access to road, rails, ports or raw materials, are now increasingly dependent instead on the ability to link often scarce human resources. Location will not be the key to most business decisions. Companies could locate any screen-based activity anywhere on earth, wherever they can find the best bargain of skills and productivity.

It is contended that with the digital revolution 'place' has never been more important. Today people can search the whole world to find the places most desirable to them. Freed from old ties to raw materials or pools of cheap labour, the Information Age businesses that drive the economy – and their employees – can be anywhere they want but are likely to remain communities, albeit in different configurations, rather than work anywhere singularly. Common interests, experiences and pursuits rather than proximity will bind the communities together.

The tower as a matrix .

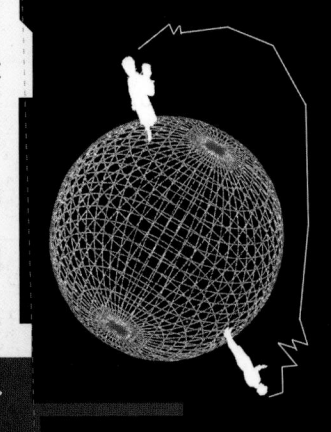

GPS for the electronic tracking of people within towers, using smart cards and GPS hand phones.

Mass House Tower, Birmingham.
[© T. R. Hamzah & Yeang, 2002]

It is contended that our cities will become highly specialised places almost totally dependent on the information industries, on high-end services and tourism. People will still occupy physical space although their work may become increasingly electronic, and they will continue to be gregarious and seek communities as work environments. Electronic location tracking will allow inhabitants to build new kinds of relationships because they will be able to permit others to follow their travel.

▷ 196|197

CAAG Tower, Deptford.
[© T. R. Hamzah & Yeang, 2001]

004
006
008
033
056
072
088
101
126
138
148
173
180
212
218
220

The New Skyscraper

Shopping education + religion

Bank

Services + personal business

24%

15%

7.7M

5M

33%

20%

work + related

10.6M

10.7M

Social, recreational + other

The increasingly pervasive presence of entertainment and IT in the home has turned the domestic environment into a self-contained media shell. It could, in theory, occupy all of our leisure time without our ever having to walk out of the front door but this does not mean the large-scale closure of public entertainment facilities. DVD, online services, pay-per-view, digital music, electronic games and so on – all of these allow us to see and experience what we want, when we want it, without leaving home. Couple this with the fact that 40 million Americans (that is 30 per cent of the work force) work at home, and what we have is, in theory, a recreationally and vocationally self-sufficient mass audience – but this is a lonely existence.

Cityscape of Ayjad complex, Mecca.
[© T. R. Hamzah & Yeang, 2001]

Roofscape of Ayjad Complex, Mecca.
[© T. R. Hamzah & Yeang, 2001]

While consuming entertainment and other media products allows us to feel as if we are part of something that is bigger than ourselves, the experience can also be isolating, solitary and ultimately alienating. Recent studies show that despite increasing visits to the putatively interactive Internet, frequent users are more likely than others to be afflicted by anxiety and depression, the diseases of loneliness. The very fact that we can have a widening variety of entertainment and work experiences at home drives the fun-focused consumer out of the home in search of real, not virtual, interpersonal contact. The solution could lie in mini theme parks, megaplexes and retail stores as mass entertainment venues that straddle the border between entertainment and commerce while offering the consumer a renewed sense of being part of a human enterprise that is larger than the individual. Inescapably, people feel part of a mass activity in these hybrid venues. They may be anonymous in a crowd, but they are at least part of something.

004
006
008
033
056
072
088
101
126
138
148
173
180
▷ 198|199
212
218
220

▷ The 3D matrix of urban space.
[Source: *Manmachine Interface*, Shirow Masamune]

The New Skyscraper

Roads-in-the-sky using electric cars.

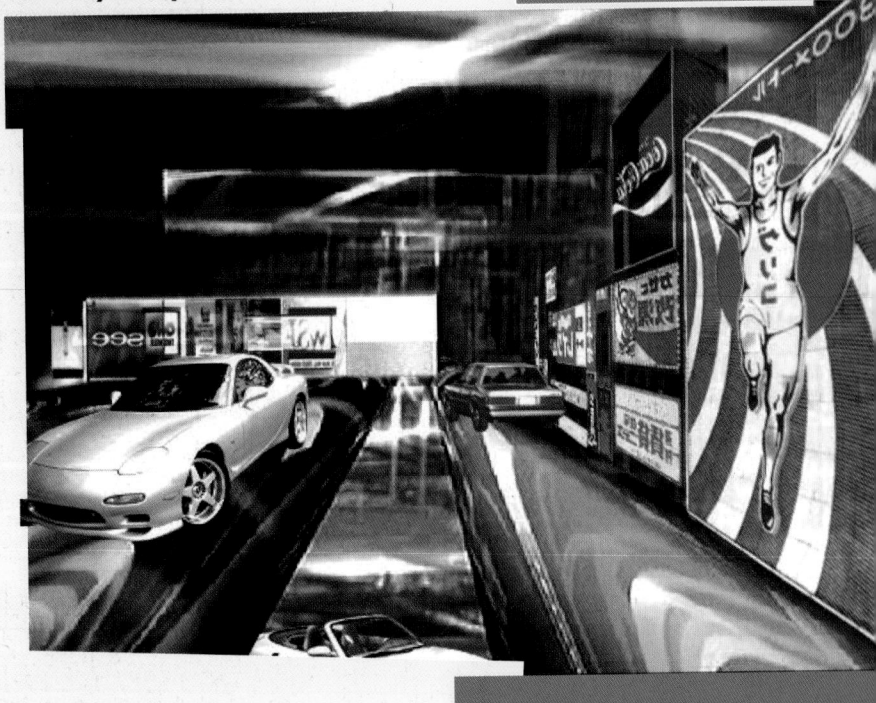

Telecommunications could undermine the benefits of concentration but the evidence is that the principal financial centres in our cities are gaining rather than losing in importance. Decision-makers benefit collectively from living and working in close geographical proximity and from the resulting opportunities for generating and accessing business information. Personal contact enables the characteristics of associates, partners and competitors to be scrutinised and assessed, and contributes to the building of 'confidence' which is an essential prerequisite for successful business.

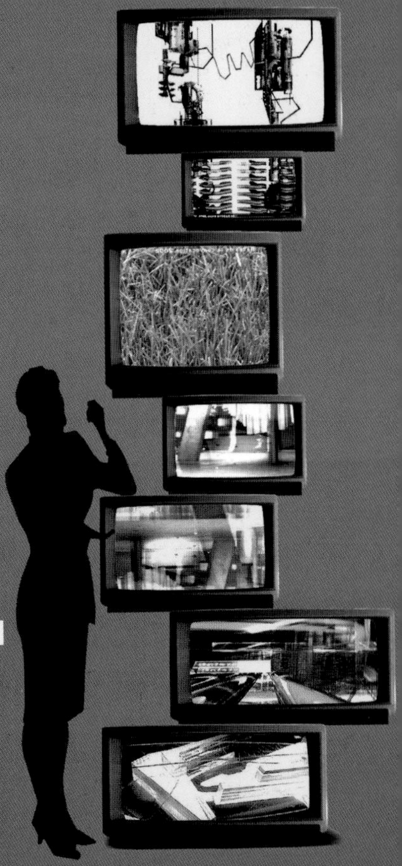

Multiplicity of land uses in the skyscraper.

Contrary to initial predictions, the growth of this new breed of industries for IT has not led to a mass migration to rural communities linked by an electronic superhighway. Inevitably IT does allow greater flexibility in terms of locations, particularly for back office functions, but it is also resulting in new urban concentrations for face-to-face activity. Thus the main hubs of economic activity, particularly the head office functions (of command and control), will remain within larger towns and cities where good linkages will make communications easy.

◁ The new skyscraper as a system of vertical flows, energy, people, materials, waste, vegetation, wind, etc.].

004
006
008
033
056
072
088
101
126
138
148
173
180
▷ 200|201
212
218
220

The New Skyscraper

The emergence of world cities as financial centres has largely been made possible by telecommunications. London, New York and Tokyo have long been regional financial centres, but the introduction of international telecommunications and computer systems has enabled them to develop global banking and financial trading functions. Of particular importance is the interlinkage of dealing rooms through dedicated and secure telecommunications networks so that currencies, stocks and shares, and commodity prices and volumes in every significant business centre are simultaneously displayed on computer screens around the world. On this basis, 24-hour global trading can be conducted at the touch of a button, with financial settlements being made by electronic funds transfer.

▷ The rooftop park. Reference Trump Tower, Stuttgart.
[© T. R. Hamzah & Yeang, 2001]

It is important to emphasise that telecommunications create and enhance rather than erode our urban functions. Although they enable interaction to take place without participants travelling to central meeting places, they are not appropriate media through which to conduct the types of 'orientation' meeting that take place in world cities. The purpose of such meetings is to evaluate options, to negotiate deals and to take decisions. They typically involve top-level personnel and their advisers. It is essential for participants to be present in person since the aim is to float ideas, gauge reactions, cajole, persuade and decide. None of these activities can adequately be performed remotely. The face-to-face activities that take place in boardrooms and on the dealing floors in major financial centres have not been, and are unlikely to be, made obsolete by new technology; rather, technology has extended the global reach of those who transact such business and so has reinforced the status of world cities.

▷ Ecological design is not an assemblage of eco-gadgets [eg double-skin walls, photovoltaics, solar collectors, etc].

004
006
008
033
056
072
088
101
126
138
148
173
180
▷ 202|203
212
218
220

The New Skyscraper

Our urban environments and centres are likely to be maintained
and enhanced by the way in which new communications
technologies are introduced. These environments benefit most
from advances in telecommunications because, as established
locations for global business, they are the places which first
received and derived the advantages of new services and
applications. Telecommunications, in common with many
innovations, diffuse hierarchically through urban systems.

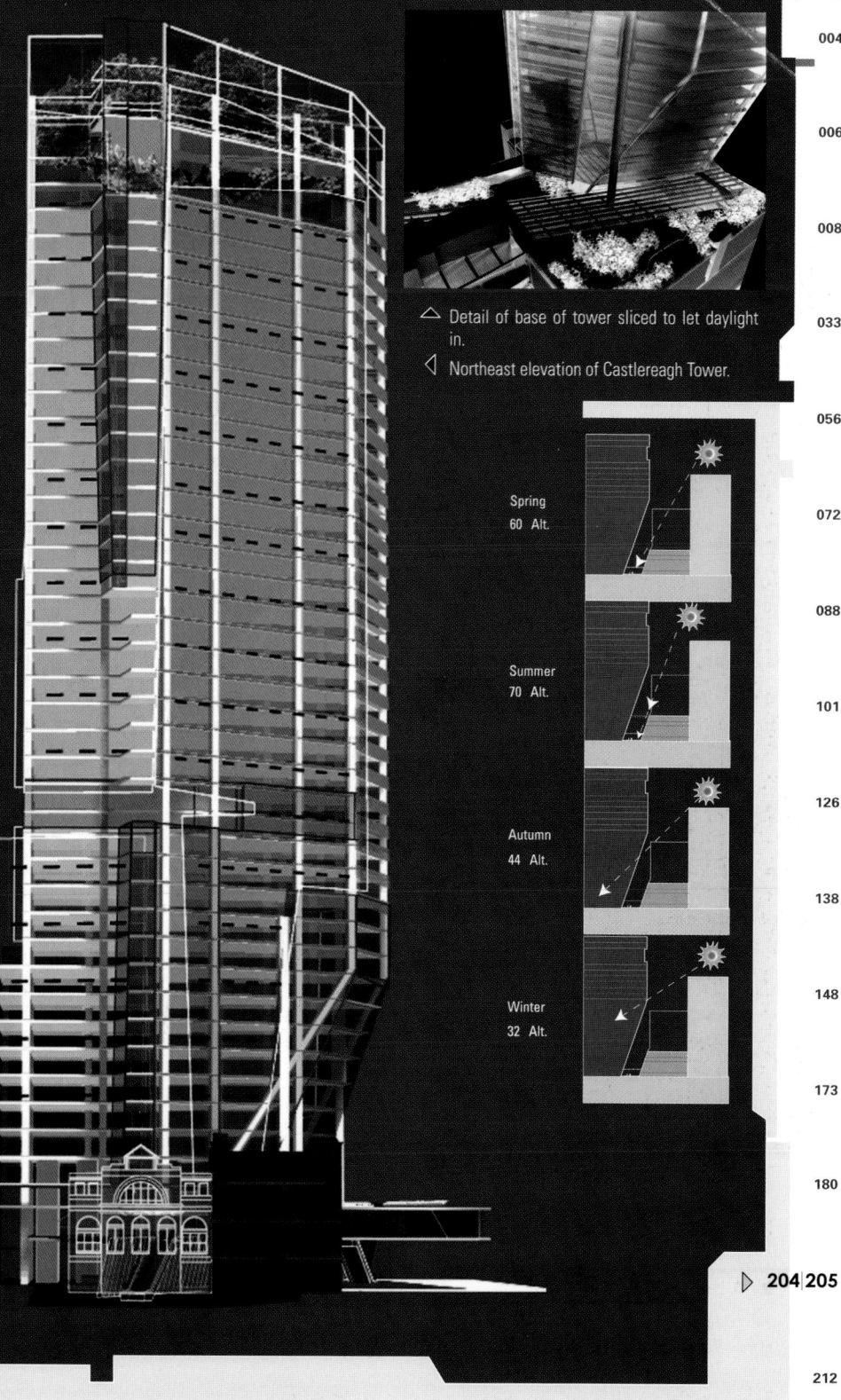

△ Detail of base of tower sliced to let daylight in.

◁ Northeast elevation of Castlereagh Tower.

Spring
60 Alt.

Summer
70 Alt.

Autumn
44 Alt.

Winter
32 Alt.

004
006
008
033
056
072
088
101
126
138
148
173
180
▷ 204|205
212
218
220

We might speculate on what the new high-rise might be as a consequence of adopting the vertical theory of urban design. How will the theoretical ideas and concepts discussed here impact, not just on the built form of the high-rise building type but also on the city?

The New Skyscraper

We contend that the new high-rise as urban design should encourage more people to return to living in city centres. Urban environments with attractive spaces and places, and plenty of shops and cafés providing lively street-life-in-the-sky, will delight those who relish the bustle and the anonymity of living in a crowd. The precincts-in-the-sky will become even more attractive as they become safer with wider use of electronic surveillance.

△ Provision of multipurpose spaces for multimedia communal activities within the high-rise.

△ Provision of internal cranes to move equipment and goods within the high-rise.

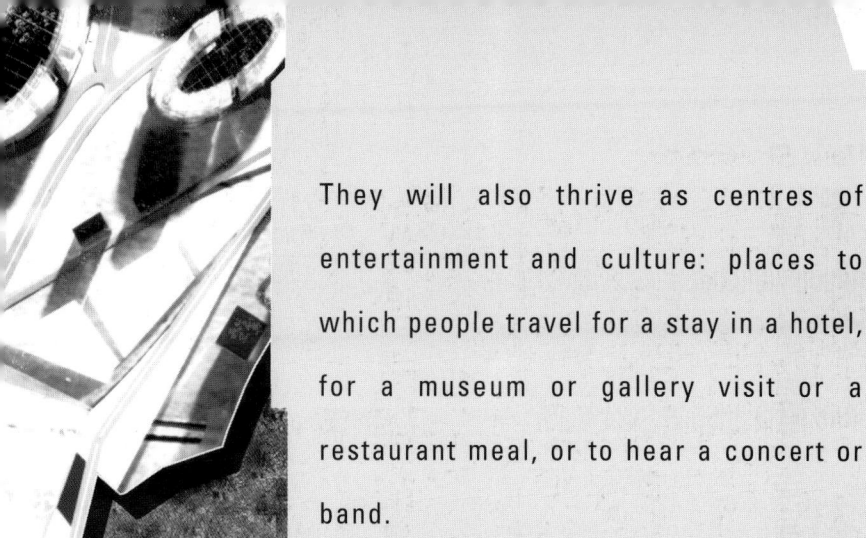

They will also thrive as centres of entertainment and culture: places to which people travel for a stay in a hotel, for a museum or gallery visit or a restaurant meal, or to hear a concert or band.

It is likely that the new high-rise's built form will have greater hybridisation with myriad building programmes, construction methods and construction details. These will enable the greater poetic expression of individual situations and communities. We will see the rejection of a mindless and strict adherence to functionalism as a primary determinant of the high-rise built form because of its denial of the complexity of life at the ground and because of its inability to explain the persistence of certain forms once their function has changed or become obsolete.

◁ The seamless integration of the man-made built environment with its organic host the biosphere and its processes.

004
006
008
033
056
072
088
101
126
138
148
173
180
▷ 206|207
212
218
220

The New Skyscraper

▷ Development of structural systems that permit change and growth.

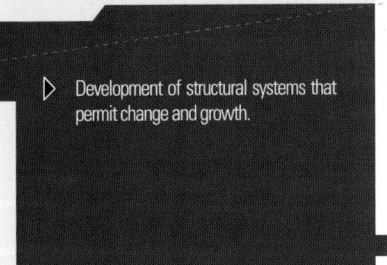

The new high-rises in our world's major cities must now adapt to the new functions of these cities in four ways: first, as highly concentrated command points in the organisation of the world economy; second as key locations for financial and specialised service firms, which have replaced manufacturing as the leading economic sectors; third, as the site of production, including the production of innovations in industries; and fourth, as markets for the products and innovations produced.

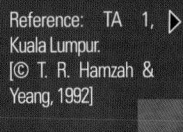

Reference: TA 1, ▷
Kuala Lumpur.
[© T. R. Hamzah & Yeang, 1992]

△ The multimedia personal space within the high-rise.

004
006
008
033
056
072
088
101
126
138
148
173
180
208 | 209
212
218
220

The high-rise as an integrated work frame of multiple structural systems.

The following three factors will determine how the new high-rise will be built and used in the future.

• Culture: If people are used to living and working in one way, they may be slow or reluctant to change. Thus it is important not to become reactionary but to be quick to spot and take advantage of new possibilities in the new high-rise as urban design.

• Convenience: Some high-rise internal configurations can be readily used in one situation but not in another. It may take an effort to master the use of the new built configuration and linkages.

• Cost: The design of the new skyscraper as vertical urbanism will be enhanced if the new built form cuts costs.

The New Skyscraper

With the continued intensification of our cities today, the proposition of designing of the new high-rise as urban design will lead to a more humane and habitable urban environment. But in order to be successful, the design must be in harmony with the social, economic and political aspects of the locality. At the same time it must address the limitations of the ecological environment.

▷ The new skyscraper as a garden city.
Reference: Waterfront House, Kuala Lumpur.
Side spikes are passive light pipes to bring daylight into upper parts of the skyscraper floors.
[© TR Hamzah & Yeang, 2000]

004

006

008

033

056

072

088

101

126

138

148

173

180

The new high-rise as urban design will be spatially decompartmentalised in contrast to the spatial segregation of the contemporary high-rise. It will be designed and planned in a three-dimensional matrix with diverse land uses, public realms, places, parks and open spaces in its upper parts. The spaces are not designed as stacks of floor plates but as precincts and neighbourhoods with a high level of optimal accessibility. In aggregate, the urban design will recreate in the sky the ideal and pleasurable conditions that we find at the ground. ▷ **210|211**

◁ The skyscraper as a free zone within a circular grid, for the colonisation of spaces.

General Planning Characteristics :
The City-in-the-Sky

Economy and Technology

• *Three-dimensional matrix.*

• *Generally, information and services oriented.*

• *Heavy industries mostly in eco parks or in small rural towns (global economy).*

Social Organisation

• *Local, community-based but globally linked.*

Transportation

• *Walking, cycling and elevators (local), transit (interbuilding and across city), cars (supplementary), air (global).*

• *Reduce car use per capita.*

• *Increase transit, walk/bike, elevators, local electric vehicles and car-pooling, decrease sole car use.*

• *Reduce average commute to and from work.*

• *Increase average speed of transit relative to cars.*

• *Increase service-kilometres of transit relative to road provisions.*

• *Increase cost recovery on transit from fares.*

• *Decrease parking spaces per 1000 workers in central business district.*

• *Increase kilometres of separated cycleways.*

Urban Form

• *Local urban villages (high-density mixed) linked across city by transit; medium and low-density areas around villages; no more urban sprawl at ground level.*

• *Urban forms within high-rise built form.*

Environment, Resource Use, Biodiversity

- Use ecological corridors within cityscape.
- Preserve agricultural land and natural landscape at the urban fringe.
- Increase amount of green space (eg as local or regional parks) per capita.
- Increase proportion of urban redevelopment to new development.
- Increase number of specially zoned transit-oriented locations.
- Increase density of population and employment in transit-oriented locations.
- Public health: decrease infant mortality per 1000 births.
- Socioeconomic objective: increase educational attainment (average years per adult).
- Increase local leisure opportunities by design.
- Public education: decrease transport fatalities per 1000 population.
- Public administration: decrease crimes per 1000 population.
- Decrease proportion of substandard residential units and housing.
- Increase pedestrian-friendly nodes (based on specific indicators).
- Increase proportion of city intensification in the suburbs with urban design guidelines to assist communities in development.
- Increase proportion of built environment allowing mixed-use, higher density urban villages.

004

006

008

033

056

072

088

101

126

138

148

173

180

193

▷ 212 213

218

220

The Goals for Reduced Metabolic Flows in the New Skyscraper

Energy Flow

• *100% renewable-based energy (eg, electricity and heating).*

• *Energy use not to exceed 60 kwh/sq. m. reducing to 50 kwh/sq.m.*

• *Reduce total energy use per capita.*

• *Decrease energy used per dollar of output from industry.*

• *Increase proportion of bridging fuels (natural gas) and renewable fuels (wind, solar, biofuels).*

• *Reduce total quantity of air pollutants per capita.*

• *Reduce total greenhouse-gas emissions.*

• *Achieve zero days where air-quality health standards are not met.*

• *Reduce average external-fleet average and new-vehicle fuel consumption.*

• *Reduce number of vehicles failing emission standards externally and internally for building.*

• *Reduce number of households complaining of noise.*

Transport, People and Vehicular Flows

• *80% commuting people flows by nonautomobile means.*

• *Less traffic by 2005 and 40% less by 2015.*

• *1More vehicles using biofuels by 2005 and 25% by 2015.*

• *100% of freight vehicles electric or low-emission vehicles.*

Water, Materials and Waste Flows

- *100% of solid waste recycled.*
- *Reduction in waste.*
- *Water consumption reduced.*
- *Sewage used for energy extraction and nutrients for farm soil.*
- *No PVC or nonrecyclable materials to be used.*
- *No rainforest timbers to be used.*
- *New building materials– less than 50% of construction.*
- *No 'sick building' chemicals to be used in carpets and furniture glues.*
- *Reduce total water use per capita.*
- *Achieve zero days where drinking water quality standards are not met.*
- *Collect rain water and recycle grey water.*
- *Increase proportion of sewage and industrial waste treated to reusable quality.*
- *Decrease amount of sewage and industrial waste discharged to streams or oceans and use of algae treatment ponds .*
- *Reduce consumption of building materials per capita (including declining proportion of old-growth timber to plantation timber).*
- *Reduce consumption of paper and packaging per capita.*
- *Decrease amount of solid waste (including increasing recycle rates for all components).*
- *Provide natural distribution centres to buildings and natural recycling centres.*
- *Increase amount of organic waste returned to soil and food production.*

Landscape Flows

- *Continuous landscape between high-rise and ground plane.*
- *High sky-gardens ratio to inorganic spaces.*

004
006
008
033
056
072
088
101
126
138
148
173
180
193
▷ 214|215
218
220

Key Design Issues in the 3D Spatial Urban Design of the New High-Rise

Urban Form and Places

• *Relationship between the high-rise and its context in the 3D planning matrix.*

• *Urban structure and grain of streets and public routes in the sky.*

• *Identity and sense of place within high-rise built-form.*

• *Design, shape and scale of major public spaces within high-rise built-form.*

• *Variety of built spaces and urban structure in the high-rise,*

• *Location of entrances along sky streets and public spaces.*

• *Distribution of residential, commercial and community facilities within the high-rise built form.*

• *Development densities, plot sizes and ratios within the high-rise built form.*

• *Intensification of public realms.*

• *Landmarks and public buildings.*

• *Public art.*

• *Use of natural features including trees, planting and water.*

• *Design and materials of hard and soft landscaped areas.*

• *Pavement widths and street furniture in the high-rise built form.*

• *Lighting and safety.*

• *24-hour use.*

Movement

• *Integration with existing pedestrian, mechanical, electric cars, communal transport routes, elevators, etc (primary, secondary, tertiary movement systems).*

• *Location of communal transport facilities and stops.*

• *Integration between different movement modes (foot, cycle, car, communal transport, elevator).*

• *Accessibility of facilities within five and ten minute walking distances.*

• *Electric car parking standards and location of parking spaces within high-rise.*

• *Traffic-calming measures.*

Built Form Configuration

• Built form layouts and orientation.

• Variety of massing, materials and architectural expression within high-rise built-form.

• Flexibility of internal layouts.

• Work/ live and lifetime dwellings.

• Disabled access.

• Materials and maintenance.

• Visual link between spaces and streets (openings and entrances, etc).

• Use of external and transitional spaces – balconies, roof terraces, porches, sky courts.

• Overlooking distances.

Environmental Aspects

• Massing and thermal performance.

• Passive environmental design.

• Exposure to sunlight and natural daylight penetration.

• Energy efficiency.

• Renewable energy sources.

• Combined Heat and Power (CHP) provision.

• Grey water recycling.

• Thermal and acoustic insulation.

• Dwelling unit waste management.

• General waste management.

• Landscape continuity, biodiversity and ecology.

• Balance of inorganic with organic within high-rise built-form.

Community Aspects

• Play areas and community facilities at the upper levels.

• Proximity to education facilities within high-rise built-form.

• Adult education and family learning opportunities.

• Sports and childcare facilities at the upper levels.

• Training opportunities and job creation.

• Management and stewardship.

• Wired community and multi-media spaces.

• Complementary community initiatives.

004
006
008
033
056
072
088
101
126
138
148
173
180
193
216 217
218
220

Bibliography

- Bacon, E N (1995), *Design of Cities: A superbly illustrated account of the development of urban form, from ancient Athens to modern Brasilia*, London: Thames & Hudson

- Barley, N and Ireson, A (2000), *City Levels*, Basel: Birkhauser

- Burnie, D (1994), *Nature-Concise Encyclopedia*, London: Dorling Kinderskey

- *Business Week: 18*, February 2002

- Clark, D (1996), *Urban World/Global City*, London: Routledge

- *CE Magazine*: January 2001

- Damacion, MC (1992), *Office Access*, Toronto: HarperCollins Publishers

- Eley, J and Marmot, A (1995), *Understanding Offices: What every manager needs to know about office buildings*, London: Penguin UK

- Gattuso, J (1996), *Insight Pocket Guides: New York City*, Kowloon: APA Publications (HK) Ltd

- Gehl, J and Gemzoe, L (1996), *Public Spaces Public Life, Copenhagen 1996*, Copenhagen: The Danish Architecture Press and The Royal Danish Academy of Fine Arts, School of Publishers

- Goos, G, Hartmanis, J and van Leeuwen, J (1999), *Cooperative Buildings: Integrating Information, Organizations and Architecture — Second International Workshop, CoBuild'99*, Pittsburgh, USA, October 1999 Proceedings, Berlin, Heidelberg & New York: Springer-Verlag

- *Far Eastern Economic Review*: 4 April 2002

- *Frame*: Jan/Feb 2002

- Jenks, M and Burgess, R (eds) (2000), *Compact Cities: Sustainable Urban Forms for Developing Countries*, London: Spon Press

- Lenne, F (2001) *Spécial Aménagement Tertiaire 2002*, Paris: AMC Le Moniteur Architecture

- Lepik, A and Schmedding, A (1999), *Architektur in Berlin*, Cologne: Dumont

- *Le Prestige*: September

- Martin, L (May 1967), 'Approach to Architecture: Sir Leslie Martin', *RIBA Journal*, Vol 74, No 5, May 1967

• Martin, L (May 1967), 'Approach to Architecture: Sir Leslie Martin', RIBA Journal, Vol 74, No 5, May 1967

• Mori, J and Taniguchi, J (1996), Benkei in New York, San Francisco: Viz Communications, Inc

• Muhammad, A (2001), Silverfish New Writing, Kuala Lumpur: Silverfishbooks

• Reiter, J (1995), Insight Compact Guides: Barcelona, Kowloon: APA Publications (HK) Ltd

• Richards, B (2001), Future Transport in Cities, New York: Spon Press

• Rogers, R (1999), Towards an Urban Renaissance: Final Report of the Urban Task Force, Chaired by Lord Rogers of Riverside, London: E & FN Spon

• Rogers, R (1997), Cities for a Small Planet, London: Faber and Faber

• SilverKris: January 2002

• SilverKris: March 2002

• Schueller, W (1986), High-Rise Building Structures, Melbourne, Florida: Robert E Krieger Publishing Company

• The Economist Research Department (1993), Pocket World in Figures, London: Imago Publishing Ltd

• The Straits Times: 19 January 2002 (Saturday)

• The Washington Post Company: 2001

• Time Out: 2-9 January 2002

• Time Out: 6-13 February 2002

• Trancik, R (1986), Finding Lost Space: Theories of Urban Design, New York: John Wiley & Sons, Inc

• Vischer, JC (1996), Workspace Strategies: Environment as a Tool for Work, New York & London: Chapman & Hall

• Yeang, K (1994), Bioclimatic Skyscrapers, London: Ellipsis

• Yee, R (2001), The Business of Design, Midland, Michigan: Quebecor World Pendell, Inc

• Zaknic, I (1998), 100 of the World's Tallest Buildings, Mulgrave, Victoria: The Images Publishing Group Pty Ltd

004
006
008
033
056
072
088
101
126
138
148
173
180
193
212
▷ 218 219
220

Index

Index

004
006
008
033
056
072
088
101
126
138
148
173
180
193
212
218

▶ 222|223